JAPANESE

The Easy Way

Karen Sandness, Ph.D.

Genko Translations
Portland, Oregon

BARRON'S

All inquiries should be addressed to:
Barron's Educational Series, Inc.
250 Wireless Boulevard
Hauppauge, New York 11788

Library of Congress Catalog Card No. 96-79019
International Standard Book No. 0-8120-9627-4

Printed in United States of America
9 8 7 6 5

Contents

Introduction   **vii**

1   Pronunciation and the Writing System   **1**
    Pronouncing Japanese—the Basic Sounds   1

2   More Sounds and Intonation   **10**
    Syllables, Accent, and Intonation   12

3   Dôzo yoroshiku!   (Pleased to meet you!)   **16**
    Greetings and Pleasantries   16
    Please and Thank You   18
    Introductions   21
    Farewells   23

4   Nani? Dare? Itsu? Ikura?   (What? Who? When? How Much?)   **28**
    Identifying Objects and People   28
    Numbers and Prices   39
    Telling Time   46

5   Nijô-jô wa doko ni arimasu ka?   (Where is Nijô Castle?)   **51**
    Possessions   51
    Locations   55
    Narrowing Down Locations   60

Review Chapters 1–5   **67**

6   Totemo takai desu ga, amari oishiku nai desu.   **69**
    (It's very expensive, but it's not very tasty.)
    Describing Things and People   69
    Negatives   73
    Pointing Out Where Things Are   77
    Numbers above 10,000   82

7   Mainichi shinbun o yomimasu.   (I read the newspaper every day.)   **87**
    Talking about Having Things   87
    Describing Your Daily Routine   91
    More about Telling Time   98

8   Toshokan de benkyô shimashita.   (I studied in the library.)   **102**
    Events in the Past   102
    Where Actions Take Place   107
    How Actions Are Accomplished   111
    Motion Toward a Place   112

9   Yasukatta desu kara, mittsu kaimashita.   **118**
    (Because they were cheap, I bought three.)
    How to Say "Also"   118
    The Months and Days of the Month   121
    Quantities   125
    Giving Reasons   129
    How to Say "With"   133

10 Tegami o kaite, yûbin de dashimashita. (I wrote a letter and mailed it.) 137

Another Class of Adjectives   137
Likes and Dislikes, Skills and Weaknesses   140
The All-Important -te Form   143
Sequences, Commands, and Requests   150

Review Chapters 6–10   *156*

11 Ginkô no kado o migi e magarimasu.   159
(Turn right at the corner where the bank is.)

Asking and Giving Directions on the Street   159
Describing Ongoing Actions   166
Verbs Whose Direct Objects Take *ga*   169
Talking about Probability   173

12 Go-kyôdai wa nannin desu ka?   176
(How many brothers and sisters do you have?)

Describing Your Family   176
Talking about Ages   182
Expressing What You Want   185
Making Suggestions and Offers   189

13 Sono mizu o nonde wa ikemasen. (You mustn't drink that water.)   192

Talking about Something Becoming Something Else   192
Asking, Giving, and Denying Permission   194
The Concepts of "No One," "Nowhere," and "Nothing"   198
Comparisons   201

14 Sensei ni kaigai ryokô no omiyage o sashiagemashita.   207
(I gave my instructor a souvenir from my overseas trip.)

"Anything," "Something," "Anyone," "Someone,""Anywhere," "Somewhere"   207
The Plain Negative Form   211
Giving   215
Going Somewhere for a Purpose   218

15 Dô iu imi desu ka? (What does it mean?)   222

The Past Tense of the Dictionary Form   222
Can and Cannot   226
Some More *Ko-So-A-Do* Words   229
The *no da* Construction   233

Review Chapters 11–15   *240*

16 Yoyaku shite yokatta!   242
(It's a good thing we made reservations!)

Verbs of Receiving   242
The -te Forms of Negatives and Adjectives   244
Have You Ever?   251
Comparing More than Two Things   253

17 Ame ga furu ka mo shiremasen. (It may rain.)   257

Giving Advice   257
Making Guesses and Giving Opinions   258

18 Dochirasama de irasshaimasu ka? (Who are you?)   264

How to Express Respect and to Whom   264
Talking on the Telephone   270

Answers to the Exercises   **276**

Japanese-English Vocabulary   **288**

English-Japanese Vocbulary   **298**

INTRODUCTION

THE AIM OF THIS BOOK

Japanese the Easy Way is especially designed for students who need extra practice or guidance in learning elementary Japanese and for people who have previously studied the language and would like to review. Since no two elementary Japanese textbooks present the same vocabulary and grammar in the same order, all vocabulary, grammar, and idioms are introduced here as if they were new. If you are an absolute beginner in Japanese, we would recommend using a coach, either a native speaker or a non-native speaker who can function as an adult in Japanese society, to help you as you use this book.

ABOUT THE JAPANESE LANGUAGE

"Japanese is really a difficult language, isn't it?"

Well, yes and no. The Foreign Service Institute of the U.S. State Department rates Japanese as one of the most difficult languages in which to achieve professional competency. But, on the other hand, if all you want are survival skills for a visit or a short stay, you have a rather simple task ahead of you. Japanese is relatively easy to pronounce, its irregular verbs can be counted on the fingers of one hand, and it has borrowed literally thousands of words from English and other European languages. The trick is *to accept the language on its own terms.*

The Japanese language is very different from English and other European languages. This does not mean that Japanese is "illogical," only that it follows its own logic. Instead of fretting about the differences between Japanese and English as if they were devised with the sole purpose of making your life miserable, consider the study of this language an opportunity to enter a world where sentences don't need subjects and adjectives can have a past tense.

Since the study of Japanese writing is a major task in itself, this book concentrates on the spoken language. Some of you who use *Japanese the Easy Way* as a supplement to classroom instruction will already be familiar with the *katakana* and *hiragana* syllabaries, but others will have used textbooks written entirely in the Latin alphabet. The Japanese-language materials in this book are written in the Latin alphabet, so that beginners and students who have not studied the Japanese writing system can concentrate on learning the vocabulary and structures presented without being frustrated or distracted by an unfamiliar script. In fact, getting a good grip on the vocabulary and structures will ultimately make it easier for you to master the *katakana, hiragana,* and *kanji.* Only the vocabulary lists are presented in both the Latin alphabet and Japanese script.

HOW TO STUDY EFFECTIVELY

Here are some steps to help you study and learn Japanese:

1. If you are currently taking a Japanese class at a school or college, be sure to do everything your instructor suggests, even if you don't have to turn it in for a grade. If you were on an athletic team and your coach told you to run and lift weights in addition to attending the scheduled practices, you would do it, even if your coach had no way of supervising you directly. Why? Because you realize that the coach knows what kind of conditioning you need in order to be good at that particular sport. Your classroom teacher is a type of coach. He or she knows what you need to do in order to learn. So if your instructor tells you to listen to tapes every day or tells you that copying sentences over and over will help you memorize the kanji, follow this advice, even if you aren't required to hand in any written work for a grade.

2. You'll get the best results if you put in some study time every day. You can't cram even one chapter's worth of Japanese into your head in one sitting, any more than an athlete can make up for a lack of steady training by practicing for 24 hours straight before the big event. People have different learning styles, but whichever approach works best for you, the key to successful learning is repetition.

3. Practice with a native speaker, if you can, but be aware that an untrained native speaker will most likely find it difficult to explain Japanese grammar in a way that makes sense to you. (Could you explain the difference between "a" and "the" to a Japanese person?) The best uses of your time with a native speaker are working on correct pronunciation, role-playing, having your handwriting critiqued, and free conversation. You can also have your written exercises checked for accuracy, because a native speaker can tell you whether you have done them correctly, even if he or she cannot explain why they are right or wrong.

    If you can't find a native speaker to practice with, find someone who has lived in Japan *within a Japanese-speaking environment.* Some—not all—military and business people live in Japan for years without ever venturing outside the English-speaking "foreigners' ghetto," but returned exchange students, missionaries, and teachers have usually had to learn to communicate with the Japanese people in their own language.

4. Get as much listening practice as you can, even if you understand no more than a few words. If you live in a major city, you may be able to see Japanese-language television programs, and most large video stores carry a few Japanese movies. Be aware, however, that in modern life, nobody talks like a samurai, so for language practice, concentrate on movies that take place in recent times.

5. Read as much as you can about Japanese history and culture, and watch the documentaries that are shown occasionally on public television or the cable channels. You may be interested in Japanese only for business purposes, but there's a lot more to Japan than its economic system. You need to develop personal relationships with Japanese people to be successful in business in Japan—and they will appreciate your interest in their culture.

Any experienced teacher will tell you that average students who are enthusiastic and hard-working can outperform talented students who are apathetic and lazy. If you *ganbaru* (a wonderful Japanese verb that means "give it all you've got and hang in there"), you will make more progress than you ever thought possible.

To the Classroom Instructor

If you are a classroom instructor looking this book over, you may find it to be more structurally oriented than the textbooks you are used to. The reason is that it is not intended to be a principal textbook but a supplement for students who are having problems with the language or who want more information than their classroom textbook provides. When students have trouble with role-playing, information gap exercises, free conversation, and other enjoyable classroom activities, it is often because they have somehow missed the basics of how to put a sentence together. Therefore, instructions to "ask the policeman where the hotel is" throw them into a panic, and they produce "word salad" on the order of *Doko wa hoteru wa arimasu desu ka?* ("As for where, as for the hotel, exists is it?") instead of the correct *Hoteru wa doko ni arimasu ka?* Sometimes an explanation from another angle, particularly one that points out the consistent patterns operating within the language, can work wonders on their understanding and self-confidence.

A word about the "English-like" hints for pronunciation: while English and Japanese sounds are not completely equivalent, some students are incapable of learning correct pronunciation by ear alone. A student who pronounces *jôzu* as *zhozhu* may be enlightened by seeing it written as *Joad Zoo*, and a student who mispronounces *shitsurei* as *shucheray* may do better after seeing it written out as *sheet-soo-ray*. Admittedly, these are not exactly the Japanese pronunciations, but they are much closer than *zhozhu* and *shucheray*.

Given clear, concise explanations, patient coaching, and plenty of opportunities for practice, any student who is willing to work hard can learn the basics of the Japanese language.

CHAPTER 1

PRONUNCIATION AND THE WRITING SYSTEM

Japanese is normally written in a mixture of Chinese characters (*kanji*), which represent units of meaning, and syllabic characters (*kana*), which represent the sounds of syllables. The *kana* are further divided into *hiragana*, which are used to write Japanese words, and *katakana*, which are used mostly to write foreign words, although both *hiragana* and *katakana* cover exactly the same repertoire of sounds.

Japanese schoolchildren first learn the *hiragana* and *katakana*, after which they can write phonetically anything they can say. However, they still face several grueling years of memorizing the 1,945 officially recognized *kanji*. (The situation could be worse: Chinese schoolchildren need to learn about 3,000 *kanji*, and they have no *hiragana* to fall back on when they're stuck!)

PRONOUNCING JAPANESE—THE BASIC SOUNDS

The words that the Japanese have borrowed from foreign languages rarely survive the experience unscathed. "Ice cream" becomes *aisu kuriimu*, "helicopter" becomes *herikoputaa*, "consultant" becomes *konsarutanto*, and "studio" becomes *sutajio*. These words in fact illustrate some of the characteristics of the Japanese sound system.

There are only five basic vowels, and they are always listed in the same order as on the chart on page 2 and pronounced the same way every time. Remember that these descriptions of the sounds are *only an approximation*. If at all possible, you should ask a native speaker to pronounce these syllables for you and coach you in pronunciation. Even if that is impossible, you will still be better off pronouncing Japanese words according to these approximations than making up your own pronunciation according to what you *think* the words should sound like.

The syllables in these charts are given in both the Latin alphabet and *hiragana*. The *hiragana* are for the benefit of any Japanese people who may be helping you with pronunciation.

English Letter	Hiragana	Sound
a	あ	like "ah," but shorter. (never pronounced like the "a" of "ape")
i	い	like the "i" of "machine," but shorter. (never pronounced like the "i" of "ice")
u	う	like the "oo" in "food," but with the lips unrounded and held for a shorter time. (never pronounced like the "u" of "uniform")
e	え	like the "e" in "set." (never pronounced like the "e" in "evil")
o	お	like "o" in "note," but shorter. (never pronounced like the "o" of "dot")

It is important to understand that Japanese vowels are held for a much shorter time than the English vowels they resemble. For example, the "oo" of "food" is held about twice as long as the Japanese *u*. In fact, in Japanese terms, it would be a *long u*, and each Japanese vowel has a long counterpart:

English Letter	Hiragana	Sound
aa	ああ	like " ah."
ii	いい	like the "i" of "machine."
û	うう	like the "oo" in "food," but with the lips unrounded.
(usually written "ei," sometimes "ee")	えい or ええ	Like "e," but held longer. (never pronounced like the "ei" of "receive" or the "ei" of "Heidi")
usually written "ô," sometimes "oo")	おう or おお	like the English word "go."

English speakers have a hard time hearing and producing the difference between the long and short vowels, but it is a very important distinction. For example, *koko* (ここ) means "here," *kôkô* (こうこう) means "high school," *kôko* (こうこ) means "municipal treasury" and *kokô* (ここう) means "arc light." You can live in Japan for years without ever hearing the last two words, but the first two are very common.

Note that there are two ways to write long *o* and long *e* in *hiragana*. For the benefit of students who are familiar with Japanese writing, we will preserve this distinction in our Latin alphabet transcriptions. The long *o*'s that are written おう in hiragana will be written *ô* in this book, while the long *o*'s that are written おお in *hiragana* or *katakana* will be written *oo*. The long *e*'s that are written えい in *hiragana* will be written *ei* in this book, while the long *e*'s that are written ええ in *hiragana* or *katakana* will be written *ee*. Note, however, that the two spelling variants of each long vowel are pronounced exactly the same.

WATCH OUT

English speakers tend to not pronounce vowels clearly in unaccented syllables, turning them into a sort of "uh" sound. (Try saying "difficult," "eligible," or "ignorant," and you'll hear those "uh" sounds.) There's nothing wrong with that kind of pronunciation—so long as you're speaking English. When you're speaking Japanese, however, always pronounce the vowels clearly.

The consonants are a lot simpler, but there are a few quirks in the system that you need to be aware of. You should have no trouble with the following syllables, so we'll get them out of the way.

ka か	ba ば	pa ぱ	na な	ma ま	ya や	wa わ
ki き	bi び	pi ぴ	ni に	mi み		
ku く	bu ぶ	pu ぷ	nu ぬ	mu む	yu ゆ	
ke け	be べ	pe ぺ	ne ね	me め		
ko こ	bo ぼ	po ぽ	no の	mo も	yo よ	wo を

Note that there are gaps in the chart. The syllables *yi, ye, wi,* and *we* are no longer used in modern Japanese, and so far as we know, there was never a syllable *wu*. The syllable *wo* (を) is now pronounced *o* and used only as a grammatical particle, not in spelling out words.

The g-syllables are always pronounced with the *g* of "get," not the *g* of "germ." In some parts of Japan, including Tokyo, -*g*- in the middle of a word or in the sentence particle *ga* is pronounced like the -*ng* in "ring" (not the -*ng*- in "finger"), but people will still understand you if you stick to the plain old *g*.

English	Hiragana	Sound
ga	が	"gah"
gi	ぎ	"ghee"
gu	ぐ	"gooh"
ge	げ	"gheh"
go	ご	"go"

The s-initial syllables are pretty straightforward, except that they are pronounced with the tongue farther forward than when pronouncing the English *s*. However, in the slot where we would expect to find *si*, we find something different:

sa	さ	"sah"
shi	し	"shee" (your tongue should be almost touching your teeth)
su	す	"sooh"
se	せ	"seh"
so	そ	"so"

The z-syllables work in a similar way, since they are simply the s-syllables with *nigori*, two small marks that indicate voicing. Note that when people are speaking slowly, you may hear a bit of a *d* sound before the z, because the tongue is farther forward than the position for pronouncing the English *z*.

za	ざ	"(d)zah"
ji	じ	"jee"
zu	ず	"(d)zooh"
ze	ぜ	"(d)zeh"
zo	ぞ	"(d)zo"

The t-initial syllables, pronounced with the tip of the tongue hitting the gum and base of the upper teeth, hold even more surprises.

ta	た	"tah"
chi	ち	"chee"
tsu	つ	"tsooh" (Start with a "t" and release it with a hiss.)
te	て	"teh"
to	と	"toh"

WATCH OUT

North Americans tend to change *t* to *d* in the middle of a word, so that "matter" and "madder" sound exactly the same. That's fine if you're speaking English, but not if you're speaking Japanese. The ancient capital of Japan is Kyôto, not Kyôdo, and *mata* "again" and *mada* "still, not yet," are clearly distinguished.

Meanwhile, the d-syllables partly overlap with the z-syllables. When writing in *hiragana*, じ and ず are used 99 percent of the time. The ぢ and づ alternatives are used in a few isolated words for historical reasons, but they are pronounced exactly the same.

da	だ	"dah"
ji	ぢ	"jee"
zu	づ	"(d)zooh"
de	で	"deh"
do	ど	"doh"

The Japanese language does not have any native words containing the sounds *ti, tu, si, di, zi,* or *du,* although words borrowed from foreign languages may contain these sounds. In such cases, the *katakana* syllabary handles the words with special spelling rules, which are given in Chapter 2.

The h-syllables are pretty predictable, but *hu* is usually transcribed into English as *fu,* as in *Mt. **Fuji**.* The English *f* is formed by placing the lower lip against the upper front teeth, but the *hu* syllable is formed by bringing both lips together as if you are about to blow out a candle.

ha	は	"hah"
hi	ひ	"hee"
fu	ふ	"fhooh"
he	へ	"heh"
ho	ほ	"ho"

You're probably aware of the stereotype that says that Japanese people have trouble telling the difference between *r* and *l*. This stereotype happens to be absolutely true. Unless they have learned a foreign language in childhood, most Japanese can neither hear nor produce the difference between these two consonants. The reason is that the Japanese sound usually transcribed as *r* is really halfway between *r* and *l*, and as people speak, the sound drifts sometimes closer to *r* and sometimes closer to *l*, but it doesn't make any difference which direction the sound drifts in. (Of course, English speakers have trouble with the difference between the long and short vowels and the difference between *su* and *tsu*, so it all comes out even in the end.)

To produce an authentic-sounding Japanese *r*, start to say an *l*, but make your tongue stop short of the roof of your mouth, so that it flaps in empty space. If you can't manage that, a flapped *r* (not a rolled *r*) or an *l* is a better option than an American English *r*.

ra	ら	"rah" or "lah"
ri	り	"ree" or "lee"
ru	る	"rooh" or "looh"
re	れ	"reh" or "leh"
ro	ろ	"ro" or "lo"

The final syllable in the repertoire is the so-called syllabic nasal, represented by the *hiragana* ん. It is usually transcribed *n*, but it is different from the *n-* of *na, ni, nu, ne, no* in that it can come only at the end of a syllable, so you can't spell *na* as んあ, only as な. Another point to note is that the syllabic nasal is held as long as any other syllable. In the word *anzen* "safety," for example, the two syllabic nasals each take as much time to say as the *a* and the *ze*. In songs, the syllabic nasal can even be sung on its own note, separately from the other syllables. Finally, the syllabic nasal is a bit of a chameleon, because it is pronounced as *m* when it appears before *-b-, -p-,* or *-m-; ng* when it appears before *-k-* or *-g-;* and simple nasalization (like talking with a stuffy nose) when it appears before a vowel. Here are some examples:

> *kantan* (かんたん) "simple" (kah-n-tah-n)
> *shinbun* (しんぶん) "newspaper" (shee-m-booh-n)
> *nanpa* (なんぱ) "shipwreck" (nah-m-pah)
> *manga* (まんが) "comic book" (mah-ng-gah)
> *genki* (げんき) "healthy" (gheh-ng-kee)
> *zen'in* (ぜんいん) "the whole staff" (zeh-ⁿ-ee-n)[1]
> (compare: *zenin* [ぜにん] "endorsement" [zeh-nee-n])
> *han'ei* (はんえい) "reflection" (hah-ⁿ-eeh)

---

1 The small raised *n* indicates nasalization.

A SPIRITUAL LAND

Torii Gate, Miyajima Yashima

Kasuga Shrine, Nara

All photos courtesy of Japan National Tourist Organization (JNTO)

Heian Shrine, Kyoto

The Great Bronze Buddha in Kamakura

CHAPTER 2

MORE SOUNDS AND INTONATION

Now that we have our full repertoire of sounds, here are some variations on them. First of all, consonants as well as vowels can be doubled. When doubling a consonant, hold it for twice as long as a single consonant before releasing it, almost as if you're bouncing off the sound. (If you speak Italian, you already know how to do this.) Don't stop the first consonant and start over; just delay the release for a bit. Ask your language coach to demonstrate the difference by pronouncing the following pairs of words for you.

> *mata* （また）"again" (mah-tah)
> *matta* （まった）"waited" (mah-ttah)
> *saka* （さか）"hill" (sah-kah)
> *sakka* （さっか）"author" (sah-kkah)
> *kona* （こな）"powder" (koh-nah)
> *konna* （こんな）"this kind of" (koh-n-nah)

The final variation is palatalization, or putting a bit of a *y* sound after the consonant.

kya	hya	nya	mya	rya	gya	bya	pya
きゃ	ひゃ	にゃ	みゃ	りゃ	ぎゃ	びゃ	ぴゃ
kyu	hyu	nyu	myu	ryu	gyu	byu	pyu
きゅ	ひゅ	にゅ	みゅ	りゅ	ぎゅ	びゅ	ぴゅ
kyo	hyo	nyo	myo	ryo	gyo	byo	pyo
きょ	ひょ	にょ	みょ	りょ	ぎょ	びょ	ぴょ

Be careful when pronouncing these palatalized syllables, because they are *one* syllable each. The name of the southernmost major island of Japan, Kyûshû, is pronounced almost as if it were spelled "Q-shoe." Looking at the name of the ancient capital of Japan, English speakers tend to pronounce it "Kee-yoh-do," when it's actually pronounced "Kyo-oh-to." If you have trouble producing the *kyo* syllable, it may help to start by saying "q" and change the vowel at the end from "oo" to "oh." There, you have it!

Once again, these are all *single* syllables. The traditional Japanese inn, the *ryokan*, is not a "rye-oh-can," which sounds like an over-the-counter medicine, but a "ryo-kah-n." Also remember that the g-syllables are always, invariably, 100 percent of the time pronounced with the hard *g* of "get," no exceptions, no bending the rules, none of this pronouncing them with *j* sounds.

Ask your language coach to demonstrate the differences between the following pairs of syllables:

kyô (きょう) "today" (kyo-oh)
kiyô (きよう) "bulletin" (ki-yoh-oh)
ryû (りゅう) "dragon" (ryoo-oo)
riyû (りゆう) "reason" (ree-yoo-oo)
hyô (ひょう) "chart" (hyo-oh)
hiyô (ひよう) "expenses" (hee-yo-oh)

When you palatalize *t-*, *s-*, and *z-* syllables, something quite different happens. You get *ch-*syllables, *sh-*syllables, and *j-*syllables. (Yes, this is how you spell the j-syllables.)

cha ちゃ	sha しゃ	ja じゃ
chu ちゅ	shu しゅ	ju じゅ
cho ちょ	sho しょ	jo じょ

WATCH OUT

Some students of French have learned their lessons too well: they pronounce the Japanese j-syllables as if they were French j-syllables, that is, as "zh." Save that sound for Paris, because it won't get you anywhere in Tokyo. While you're at it, lose the French "u," too.

Since the end of World War II, the Japanese have developed **katakana** spellings for several foreign syllables that don't occur in their own language:

フア fa	フィ fi		フェ fe	フォ fo
	セイ si			
	ティ ti	トゥ tu		
	ディ di	ドゥ du		
	ウィ wi		ウェ we	ウォ wo
ヴァ va	ヴィ vi	ヴ vu	ヴェ ve	ヴォ vo
ツァ tsa	ツィ tsi		ツェ tse	ツォ tso
			チェ che	
			シェ she	
			ジェ je	

SYLLABLES, ACCENT, AND INTONATION
(OR, WHY THE JAPANESE TALK SO FAST)

Some textbooks tell you that the Japanese speak in a monotone. The trouble with that description is that it calls to mind an electronically synthesized robot-like voice, which is not what Japanese speech sounds like at all. What those textbook writers are trying to do is contrast Japanese speech patterns with English, so it may help to know something of how linguists describe English accentuation.

When English speakers accent a syllable, they pronounce it louder and hold it longer than they would an unaccented syllable. Also, they unconsciously speed up between accented syllables, giving their speech a kind of uneven, stop-and-start feel. On the other hand, Japanese speakers spend an equal amount of time on each syllable and don't speed up between accented syllables. In fact, Japanese accentuation consists of saying the syllable on a slightly higher pitch, without slowing down or getting louder. As a result, compared to the irregular rhythm of English, Japanese sounds like a steadily flowing stream.

This is one reason that students believe that Japanese people talk too fast. The other reason is that all unfamiliar languages sound fast to an outsider. Actually, just about any Japanese person will tell you that North Americans speak English too fast.

Despite the fact that each syllable is supposed to take the same length of time, *i* and *u* can virtually disappear if they're stuck between any two of the so-called voiceless consonants, *t*, *s*, *f*, *p*, or *k*, and sometimes if they are at the end of a word. Technically speaking, the vowels get "whispered," but to an English speaker it sounds as if they have disappeared. Here are some examples:

Rômaji Spelling	Hiragana	Pronunciation	Meaning
suki	すき	s'kee	"liked"
shite	して	sh'teh	"doing"
kusuri	くすり	k'suree	"medicine"
tasukeru	たすける	tah-s'keh-rooh	"to rescue"
fukin	ふきん	f'kee-n	"vicinity"
shikata	しかた	sh'kah-tah	"way of doing"
yoshi	よし	yoh-sh	"okay"
desu	です	dess	"it is"
~masu	~ます	~mahs	(polite verbal ending)
~mashita	~ました	~mah-sh'tah	(past tense of *~masu*)
deshita	でした	desh'tah	"it was"

The final area of Japanese pronunciation that you need to concern yourself with is accent and intonation. If you speak Japanese with English intonation, Japanese people will hear your "sentence melody" before they hear your words, and they will simply assume that you are speaking English. The aspect that gives English speakers the most trouble is the intonation of questions. Here are the typical question intonation patterns for North American English: (The raised and lowered letters represent high and low pitch.)

For questions beginning with wh-words:

Where ^{is} it?

What are you ^{do}-ing?

Why $^{can't}$ you?

The intonation on the corresponding Japanese sentences is like this:

^{Do}-ko $_{desu}$ ^{ka}?

^{Na}-ni $_{o\ shite\ imasu}$ ^{ka}?

^{Do}-oshite dekinai n desu ^{ka}?

For yes-no questions, the typical English intonation is:

Do you under$^{stand?}$

Is it $^{yours?}$

Can you $^{swim?}$

The intonation on the corresponding Japanese sentences is like this:

$_{Wa}$*karimasu* $^{ka?}$

A ^{na} *ta no desu ka?*

$_{O}$*yogemasu* $^{ka?}$

No accentuation or intonation will be marked in the Japanese materials within this book. In most cases, accentuation does not differentiate words, and anyway, it differs from region to region. For example, a certain large city in central Japan is called *Na-*^{go}*-ya* by its inhabitants and ^{Na}*-go-ya* by people in the Tokyo-Yokohama area. Just listen to and imitate spoken Japanese as much as possible, and soon you will be accenting words in an acceptable manner without thinking about it.

The Japanese-language material in this book is written in the Latin alphabet, but the Japanese script version will be given in the vocabulary boxes. You should not try to copy these on your own unless you have already learned the basic principles of Japanese writing or have someone who can act as your writing coach. Untrained English-speakers tend to "draw" rather than write *kanji,* and doing so can result in characters that are unreadable by a native speaker. However, if you learn to recognize a few words, so much the better.

Here are some Japanese words that you may have seen in print or heard people use, along with their customary North American pronunciations and their real Japanese pronunciations:

Word	Typical American Pronunciation	Actual Japanese Pronunciation
karaoke カラオケ	carry-okie	kah-rah-oh-keh
geisha げいしゃ	ghee-shuh or guy-shuh	ge-eh-sha
shôgun しょうぐん	shoh-g'n	sho-oh-gooh-n
sukiyaki すきやき	sooky-yocky	s'kee-yah-kee
kamikaze かみかぜ	comma-cozzy	kah-mee-kah-zeh
hibachi ひばち	huh-botchy	hee-bah-ch'
samurai さむらい	sammer-eye	sah-moo-rah-ee
futon ふとん	foo tahn	f'toh n
harakiri はらきり	harry carry	hah-rah-kee-ree
sake さけ	socky	sah-keh
karate から て	kuh-roddy	kah-rah-teh
ikebana いけばな	icky-banna	ee-keh-bah-nah
kimono きもの	kuh-mona	kee-mo-no

And now, before you move toward the new chapter, look at the map of Japan and learn the names of the main cities.

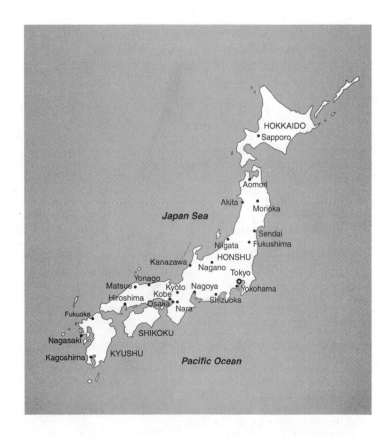

CHAPTER 3

DÔZO YOROSHIKU! PLEASED TO MEET YOU!

In this chapter you will learn to:

1. greet people and exchange pleasantries
2. ask for and acknowledge favors
3. introduce yourself
4. say good-bye

GREETINGS AND PLEASANTRIES

When Japanese people run into an acquaintance out in public, they typically make a vague comment about the weather. They don't inquire about the other person's health unless they really want to know, such as when meeting an acquaintance who has recently been ill. The typical pattern is:

A: (appropriate greeting for the time of day)
B: (appropriate greeting for the time of day)
A: (comment about the weather)
B: (agrees with A's comment)

Let's take a look at some of the phrases used in these encounters. At this point, don't worry about the individual words or grammar involved.

At different times of the day:

Ohayô [gozaimasu*]	Good morning
Konnichi wa	Good day, good afternoon (used after about 10:00 A.M.)
Konban wa	Good evening

---

*The form with *gozaimasu* is more polite. Use it with everyone who is not a family member, a close friend, or a child.

Comments about the weather:

Ii o-tenki desu nee.	It's nice weather, isn't it?
Atsui desu nee.	It's hot, isn't it?
Samui desu nee.	It's cold, isn't it?
Yoku furimasu nee.	It's really coming down, isn't it? (rain, snow)
Sô desu nee.	It sure is, isn't it?

Just in case you need to inquire about someone's health, here's how you do it:

O-genki desu ka?	Are you in good health?
Ee, okagesama de.*	Yes, thank you for asking.

Okagesama de can be used whenever you can announce good news in answer to someone's concerned inquiry, such as when someone asks if you have found a job, and indeed you have found one.

If you happen to disagree with the other person's comment about the weather, don't argue. That's not the point—it's just a greeting, not the beginning of a serious discussion about the current barometric pressure.

The intonation on these comments is like this:

I_{-i} o-^{te}-n-ki $desu$ ^{ne}-e.

A-^{tsu}-i $desu$ ^{ne}-e.

So-$_o$ $desu$ ^{ne}-e.

If you can, have a Japanese person pronounce these phrases for you and coach you on your intonation.

Practice 3.1

Mr. Tanaka and Ms. Suzuki live in the same neighborhood and commute to work from the same subway stop. Here are three of the encounters they had last week. For each one, tell what time of the day it was and what the weather was like.

1. Tanaka: Ohayô gozaimasu.
   Suzuki: Ohayô gozaimasu.
   Tanaka: Ii o-tenki desu nee.
   Suzuki: Sô desu nee.

2. Suzuki: Konnichi wa.
   Tanaka: Konnichi wa.
   Suzuki: Atsui desu nee.
   Tanaka: Sô desu nee.

3. Tanaka: Konban wa.
   Suzuki: Konban wa.
   Tanaka: Yoku furimasu nee.
   Suzuki: Sô desu nee.

1._____ 2._____ 3._____

Practice 3.2

Now make up your own dialogue for Mr. Tanaka and Ms. Suzuki. Use today's actual weather and the time of day you are working on this exercise.

_____

_____

_____

_____

PLEASE AND THANK YOU

Here are some expressions used when requesting and acknowledging favors. Again, don't try to analyze the grammar or individual words at this point.

[Chotto] o-negai shimasu.	Please [help me a little].
_____ o-negai shimasu.	Please give me _____. Please do _____ for me.
Dôzo.	Please feel free. Please accept this. Here is what you asked for.
_____ o dôzo.	Here is a/some _____ for you. Have some_____.
_____wa?	How about some _____?
Arigatô [gozaimasu].*	Thank you.
Dômo arigatô [gozaimasu]	Thank you very much.
Sumimasen.	I'm sorry [to have made you go to all this trouble]. Thank you [for the unexpected favor].
Okamai naku.	Don't bother; don't go to any trouble.
Iie.	No; it's nothing (as a response to thanks or an apology).
Hai or Ee	Yes.
Dewa, itadakimasu.	Well then, I accept.
Iie, kekkô desu.	No, I'm fine. I don't want any.
Dômo.	Thanks!
Dô itashimashite.	You're welcome.

*As with the greetings, the forms with _gozaimasu_ are more polite.

If you are visiting in a private home and your hosts offer you food or drink, it is considered polite to refuse at first. _Okamai naku_ is the standard phrase for these polite refusals. Your hosts will ask you again, and then you may accept. If you really don't want the food or beverage, take a little bit just to be polite, or, if you really cannot eat or drink what is offered for reasons of health or because of your religious beliefs, accept anyway and leave it untouched. If you are living with a family and eating meals with them regularly, you don't have to be so formal, and you can refuse with phrases such as _iie, kekkô desu._

Here are some examples of how these phrases are used.

1. Mr. Yamada and Mr. Satô are in their company's reference library. Mr. Yamada needs a book from the top shelf, so he asks Mr. Satô, who is taller, for some help.

Yamada:	Chotto o-negai shimasu.
Satô:	Dôzo.
Yamada:	Arigatô gozaimasu.
Satô:	Iie.

Yamada:	Could you get that for me?
Satô:	Here you go.
Yamada:	Thank you.
Satô:	No problem.

2. Ms. Itô is presenting Ms. Kimura, a co-worker, with a souvenir that she brought back from her vacation.

Itô:	Dôzo.
Kimura:	A, dômo arigatô gozaimasu.
Itô:	Iie, dô itashimashite.

Itô:	This is for you.
Kimura:	Oh, thank you very much.
Itô:	You're welcome.

3. Amanda Smith, a Canadian exchange student, has been invited to the home of Professor Takahashi for lunch. Professor Takahashi's wife brings out some iced coffee.

Takahashi:	Aisu koohii o dôzo.
Smith:	Okamai naku.
Takahashi:	Dôzo, dôzo.
Smith:	De wa, itadakimasu.

Takahashi:	Please have some iced coffee.
Smith:	Don't go to any trouble.
Takahashi:	Please feel free.
Smith:	All right, I'll have some.

INTRODUCTIONS

Watakushi OR Watashi OR Boku	(wa)_____ desu. OR (wa)_____ de gozaimasu.	I am_____. (*Watakushi* is formal. *Boku* is the least formal of the three and is used only by males, but both males and females use *watashi*.)
(Company/school) no (Name) desu.		I am (Name) from (Company/School)
Hajimemashite.		Pleased to meet you.
(Dôzo) yoroshiku (o-negai itashimasu).		Please treat me well in our future encounters.
Kochira koso.		Same here.
Shitsurei desu ga		Excuse me for asking, but...
(Name)+-san		Mr./Ms. (Name)
daigaku		college, university
kôkô		high school
_____ -san desu ka.		Are you Mr./Ms. _____?
Iie, chigaimasu.		No, you're mistaken.
Shitsurei shimashita.		I'm sorry (to have done that).

• As with the other expressions, the forms with *gozaimasu* are more polite.

• Your school or work affiliation is considered very important in Japanese society. In fact, if you call a business office and give only your name, the receptionist will ask you what company you represent.

• In Japan, the family name comes before the given name. Thus Tanaka Akira is a man named Akira who belongs to the Tanaka family. (Japanese people do not have middle names.) However, everyone knows that people in Western countries put the given name first, so you can introduce yourself without reversing your name.

• The title -*san* is used for both males and females, and it may be attached either to the family name or the given name. It is a respectful title, so you must not attach it to your own name or to the name of one of your family members.

• Outside their families or circle of closest lifelong friends, Japanese adults are rarely addressed by their given names, even by neighbors or co-workers. Thus if you are introduced to Tanaka Akira, you should address him as *Tanaka-san*, not *Akira-san*. If you go to Japan as a student, people will probably address you by your given name, but if you go to Japan on business, introduce yourself with your last name only.

• When Japanese people introduce themselves, particularly in business situations, they exchange business cards called *meishi*. Treat another person's *meishi* respectfully, and after studying it carefully, put it in your wallet or credit card holder; don't cram it into a pocket.

Here are some examples.

1. Ms. Blake of Widgetronics, an Australian high tech company, has just arrived at the offices of Technopoly, a potential client in Tokyo. Mr. Murakami greets her. They present their business cards to each other.

Blake:	Watakushi wa, Uijetoronikkusu no Bureeku de gozaimasu. Hajimemashite. Dôzo yoroshiku o-negai itashimasu.
Murakami:	Hajimemashite. Tekunoporii no Murakami de gozaimasu. Kochira koso yoroshiku o-negai itashimasu.

Blake:	I'm Ms. Blake from Widgetronics. I'm glad to meet you. I hope our dealings go well.
Murakami:	Pleased to meet you. I'm Mr. Murakami from Technopoly. I, too, hope that things go well between us.

2. Thomas Wilson, an American student from Academia University, arrives at Tokyo's Narita Airport to begin a junior year abroad. He has been told that Ms. Hasegawa, a representative of Intergaku Student Exchange Agency will meet him there. All he knows about Ms. Hasegawa is that she is short, wears glasses, and has long hair. He approaches a woman who matches that description.

Wilson:	Shitsurei desu ga, Intaagaku no Hasegawa-san desu ka.
Woman:	Iie, chigaimasu.
Wilson:	A, shitsurei shimashita.
Woman:	Iie.

Wilson:	Excuse me, but are you Ms. Hasegawa from Intergaku?

Woman: No, you're mistaken.
Wilson: Sorry to have bothered you.
Woman: It's nothing.

He spots another woman who matches the description, and she is surveying the crowd of international travelers. He approaches her.

Wilson: Shitsurei desu ga, Intaagaku no Hasegawa-san
           desu ka.
Hasegawa: Hai, sô desu.
Wilson: Watakushi, Akademia Daigaku no Tomasu Uiruson
           desu. Dôzo yoroshiku o-negai itashimasu.
Hasegawa: Intaagaku no Hasegawa desu. Kochira koso
           yoroshiku o-negai itashimasu.

Wilson: Excuse me, but are you Ms. Hasegawa from
           Intergaku?
Hasegawa: Yes, that's right.
Wilson: I'm Thomas Wilson from Academia University. I
           hope things go well.
Hasegawa: I'm Ms. Hasegawa from Intergaku. I, too, hope that
           things go well.

FAREWELLS

Most people know that *sayonara* is a Japanese word for "good-bye," but it is not appropriate for all circumstances. Here are some other phrases commonly used.

Ki o tsukete.	Take care.
Sayonara OR Sayônara	Good-bye.
(Kore de) shitsurei shimasu.	I'm going to [be rude and] leave now.
Itte mairimasu. Itte kimasu.	Good-bye. (Said by a person leaving home: "I'll go and come.") Itte kimasu is informal.
Itte irasshai.	Good-bye. (The response to *itte kimasu* given by the people remaining at home: "Please go and come.")
Ja, mata.	See you later. (informal)
Ja, ne.	'Bye! (extremely informal)
Gochisôsama deshita.	Thank you for the food/drink.

- *Shitsurei shimasu* is a formal expression used when announcing that you are leaving someone's presence or when you are leaving before someone else.
- People do not normally say *Sayonara* when leaving their own homes or places of temporary residence unless they are leaving for a very long time.

Here are some examples of how these phrases are used.

1. Amanda Smith has finished having lunch at Professor Takahashi's house. After staying and talking for a while, she decides that it's time to go home. Here is the conversation they have at the door.

Smith:	Kore de shitsurei shimasu. Gochisôsama deshita.
Takahashi:	Iie. Ki o tsukete. Sayonara.
Smith:	Sayonara.

Smith:	I'm going to leave now. Thank you for the food.
Takahashi:	You're welcome. Take care. Good-bye.
Smith:	Good-bye.

2. Eric Jones, an American student, is living with a host family, the Yamadas. As he leaves for class in the morning, his host mother, Mrs. Yamada, sees him off at the door.

Jones:	Itte kimasu.
Yamada:	Itte irasshai.

Jones:	Good-bye.
Yamada:	Good-bye.

3. Kobayashi Mayumi and Nakamura Takashi are students in the same class. After class they talk for a while, and then they have to go off to different club meetings.

Nakamura:	Ja, mata.
Kobayashi:	Ja, ne.

Nakamura:	See you later.
Kobayashi:	'Bye!

Cultural Note: How to Bow

The bow (*ojigi*) is an essential part of Japanese daily life. People bow when saying hello, when thanking someone, when apologizing, when saying good-bye, and when introducing themselves.

The deeper you bow, the more respect you are showing. Men and women bow differently. Men bow with their hands held at their sides, palms facing inward. Women bow with their hands crossed in front of them. You may see parents coaching small children on the proper form, placing their hands in the correct position and "folding" them at the waist.

There is also a "bow on the run" called an *eshaku*. This consists of bobbing forward briefly as you turn your head toward the person you are greeting.

If you live in Japan for any length of time, you will begin bowing automatically as you say certain expressions. Like the Japanese people around you, you will even bow as you talk on the phone, simply because the action is so closely linked to the words.

SUMMING UP
MATOME
まとめ

A. What would you say in response to each of these phrases?

1. Ii o-tenki desu ne.

2. Arigatô gozaimasu.

3. O-genki desu ka.

4. Dôzo yoroshiku o-negai itashimasu.

5. Itte kimasu.

B. Complete the following dialogues according to the cues given.

1. Your last name is Miller, and you are going to Japan either on business or for school. You know that Mr. Sonoda is scheduled to meet you at the airport. You are the only non-Japanese in the crowd, so Mr. Sonoda walks up to you and starts talking. Write in your half of the dialogue.

Sonoda:	Shitsurei desu ga, Miraa-san desu ka.
You:	(confirm his guess)
Sonoda:	Watakushi wa, Sonoda de gozaimasu. Dôzo yoroshiku onegai itashimasu.
You:	(give your name, using the name of your actual school or employer and saying that you hope all goes well.)

2. You are visiting the Tomitas.

Tomita:	Kôhii o dôzo.
You:	(refuse politely for the sake of form)
Tomita:	Dôzo, dôzo.
You:	(accept)

3. You're at work. Your colleague Ms. Wada points at the eraser that is on your desk.

Wada:	Chotto o-negai shimasu.
You:	(hand it over to her)
Wada:	Dômo.
You:	(respond)

4. You are leaving the Tomitas' house.

Tomita: Sayonara. Ki o tsukete.
You: (thank them for the food and say goodbye)

CHAPTER 4

NANI? DARE? ITSU? IKURA? (WHAT? WHO? WHEN? HOW MUCH?)

In this chapter, you will learn to:

1. ask basic informational questions to identify objects and people
2. count in Japanese and ask prices
3. tell time on the hour

IDENTIFYING OBJECTS AND PEOPLE

One of the most important foreign language skills is asking questions, and you definitely need to know the great vocabulary-building question, the basic form of which is:

Nan	desu	ka?
what	is/are	(question mark)
What is it?		

WATCH OUT

As an English speaker, you will be tempted to give the question the intonation Nan ^{desu} ka, but unless you use the Japanese intonation, ^{Na}-$_n$ $desu$ ^{ka}, people may think you are speaking English.

Nan, which is also pronounced $nani$ in other contexts, is "what." Ka is a spoken question mark. $Desu$ can be translated as "is, are," but it's a special kind of "is, are," one that acts as an equal sign. The Japanese equivalents of these English sentences would contain $desu$.

We are students. (we = students)
Tokyo is the capital of Japan. (Tokyo = capital of Japan)
Tempura is delicious. (tempura = delicious)

The Japanese equivalents of these sentences would **not** contain *desu*.

> There are volcanoes in Japan.
> I am practicing Japanese.

The bare question *nan desu ka* is rarely used all by itself, except when responding to one's name or reacting to something startling. Let's say that you've encountered some unrecognizable object during your travels in Japan, so you want to ask what it is. In English you might say, "What is this?" or "What is that?" In Japanese, you need one of these three words plus a question word:

kore	sore	are	dore
this thing, this one	that thing by you or near both of us, that one by you or near both of us	that thing over there, that one over there	which one? which thing?

Put the first three together with *nan desu ka*, and you get:

Kore this thing					What is this?
Sore that thing	wa topic marker	nan what	desu is/are	ka ?	What is that nearby?
Are that thing over there					What is that over there?

Wa, spelled は in *hiragana*, has no English equivalent. It tells you that the noun in front of it is the **topic** of the sentence. What comes after *wa* is the **comment**. In other words, the part before the *wa* tells you what you're talking about, and the part after *wa* contains the question or information about the **topic**.

Kore	wa	nan	desu	ka
Sore				
Are				
NOUN	wa	question word	desu	ka
TOPIC	wa	COMMENT		

To reply to a "what" question, simply substitute the answer for *nan*. Often students get confused at the early stages because they can't believe it's that simple, so they try to rearrange the words. Also remember to change *kore*, *sore*, or *are*, depending on where the object is in relation to you. And don't forget to take the *ka* off, since your answer is a statement, not a question.

Sore	wa	nan	desu	ka
↓	↓	↓	↓	
Kore	wa	obi	desu	

What is that?
This is an *obi* (*kimono* sash).

Kore	wa	nan	desu	ka
↓	↓	↓	↓	
Sore	wa	nattô	desu	

What is this?
That is *nattô* (fermented soybeans).

Are	wa	nan	desu	ka
↓	↓	↓	↓	
Are	wa	o-tera	desu	

What is that over there?
That over there is a [Buddhist] temple.

You can change that last answer, or virtually any Japanese sentence, into a question, simply by adding *ka*.

Are	wa	o-tera	desu	
↓	↓	↓	↓	
Are	wa	o-tera	desu	ka.
Is that one over there a temple				?

Is that-thing-over-there a temple?

If it indeed is a temple, two possible answers are:

Hai, OR Ee,	o-tera	desu.
Yes, it's a temple.		

Hai, OR Ee,	sô	desu.
Yes, that's right. (That's so.)		

If it's not a temple, but a shrine (a Shinto place of worship), a possible answer is:

Iie, No	jinja desu.
Chigaimasu. You're mistaken; It's different from what you said;	It's a shrine.

No, it's a shrine.

If you first want to say that it's *not* a temple or an *obi* or *nattô* or whatever, you need to know how to negate a sentence with NOUN + *desu.* Here's the pattern:

NOUN	desu.
↓	↓
NOUN	de wa arimasen.
	de wa nai desu.
	ja arimasen.
	ja nai desu.

It isn't NOUN.

At this point, you may be wondering, "*De wa arimasen* and *ja nai desu* are the negative forms of *desu*? I don't see any connection! What a weird language! I give up!" But never fear: *desu* is irregular, and those of you who have studied a European language will be delighted to know that nearly all Japanese verbs are regular. *De wa* is more formal than *ja*, which is more common in ordinary conversation. Similarly, *arimasen* is slightly more formal than *nai desu.*

You may have also noticed that a number of the examples above contain "it" in the English version but there's no corresponding word in the Japanese version. That's because Japanese has no word that means "it," and it uses very few pronouns in general. More on that later.

You can also put other question words into the slot occupied by *nan*, and you answer these questions by substituting the answer for the question word. The parentheses around the topics indicate that they are normally omitted, except in very careful, precise speech. You don't need them, because you already know what you're talking about.

O-matsuri	wa	**itsu**	desu	ka?
↓	↓	↓	↓	
(O-matsuri	wa)	**kyô**	desu.	

When is the festival?
The festival is **today.**

Sono	kôhii	wa	**ikura**	desu	ka
↓	↓	↓	↓	↓	
(Kono	kôhii	wa)	**ichi doru**	desu.	

How much is that coffee?
This coffee is **one dollar**.

Ano	hito	wa	**dare**	desu	ka
	kata		**donata**		
↓	↓	↓	↓	↓	
(Ano	hito/kata	wa)	**Katô-san**	desu.	

Who is that person?
(That person) is **Mr./Ms. Katô.**

Donata and *kata* are more polite than *dare* and *hito*. Use them when you have some reason to believe that the person you are asking about is someone you would have to be polite to.

You've undoubtedly noticed that we have *sono* and *ano* here instead of *sore* and *are*. So what's the difference? The difference is that the words ending in *-re*—*kore, sore, are*, and *dore*—are nouns. They are always used by themselves, **without** any other noun following them. The ones ending in *-no*—*kono, sono*, and *ano*—always come **with** a noun following them.

kono	obi	this kimono sash
kore		this one; this thing

sono	kôhii	that coffee
sore		that one, that thing, that stuff

ano	o-tera	that temple over there,
are		that one over there that thing over there

dono	jinja	which shrine?
dore		which one? which thing?

Vocabulary

kyô	今日	きょう	today
ashita	明日	あした	tomorrow
asatte	明後日	あさって	the day after tomorrow
chokoreeto		チョコレート	chocolate
anko		あんこ	*anko*, sweet bean paste
komarimashita	困りました	こまりました	Oh, no! I'm upset!
sensei	先生	せんせい	teacher, professor, a respectful title
shiken	試験	しけん	test
anô		あのう	uh, umm (a hesitation noise)
hora		ほら	Look there! You see? etc.
naruhodo		なるほど	of course, I see; Oh, I knew that, etc.

Here are some examples of how these words and phrases are used:

1. Ms. King, who has just started working at a Japanese company, is on her way back from lunch with Ms. Shimizu, a co-worker. They stop to look at some cakes and sweet rolls in a bakery window. One of the rolls has been cut open to show a dark brown filling.

Kingu: Sore wa chokoreeto desu ka?
Shimizu: Sore desu ka? Iie, chigaimasu. Anko desu yo.

King: Is that chocolate?
Shimizu: That? No, you're mistaken. It's *anko*.

2. Eric Jones has been sick for a while, and this is his first day back on campus. He vaguely remembers hearing that there is supposed to be an important test in his Japanese language class sometime soon, but he can't remember exactly when it was. He approaches Professor Koyanagi before class.

Jones:	Koyanagi Sensei, ohayô gozaimasu.
Koyanagi:	A, Joonzu-san, ohayô. O-genki desu ka?
Jones:	Ee, okagesama de. Anô, Sensei, shiken wa itsu desu ka?
Koyanagi:	Shiken desu ka? Ashita desu yo.
Jones:	Ashita desu ka? Komarimashita!

Jones:	Good morning, Professor Koyanagi.
Koyanagi:	Oh, Mr. Johnson, good morning. Are you all right?
Jones:	Yes, thanks for asking. Uh, Professor, when is the test?
Koyanagi:	The test? It's tomorrow.
Jones:	Tomorrow? Oh, no!

3. Mr. Tanaka has been talking to a fellow employee from another department. He can't remember the other man's name, and that bothers him. After the unknown man has walked away to talk to someone else, Mr. Tanaka calls Ms. Ishida over to ask if she knows who he is.

Tanaka:	Ano hito wa dare desu ka?
Ishida:	Dono hito desu ka?
Tanaka:	Hora, ano hito desu.
Ishida:	Ano hito desu ka? Saa, Morimoto-san ja arimasen ka?
Tanaka:	A, naruhodo!

Tanaka:	Who is that person over there?
Ishida:	Which person?
Tanaka:	You see? That person over there.
Ishida:	That person? Hmm, isn't it Mr. Morimoto?
Tanaka:	Oh, of course!

• Reading over these dialogues, you're probably asking yourself, "Is there an echo in here?" No, that repetition you see is just a natural Japanese speech pattern. People often echo part of your question before answering it.

• The particle *yo* has no English equivalent. If you put *yo* at the end of a sentence, you are telling your listener either that you think this is new information or that you are contradicting what your listener said. Thus Ms. Shimizu contradicts Ms. King's assumption that the roll filling is made of chocolate by saying *Anko desu yo.* By the way, *anko* is made from sweetened beans, and it doesn't taste the least bit like chocolate.

• Professor Koyanagi says *ohayô* instead of *ohayô gozaimasu* because as an instructor, she ranks above Eric Jones in the Japanese social scheme. Eric Jones uses the longer form, because students are expected to speak politely to instructors. She also calls him *Joonzu-san,* because instructors address university-level students by their family name plus -*san,* not by their given name. This comparative formality has nothing to do with whether the instructor and student like each other or not; it's simply the way the system works.

• Because he's addressing an instructor, Eric Jones expresses his dismay with the formal form of the verb that means "to be upset," "to be a hassle." If he were talking to himself or to a close friend or family member, he would use the plain form, *komatta!*

• *Hora* is an exclamation used when directing someone's attention.

• You can't use *naruhodo* for all the meanings of "of course." It's a comment made when the speaker has been reminded of something or is expressing noncommittal agreement with what the previous speaker has said.

Practice 4.1

Here are some items and places typically found in Japan:

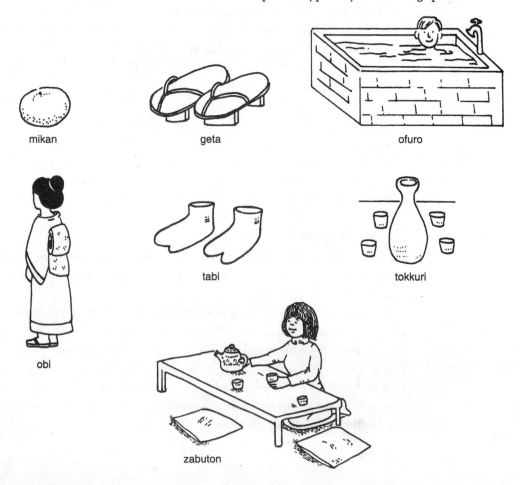

mikan

geta

ofuro

obi

tabi

tokkuri

zabuton

Now here is some additional vocabulary you will need to complete the exercises. Some of these words will be very familiar to you.

orenji	オレンジ		orange
sandaru	サンダル		sandals
puuru	プール		swimming pool
beruto	ベルト		belt
sokkusu	ソックス		socks
kabin	かびん	花瓶	vase
mikan	みかん		Mandarin orange
makura	まくら	枕	pillow

WATCH OUT

Given words like *beruto* and *sokkusu* you may be tempted to pronounce them exactly like the English words they came from. There are two reasons why you shouldn't do that. One is that Japanese people may not recognize such words when they are pronounced in the English manner, and the other is that the words may change their meaning in the process of being borrowed into Japanese, so they aren't really the same words anymore.

Here are some questions about the numbered items on page 36. Answer as indicated in the example.

EXAMPLE:

Kore wa orenji desu ka?
Iie, chigaimasu. Sore wa orenji ja (OR de wa) nai desu (OR arimasen). Mikan desu.
Is this an orange?
No, you're mistaken. That's not an orange. It's a Mandarin orange.

NOTE: You may use any of the variations of the negative.

1. Kore wa sandaru desu ka?

2. Kore wa puuru desu ka?

3. Kore wa beruto desu ka?

4. Kore wa sokkusu desu ka?

5. Kore wa kabin desu ka?

6. Kore wa makura desu ka?

Practice 4.2

Answer the questions on page 39 according to the hints given in the parentheses.

Here are some words you may need:

matsuri	まつり	祭	traditional festival
kaigi	かいぎ	会議	meeting
hito	ひと	人	person
kata	かた	方	person (honorific form)
kyandii	キャンディー		Western-style candy
sashimi	さしみ	刺身	*sashimi*, slices of raw fish
dare	だれ		who?
donata	どなた		who? (honorific form)
itsu	いつ		when?
ikura	いくら		how much? (price)
NAME +sensei	NAME +せんせい	NAME +先生	Dr./Professor NAME
kyô	きょう	今日	today
ashita	あした	明日	tomorrow
asatte	あさって	明後日	the day after tomorrow

WATCH OUT

Ikura is **not** pronounced "ick-YOO-ra," but more like "EE-koo-ra."

• A lot of people in Western countries think that *sushi* is just raw fish, but actually, the word for sliced raw fish served by itself is *sashimi. Sushi* always includes vinegared rice in some form, and it may contain vegetables or a slice of omelet instead of fish.

EXAMPLE:

Matsuri wa itsu desu ka? (today)
(Matsuri wa) kyô desu.
When is the festival?
It's today.

1. Kaigi wa itsu desu ka? (tomorrow)

2. Shiken wa itsu desu ka? (the day after tomorrow)

3. Ano hito wa dare desu ka? (Ms. Suzuki)

4. Ano kata wa donata desu ka? (Professor Iwasaki)

5. Ano kyandii wa ikura desu ka? (one dollar)

6. Are wa nan desu ka? (a shrine)

7. Kore wa nan desu ka? (*sashimi*)

NUMBERS AND PRICES

You may have learned to say "How much is it?" in the previous section, but you can't really answer that question or understand other people's answers unless you have learned some numbers. Here are the basic units. We've included the kanji numerals, because they are often seen on signs.

zero OR rei	ゼロ／れい	零	zero
ichi	いち	一	one
ni	に	二	two
san	さん	三	three
shi OR yon	し/よん	四	four
go	ご	五	five
roku	ろく	六	six
shichi OR nana	しち/なな	七	seven
hachi	はち	八	eight
kyû OR ku	きゅう/く	九	nine
jû	じゅう	十	ten
hyaku	ひゃく	百	hundred(s)
sen	せん	千	thousand(s)
man	まん	万	ten thousand(s)
oku	おく	億	hundred million(s)

All the Japanese numbers that you are likely to need in daily life are made up of these fourteen elements. The alternatives for *four, seven,* and *nine* are used in different contexts. Always use the first alternatives (*shi, shichi,* and *kyû*) when counting out loud. The second alternatives for *four* and *seven* (*yon* and *nana*) are more common in most other contexts, but the first alternative for nine (*kyû*) is used except in a few words having to do with time. In most cases, Japanese people use the familiar Arabic (Western) numerals when they are writing horizontally and *kanji* numerals when they are writing in vertical columns.

WATCH OUT

Be careful with the pronunciation of *hyaku*. The *h + y* combination has to be pronounced all at once, and *hya-* is one syllable.

Practice 4.3

Telephone numbers are very easy in Japanese. Just say the digits in order with a *no* (の) in place of the dash and then add *-ban.*

555-1212 would be *go-go-go-no-ichi-ni-ichi-ni-ban*. If yo area code, put another *no* between the area code and number:

(212) 555-1212 would *ni-ichi-ni-no-go-go-go-no-ichi-ni-ichi-ni-vu*

Try saying the following (fictitious) phone numbers in Japanese:

1. 123-4567

2. 765-4321

3. 5432-1098 (Phone numbers in Tokyo have eight digits.)

4. 987-6543

5. (800) 123-7654

6. Try saying your home phone number, including the area code, in Japanese.

7. Now try saying your work or school phone number, including the area code, if it's different from your home phone number.

To ask what someone's telephone number is, just say:

> NAME san no denwa-bangô wa nanban desu ka?

If your phone number were 918-2736, you would answer the question as follows:

> Watashi no denwa bangô wa kyû-ichi-hachi-no-ni-nana-san-roku-ban desu.

Putting a smaller number in front of a larger one indicates multiplication:

nijû	にじゅう	二十	twenty
nihyaku	にひゃく	二百	two hundred
nisen	にせん	二千	two thousand
niman	にまん	二万	twenty thousand

Putting a smaller number after a larger number indicates addition:

jûichi	じゅういち	十一	eleven
jûni	じゅうに	十二	twelve
nijûichi	にじゅういち	二十一	twenty-one
sanjûni	さんじゅうに	三十二	thirty-two
yonjûsan	よんじゅうさん	四十三	forty-three
gojûyon	ごじゅうよん	五十四	fifty-four
hyaku nijû	ひゃくにじゅう	百二十	one hundred twenty
sen kyûhyaku kyûjû nana	せんきゅう ひゃく きゅう じゅうなな	千九百九十七	one thousand nine hundred ninety seven

Sen kyûhyaku kyûjû nana nen, by the way, is also how you say the year 1997.

The system is mostly easy, and the only pitfalls, other than the pronunciation of *hyaku*, are the irregular pronunciations of certain combinations. And yes, you do need to learn these, because pronouncing them wrong sounds as odd as pronouncing *twenty*, *thirty*, and *fifty* as *two-ty*, *three-ty*, and *five-ty*.

Here are the hundreds with the irregular pronunciations indicated in boldface.

hyaku	ひゃく	百	one hundred
nihyaku	にひゃく	二百	two hundred
sanbyaku	**さんびゃく**	三百	three hundred
yonhyaku	よんひゃく	四百	four hundred
gohyaku	ごひゃく	五百	five hundred
roppyaku	**ろっぴゃく**	六百	six hundred
nanahyaku	ななひゃく	七百	seven hundred
happyaku	**はっぴゃく**	八百	eight hundred
kyûhyaku	きゅうひゃく	九百	nine hundred

Now here are the thousands, again with the irregular pronunciations in boldface.

sen OR issen	せん/いっせん	千/一千	one thousand
nisen	にせん	二千	two thousand
sanzen	**さんぜん**	三千	three thousand
yonsen	よんせん	四千	four thousand
gosen	ごせん	五千	five thousand
rokusen	ろくせん	六千	six thousand
nanasen	ななせん	七千	seven thousand
hassen	**はっせん**	八千	eight thousand
kyûsen	きゅうせん	九千	nine thousand

You will be happy to know that *man* and *oku* are completely regular, except that *ten thousand* and *one hundred million* are always *ichiman* and *ichioku*, not just plain *man* and *oku*.

Perhaps you think that you will never really need to know these larger numbers, but the Japanese unit of currency, the yen (pronounced *en* in modern Japanese) has been worth approximately one United States cent or less for the past couple of years. This means that ten thousand yen (*ichiman en*) is only about 100 U.S. dollars. If you travel to Japan on business, your hotel room could easily cost *ichiman en* per night, and the business deal you negotiate could be worth *ichioku en*, or a million dollars.

You will learn more about these extra-large numbers in Chapter 6, but for now, you know the numbers you need for shopping. Here are some extra phrases that may come in handy.

Sumimasen ga...	すみませんが...		Excuse me, but... (used to get someone's attention)
Irasshaimase.	いらっしゃいませ。		(A greeting given by store or restaurant employees. You are not expected to answer.)
_____o kudasai en	＿をください。 えん	円	Please give me_____ yen (Japanese unit of currency, worth approximately one U.S. cent)
otsuri	おつり	お釣り	change [given back to a customer by a store employee]
ten'in	てんいん	店員	sales clerk
hankachi	ハンカチ		handkerchief
Arigatô gozaimashita.	ありがとう ございました。		Thank you [for your business]. (You are not expected to respond to this phrase either.)
Mata dôzo.	またどうぞ。		Please call again.

Now for an example:

Ms. Yamaguchi is walking through the train station on a hot, humid day. She feels like wiping the sweat off her face, but she has left her handkerchief at home. She spots a nice handkerchief for sale at one of the newsstands.

Ten'in: Irasshaimase.
Yamaguchi: Sumimasen ga, sono hankachi wa ikura desu ka?
Ten'in: Kore desu ka? Roppyaku en desu.
Yamaguchi: Jaa, sore o kudasai.
Ten'in: Hai, dôzo.
Yamaguchi: Hai, sen en.
Ten'in: Otsuri (wa) yonhyaku en desu. Arigatô gozaimashita. Mata dôzo.

Sales clerk: May I help you?
Yamaguchi: Excuse me, but how much is that handkerchief?
Sales clerk: This one? It's 600 yen.
Yamaguchi: Well then, I'll take it.

Sales clerk: All right, here you are.
Yamaguchi: Out of 1,000 yen.
Sales clerk: Your change is 400 yen. Thank you.
Please come again.

• The newsstands in train stations sell all sorts of convenient items, including handkerchiefs and packets of tissues. These are popular because public restrooms in Japan are rarely stocked with toilet paper or paper towels.

• Although more and more non-native speakers are learning Japanese all the time, some people still believe that their language is too difficult for outsiders. If you don't look Japanese, people may assume that you are speaking English, even if you're really speaking Japanese. If you approach an unfamiliar person to ask a question or make a request, it's a good idea to start with *Sumimasen ga....* ("Excuse me, but. . ."), pause for a second or two so the person can absorb the fact that you're speaking Japanese, and then continue with what you intended to say.

Practice 4.4

Answer the following questions according to the hints given in parentheses.

EXAMPLE:

Sono hankachi wa ikura desu ka? (600 yen)
Kono hankachi wa roppyaku en desu.

1. Kôhii wa ikura desu ka? (200 yen)

2. Sono geta wa ikura desu ka? (5432 yen)

3. Sono kyandii wa ikura desu ka? (1567 yen)

4. Sono sokkusu wa ikura desu ka? (750 yen)

5. Sono mikan wa ikura desu ka? (65 yen)

6. Kono nattô wa ikura desu ka? (418 yen)

7. Ano obi wa ikura desu ka? (8830 yen)

8. Ano sandaru wa ikura desu ka? (3340 yen)

9. Try saying these amounts of money in Japanese (rounded off to the nearest *doru* [dollar]):

(a) a semester's or quarter's tuition at your school or your monthly salary

(b) how much rent or mortgage you pay each month

(c) the price of the last car you bought or the car you would like to buy

(d) the approximate price of a large pizza with two toppings

(e) the price of a pair of jeans

(f) the price of a pair of high-quality athletic shoes

TELLING TIME

You can also use the numbers you learned earlier to tell time. The hours are quite simple, but you need to watch out for *four*, *seven*, and *nine*.

ichiji	いちじ	一時	one o'clock
niji	にじ	二時	two o'clock
sanji	さんじ	三時	three o'clock
yoji	よじ	四時	four o'clock
goji	ごじ	五時	five o'clock
rokuji	ろくじ	六時	six o'clock
shichiji	しちじ	七時	seven o'clock
hachiji	はちじ	八時	eight o'clock
kuji	くじ	九時	nine o'clock
jûji	じゅうじ	十時	ten o'clock
jûichiji	じゅういちじ	十一時	eleven o'clock
jûniji	じゅうにじ	十二時	twelve o'clock
ichijihan	いちじはん	一時半	one-thirty
nijihan	にじはん	二時半	two-thirty

You will see the 24-hour clock used on transportation schedules. But normally you can get by with the combinations listed above and the following words and phrases:

Ima nanji desu ka?	いまなんじ ですか。	今何時ですか。	What time is it now?
ima	いま	今	now
Gozen kuji desu.	ごぜんくじです。	午前九時です。	It's 9:00 A.M.
Gogo kuji desu.	ごごくじです。	午後九時です。	It's 9:00 P.M.
Gogo kuji-han.	ごごくじはん	午後九時半	9:30 P.M.
Sô desu ne.	そうですね。		Hmm, let me see. (when spoken in a quiet, thoughtful tone)
_____kara	____から		from_____
_____made	____まで		until_____
Nanji kara desu ka?	なんじから ですか。	何時から ですか。	From what time is it? (=When does it start?)
Nanji made desu ka?	なんじまで ですか。	何時まで ですか。	Until what time is it? (=How long does it last?)
Nanji kara nanji made desu ka?	なんじから なんじまで ですか。	何時から 何時まで ですか。	From what time to what time is it?

• Note that _kara_ and _made_, unlike English _from_ and _until_, **follow** the noun.

Compare:

> **from** seven o'clock
> _shichiji **kara**_
>
> **until** eight o'clock
> _hachiji **made**_

All the Japanese words corresponding to English prepositions (_from, by, to, for, with, until_, etc.) follow the noun.

Examples:

1. Mr. Tanaka is supposed to meet a business contact at a coffeehouse at 9:30 A.M. After what seems like a long time, he looks at his watch, but it hardly seems to have moved. He wonders if it has stopped, so he asks the waiter for the time.

Tanaka:	Sumimasen ga, ima nanji desu ka.
Ueetaa:	Ima jûji desu.
Tanaka:	A, arigatô gozaimasu.

Tanaka:	Excuse me, but what time is it now?
Waiter:	It's ten o'clock.
Tanaka:	Oh, thank you.

2. Ms. Ishida has been told to phone her company's branch offices in San Francisco and Singapore, but she's not sure whether it's a good time to do so. She asks Mr. Morimoto, who has traveled to both offices several times, to help her figure out the time differences.

Ishida:	Morimoto-san, San Furanshisuko wa ima nanji desu ka?
Morimoto:	Sô desu ne. Ima gozen goji desu.
Ishida:	Jaa, Shingapooru wa?
Morimoto:	Shingapooru wa ima gogo niji-han desu.

Ishida:	Mr. Morimoto, what time is it in San Francisco now?
Morimoto:	Hmm, let me see. It's 5:00 A.M. now.
Ishida:	Well, how about Singapore?
Morimoto:	It's 1:30 P.M. in Singapore.

3. Amanda Smith is living in a dormitory for students from overseas. She wants to watch the news, but when she goes to the television lounge, her friend from Hong Kong, Chan Ngan-fa, and her friend from Malaysia, Zaini Abdul, are watching something else.

Smith:	Chan-san, nyûsu wa nanji kara desu ka?
Chan:	Rokuji kara desu.
Smith:	Sô desu ka? Nanji made desu ka?
Chan:	Shichiji made desu.
Abdul:	Ee, nyûsu wa rokuji kara shichiji made desu.

Smith:	Ms. Chan, what time does the news start?
Chan:	It starts at six o'clock.
Smith:	Really? How long does it last?
Chan:	It lasts until seven.
Abdul:	Yes, the news is from six to seven.

• NOUN+*wa* with a questioning intonation means *What about NOUN*? For example, If someone says that the news starts at six o'clock, and you really want to know about the animated cartoons (*anime*), you could ask, *Anime wa*? or *What about the cartoons*?

Practice 4.5

Pick five television programs and tell how long each one lasts.

EXAMPLE:

ER wa gogo jûji kara jûichiji made desu.

1.

2.

3.

4.

5.

SUMMING UP
MATOME
まとめ

Complete the dialogues according to the cues.

1. You are guiding Aoki Takashi, a visiting Japanese student, around your university campus, when he spots a distinguished-looking faculty member.

Aoki: Ano kata wa donata desu ka?
You: (Say that it's Professor Smith).

2. You have heard people talking about the fact that your favorite singer is currently touring Japan and that they have tickets to that singer's concert (*konsaato*), but you haven't heard all the details, so you ask Ikeda Masaru.

You: (ask when the concert is)
Ikeda: Asatte desu.

You:	(ask how much the tickets [*kippu*] are)
Ikeda:	Sanzen en desu.
You:	(ask what time the concert starts)
Ikeda:	Gogo hachiji kara desu.

3. You are shopping in a department store, and you see what look like cotton kimono wrapped in plastic on a shelf.

You:	(Get the sales clerk's attention, and then ask if these are *kimono*.)
Ten'in:	Iie, chigaimasu. Sore wa nemaki desu.
You:	(Ask how much this *nemaki* is.)
Ten'in:	Nisen sanbyaku en desu.
You:	(Tell the sales clerk that you'll take this one. Hand over 3,000 yen.)
Ten'n:	Hai, o-tsuri, nanahyaku en desu. Arigatô gozaimashita.

• A *nemaki* is a lightweight cotton garment cut like a *kimono* and traditionally used as a sort of nightgown. Non-Japanese often buy *nemaki* to use as bathrobes.

Tokyo Stock Exchange

Japan National Tourist Organization (JNTO)

CHAPTER 5

NIJÔ-JÔ WA DOKO NI ARIMASU KA? (WHERE IS NIJÔ CASTLE?)

In this chapter you will learn to:

1. talk about possessions and who owns what
2. talk about where things are located
3. narrow down locations

POSSESSION

In English, we indicate possession with apostrophe + s.

> the children's books
> the dog's dish
> the city's boundaries
> the movie's plot

The Japanese counterpart to apostrophe + s is the particle *no*. All the above phrases would contain *no* if they were translated into Japanese, and so would these:

> my cat
> her shoes
> his jacket

That's right. There are no irregular possessive forms. The standard, unvarying pattern is:

NOUN₁	no	NOUN₂
Tanaka-san	no	nooto
Mr. Tanaka	's	notebook
watashi	no	kasa
my		umbrella
getsuyôbi	no	kaigi
Monday	's	meeting
dare	no	pen
whose		pen

Even when used without a second noun, *no* is still a possessive:

> *Watashi no desu.*   It's mine.
> *Dare no desu ka?*   Whose is it?
> *Amerika no desu.*   It's an American one.

Sometimes Japanese uses *no* where English uses *in, on, at,* or *of.*

> *getsuyôbi no shichiji*
> seven o'clock on Monday
>
> *Yokohama no resutoran*
> a restaurant in Yokohama
>
> *Yoji no kaigi*
> the meeting at four o'clock
>
> *Hon no kabaa*
> the cover of the book

Here are some examples, along with some words you may need to understand them.

pen	ペン		pen
nooto	ノート		notebook
Amerika	アメリカ		the United States of America
okane	おかね	お金	money
Kanada	カナダ		Canada
getsuyôbi	げつようび	月曜日	Monday
kayôbi	かようび	火曜日	Tuesday
suiyôbi	すいようび	水曜日	Wednesday
mokuyôbi	もくようび	木曜日	Thursday
kin'yôbi	きんようび	金曜日	Friday
doyôbi	どようび	土曜日	Saturday
nichiyôbi	にちようび	日曜日	Sunday
nan'yôbi?	なんようび?	何曜日	what day of the week?
kaigi	かいぎ	会議	meeting
kokusai bôeki sentaa	こくさい ぼうえき センター	国際貿易 センター	international trade center (as a building or in stituation)
messe	メッセ		trade fair (from the German word *Messe*)

1. Mr. Tanaka, Ms. Ishida, and Mr. Morimoto are the last to leave a meeting. Mr. Tanaka spots an expensive-looking pen on the table and picks it up.

Tanaka: Kono pen wa dare no desu ka? Morimoto-san no desu ka?
Morimoto: Iie, boku no ja arimasen.
Ishida: A, sore wa watashi no pen desu yo.

Tanaka: Whose pen is this? Is it yours, Mr. Morimoto?
Morimoto: No, it's not my pen.
Ishida: Oh, that's my pen!

2. Ms. Suzuki is counting out different types of foreign money, and Ms. Murayama, her colleague at the bank, approaches her curiously.

Murayama: Sore wa Amerika no okane desu ka?
Suzuki: Kore desu ka? Iie, Kanada no desu yo.

Murayama: Is that American money?
Suzuki: This? No, it's Canadian.

3. Mr. Tanaka has been out of town on business, and he needs an update about some of the events scheduled for this week. He consults Ms. Shimizu, a colleague in his department.

Tanaka: Kokusai Bôeki Sentaa no messe wa nan'yôbi kara nan'yôbi made desu ka?
Shimizu: Mokuyôbi kara nichiyôbi made desu.

Tanaka: What days does the trade fair at the international trade center run?
Shimizu: It's from Thursday to Sunday.

Practice 5.1

rajio	ラジオ		radio
hon	ほん	本	book
Suisu	スイス		Switzerland
piano	ピアノ		piano
Nihon	にほん	日本	Japan
kasa	かさ	傘	umbrella
resutoran	レストラン		restaurant

How would you say it?

1. my umbrella

2. Ms. Smith's book

3. Mr. Tanaka's telephone number

4. Ms. Chan's notebook

5. Mr. Morimoto's radio

6. tomorrow's meeting

7. Singapore dollars

8. Japanese money

9. an international trade center in Kôbe

10. the person at the hotel

LOCATIONS

As mentioned in Chapter 4, *desu* corresponds to only one aspect of the English verb "to be." In order to cover the meanings of "to exist" or "to be located," you need another pair of verbs, *aru* and *iru*. They mean essentially the same thing, but *aru* refers only to inanimate objects, while *iru* refers only to animate creatures, such as people or animals.

Iru and *aru* are the so-called "dictionary forms" (*jishokei*) of these verbs, and these dictionary forms are used in many contexts, some of which are introduced in this book, but for the time being, we will concentrate on the *-masu* forms, *arimasu* and *imasu*.

Putting a verb into the *-masu* form does not change its meaning, but it is more polite, and you use it when speaking to a stranger, a casual acquaintance, or someone who ranks above you in the Japanese social system. If you go to Japan for the first time as an adult, everyone you meet will fall into one of these three categories, and in any case, you won't offend anyone by using these polite forms. They're also more regular than the dictionary forms, which is another reason to learn them first.

To ask where a place or object is, use the pattern:

NOUN	wa	doko	ni	arimasu	ka?
NOUN	(topic)	where	at	is	?
Hoteru	wa	doko	ni	arimasu	ka?
Where is the hotel?					

To ask where a person or animal is, use the pattern:

NOUN	wa	doko	ni	imasu	ka?
NOUN	(topic)	where	at	is	?
Itô-san	wa	doko	ni	imasu	ka?
Where is the Mr./Ms. Itô?					

The word order isn't like anything you've seen before, but there's good news for those of you who have studied a European langauge such as French, Spanish, or German: Japanese verbs do not change their endings for person, gender, or number. That is, whether you are asking "Where is he?," "Where is she?," "Where are you?," or "Where are they?" the verb ending stays the same.

As you learned in Chapter 4, you can answer Japanese questions by substituting the answer for the question word. This is true here as well. Suppose that the hotel being asked about in the sample question is in Akasaka, a neighborhood of Tokyo.

Hoteru	wa	**doko**	ni	arimasu	ka?
↓	↓	↓	↓	↓	
(Hoteru	wa)	**Akasaka**	ni	arimasu.	

Where is the hotel?
It's in **Akasaka.**

Now suppose that Ms. Itô is in Yokohama. Here's how the question about her and its answer would fit together.

Itô-san	wa	**doko**	ni	imasu	ka?
↓	↓	↓	↓	↓	
(Itô-san	wa)	**Yokohama**	ni	imasu.	

Where is Ms. Itô?
She's in **Yokohama.**

Note that you don't have to repeat the topic in the answer as long as it's the same as the topic of the question. That's why *hoteru wa* and *Itô-san wa* are written in parentheses in these answers. In fact, it sounds a bit stiff to repeat the topic unless you quickly go on to compare the whereabouts of the hotel or Ms. Itô to the whereabouts of something or someone else.

Like *dore* and *dono, doko* is part of a set of words referring to locations in relation to the speaker. Here are the forms you have learned so far:

kore	kono + NOUN	koko
this one, this thing	this + NOUN	here, this place
sore	sono + NOUN	soko
that one nearby, that thing nearby	that NOUN nearby	there nearby, that place nearby
are	ano + NOUN	asoko
that one over there that thing over there	that NOUN over there	over there, that place over there
dore	dono + NOUN	doko
which one? which thing?	which NOUN?	where? which place?

If you use *iru/imasu* by itself without mentioning a place, it means "to be present," "to be here," "to be around":

> *Suzuki-san wa imasu ka?*
> Is Ms. Suzuki here?
> Is Ms. Suzuki present?
> Is Ms. Suzuki around?

WATCH OUT

It is possible to replace *PLACE ni arimasu* or *PLACE ni imasu* with *desu,* as in *Suzuki-san wa doko desu ka?*, but it is not possible to replace *arimasu* or *imasu* with *desu* in other circumstances.

> RIGHT: *Hoteru wa doko ni arimasu ka?*
> RIGHT: *Hoteru wa doko desu ka?*
> Where is the hotel?

> RIGHT: *Hoteru wa arimasu ka?*
> WRONG: *Hoteru wa desu ka?*
> Is there a hotel?

In normal sentence structure, you don't use *wa, ga,* or *o* before *desu.* (There are a few exceptions, but nothing that you have to worry about at the elementary level.)

Vocabulary

Nijô-jô	にじょうじょう	二条城	Nijô Castle, a shôgun's castle in Kyôto
daibutsu	だいぶつ	大仏	a large statue of the Buddha
Kamakura	かまくら	鎌倉	a small, historic city about an hour south of Tôkyô,
jaa	じゃあ		well, then
Nara	なら	奈良	a small city about an hour south of Kyôto, the capital of Japan in the eighth century
toshokan	としょかん	図書館	library

Examples:

1. Thomas Wilson is planning a trip for spring vacation, and there are various sights he wants to see, but he's not quite sure where they are. He goes to Ms. Hasegawa for advice.

Wilson:	Nijô-jô wa doko ni arimasu ka?
Hasegawa:	Nijô-jô desu ka? Kyôto ni arimasu yo.
Wilson:	Jaa, Kasuga Jinja wa?
Hasegawa:	Kasuga Jinja wa Nara ni arimasu.
Wilson:	Daibutsu wa?
Hasegawa:	Nara no Daibutsu desu ka? Kamakura no Daibutsu desu ka?
Wilson:	Kamakura no Daibutsu desu.

Hasegawa:	Uiruson-san, Kamakura no Daibutsu wa . . .
	Kamakura ni arimasu yo.
Wilson:	A, naruhodo.

Wilson:	Where is Nijô Castle?
Hasegawa:	Nijô Castle? It's in Kyôto.
Wilson:	Well, what about Kasuga Shrine?
Hasegawa:	Kasuga Shrine is in Nara.
Wilson:	What about the Great Buddha?
Hasegawa:	Do you mean the Great Buddha of Nara or the Great Buddha of Kamakura?
Wilson:	I mean the Great Buddha of Kamakura.
Hasegawa:	Mr. Wilson, the Great Buddha of Kamakura is in . . . Kamakura!
Wilson:	Oh, right.

• In case you're wondering, the Great Buddha of Kamakura is the one you've seen on all those travel posters.

2. Chan Ngan-fa and Amanda Smith are going shopping together, and they want to invite Zaini Abdul along, but they can't find her. They ask Kim Byong-il, a Korean student, where she is.

Chan:	Kimu-san, Abuduuru-san wa doko ni imasu ka?
Kim:	Toshokan ni imasu yo.
Sumisu:	Toshokan desu ka? Dômo!

Chan:	Mr. Kim, where's Ms. Abdul?
Kim:	She's in the library.
Smith:	The library? Thanks!

WATCH OUT

You may be confused by now. Didn't you just learn that *no* can mean "in," "on," "at," or "of"? Yes, you did. But note the difference. *Ni* is used when the main verb of the sentence is a verb of location (or motion, as you learn later).

> *Hoteru wa Tôkyô ni arimasu.*
> The hotel is in Tôkyô.

No is used when the main verb is of some other type.

> *Tôkyô no hoteru wa ikura desu ka?*
> How much is the hotel in Tôkyô?

Practice 5.2

Ask where each of the following people or objects is, and then answer the question according to the cues given.

EXAMPLE:

(Hasegawa-san)
(Intaagaku) →
Hasegawa-san wa doko ni imasu ka?
Intaagaku ni imasu.
Where is Ms. Hasegawa?
She's at Intergaku.

1. (Abuduuru-san) (asoko)

2. (kasa) (soko)

3. (nooto) (toshokan)

4. (resutoran) (Kamakura)

5. (Sumisu-san) (daigaku)

NARROWING DOWN LOCATIONS

Sometimes you need to be more specific in telling where a person or thing is. Is the car behind the house or alongside it? Is your friend inside the restaurant or in front of it? Is the dog on top of the bed or under it? Here are some words you need to know to make these sorts of statements.

mae	まえ	前	front
ushiro	うしろ	後ろ	behind, back of
yoko	よこ	横	alongside, to the side of
ue	うえ	上	top, above
shita	した	下	bottom, under
naka	なか	中	inside, middle
tonari	となり	隣	next door, neighboring
aida	あいだ	間	between, interval
mukô	むこう	向こう	beyond

All these words pattern as **nouns** in Japanese, so here is how you say "It's in front," "it's in back," etc.

Mae	ni arimasu.	It's in front.
Ushiro		It's in back.
Yoko		It's at the side.
Ue		It's on top.
Shita		It's underneath
Naka		It's inside.
Tonari		It's next door.
Aida		It's in between.
Mukô		It's beyond.

But in front of what? Behind what? Well, here's something more to add to these sentences:

Eki	no	mae	ni arimasu.	It's in front of the station.
Depaato		ushiro		It's in back of the department store.
Uchi		yoko		It's at the side of the house.
Teeburu		ue		It's on top of the table.
Isu		shita		It's underneath the chair.
Kuruma		naka		It's inside the car.
Mise		tonari		It's next door to the store.
Suupaa to hon'ya		aida		It's between the supermarket and the bookstore.
Kôen		mukô		It's beyond the park.

The same pattern holds true if you're talking about a person or animal: *Eki no mae ni imasu. Depaato no ushiro ni imasu.*

Can you guess how you add a topic to sentences like this; for example, how you say "The car is in front of the station"? That's right:

Kuruma	wa	eki	no	mae	ni	arimasu.

WATCH OUT

If you reverse the order of these location phrases, you change their meanings:

Uchi no mae
The front of the house

Mae no uchi
The house that is in front OR The previous house

Kuruma no naka
The inside of the car

Naka no kuruma
The car that is inside

Vocabulary

uchi	うち		house
kuruma	くるま	車	car, automobile
eki	えき	駅	train, bus, or subway station
teeburu	テーブル		table
isu	いす	椅子	chair
mise	みせ	店	shop, store, place of business
suupaa	スーパー		supermarket
hon'ya	ほんや	本屋	bookstore
doa	ドア		Western-style door
kôen	こうえん	公園	park
depaato	デパート		department store
o-tearai	おてあらい	お手洗い	toilet, restroom
kaidan	かいだん	階段	stairs
denwa	でんわ	電話	telephone
takushii noriba	タクシー のりば	タクシー 乗り場	taxi stand

Examples:

1. Amanda Smith is in a large train station, looking for the restroom. She approaches a newsstand and asks the sales clerk for directions.

Sumisu:	Sumimasen ga, o-tearai wa doko desu ka?
Ten'in:	O-tearai desu ka? Ano kaidan to denwa no aida ni arimasu.
Smith:	Excuse me, but where is the restroom?
Sales clerk:	The restroom? It's between those stairs over there and the phones.

2. Chan Ngan-fa's weekend host family, the Yamaguchis, have a cat named Kuro, whom Chan Ngan-fa is very fond of. She arrives at the Yamaguchis', and after a while, she realizes that she hasn't seen Kuro yet, so she asks Ms. Yamaguchi and her daughter Mariko where he is.

Chan: Kuro wa doko ni imasu ka?
Yamaguchi: Kuro desu ka? Saa...
Mariko: Teeburu no shita ni imasu yo.

Chan: Where's Kuro?
Yamaguchi: Kuro? Hmm . . .
Mariko: Oh, he's under the table.

Practice 5.3

This is a drawing of a student's dormitory room. Answer the following questions about where various things are.

EXAMPLE:

Ryukku wa doko ni arimasu ka?
Hondana no mae ni arimasu.

Where is the backpack?
It's in front of the bookshelf.

Vocabulary

beddo	ベッド		bed
bôshi	ぼうし	帽子	hat, cap
kutsu	くつ	靴	shoe
posutaa	ポスター		poster
kabe	かべ	壁	wall
kuzukago	くずかご	屑籠	wastebasket
tegami	てがみ	手紙	letter
sutando	スタンド		desk lamp
tsukue	つくえ	机	desk
hikidashi	ひきだし	引き出し	drawer
konsento	コンセント		electrical outlet
kaaten	カーテン		curtain
mado	まど	窓	window
sutereo	ステレオ		stereo
hondana	ほんだな	本棚	bookshelf
suisô	すいそう	水槽	aquarium tank
sakana	さかな	魚	fish
jiinzu	ジーンズ		jeans
seetaa	セーター		sweater
neko	ねこ	猫	cat
tansu	たんす		chest of drawers
yuka	ゆか	床	floor

1. Kutsu wa doko ni arimasu ka?

2. Bôshi wa doko ni arimasu ka?

3. Konpyuuta to sutando wa doko ni arimasu ka?

4. Konsento wa doko ni arimasu ka?

5. Kuzukago wa doko ni arimasu ka?

6. Tegami wa doko ni arimasu ka?

7. Neko wa doko ni imasu ka?

8. Sutereo wa doko ni arimasu ka?

9. Suisô wa doko ni arimasu ka?

10. Sakana wa doko ni imasu ka?

11. Seetaa wa doko ni arimasu ka?

12. Jiinzu wa doko ni arimasu ka?

SUMMING UP
MATOME
まとめ

1. Your friend Thomas Wilson is traveling around Japan, and Professor Takahashi asks you about him.

Takahashi: Uiruson-san wa ima doko ni imasu ka?
You: (say that he's in Kyôto until Friday. Hint: time always comes before place, and the verb always comes at the end.)

2. You have just arrived in an unfamiliar city, and you want to buy some postcard stamps.

You: (get the attention of a station employee [*ekiin*] and ask where the post office [*yûbinkyoku*] is.)
Ekiin: Ano depaato no tonari ni arimasu.
What has the station employee told you?

3. Teachers in Japanese high schools have their desks in a separate office room and move from classroom to classroom throughout the day. Yamaguchi Mariko, who has just started high school, needs to leave a message for her music teacher, but she isn't sure which desk is the right one. She asks you, the English teaching assistant, for help.

Mariko: Sumimasen ga, Kagawa Sensei no tsukue wa doko desu ka.
You: (it's between that wall over there and the bookshelf)

A. Match the questions or phrases in column A with the most appropriate responses in column B.

___1. Atsui desu ne.

a. Tanaka-san desu.

___2. Tanaka-san wa doko ni imasu ka?

b. Dôzo.

___3. Ano hito wa dare desu ka?

c. Eki no mukô ni arimasu.

___4. Arigatô gozaimasu.

d. Sô desu ne.

___5. O-negai shimasu.

e. Kyôto ni imasu.

___6. Yûbinkyoku wa doko ni arimasu ka?

f. Iie, dô itashimashite.

___7. O-matsuri wa itsu desu ka?

g. Sen nihyaku en desu.

___8. Itte kimasu.

h. Kyô to ashita desu.

___9. Sono hon wa ikura desu ka?

i. Itte irasshai.

B. Look at the following drawing of the area around a commuter train station and answer the following questions.

1. Denwa wa doko ni arimasu ka?

2. Takushii wa doko ni arimasu ka?

3. Daigaku wa doko ni arimasu ka?

4. Apaato wa doko ni arimasu ka?

5. Kôen wa doko ni arimasu ka?

C. The drawing on the previous page contains a number of things that you don't know how to say in Japanese. Study the following sentences and figure out what the words in bold type mean by figuring out where the objects they refer to are located.

1. **Baiten** wa eki to hon'ya no aida ni arimasu.

2. **Jitensha** wa baiten no yoko ni arimasu.

3. Depaato no resutoran wa **okujô** ni arimasu.

4. **Kagu** wa depaato no shoo-uindoo ni arimasu.

5. **Benchi** wa kôen ni arimasu.

6. **Ike** wa benchi no mae ni arimasu.

7. **Ki** wa benchi no ushiro ni arimasu.

TOTEMO TAKAI DESU GA, AMARI OISHIKU NAI DESU. (IT'S VERY EXPENSIVE, BUT IT'S NOT VERY TASTY.)

In this chapter you will learn to:

1. describe things and people
2. make verbs and adjectives negative
3. describe what or who is in a given place
4. use the numbers above 10,000

DESCRIBING THINGS AND PEOPLE

The Japanese language has two kinds of adjectives, the *-ku* adjectives and the *-na* adjectives, which you will see in Chapter 10. The *-ku* adjectives always end in *-ai, -ii, -ui,* or *-oi,* and here are some examples of them:

takai	expensive
atarashii	new
furui	old
omoshiroi	interesting

The word order for adjectives is exactly the same as in English.

Hoteru wa takai desu.	The hotel is expensive.
Takai hoteru desu.	It's an expensive hotel.
Kuruma wa atarashii desu.	The car is new.
Atarashii kuruma desu.	It's a new car.
Hon wa omoshiroi desu.	The book is interesting.
Omoshiroi hon desu.	It's an interesting book.

In other words, if the adjective comes before the noun in English, it comes before the noun in Japanese. If it comes after the noun in English, it comes after the noun in Japanese. It's really that simple.

WATCH OUT

Occasionally students ask what the difference is between sentences like: *Kore wa omoshiroi hon desu* "This is an interesting book" and *Kono hon wa omoshiroi desu* "This book is interesting." Well, what is the difference between their English counterparts? Would they be completely interchangeable in English, even though they are describing the same reality? Think about when you would use each one.

Adjectives with *desu* are polite forms, and the *-ku* adjectives are complete sentence endings in themselves when you are speaking in the dictionary form (plain) style. For example, if you were speaking to a close friend or family member about the price of a certain hotel, you would say *Ano hoteru wa takai* instead of *Ano hoteru wa takai desu,* and it would still be a complete sentence. But remember that we are working with the polite forms at this point.

Even when a sentence contains adjectives, everything else stays the same. Let's build up two sentences.

> *Hon desu.*
> It's a book.

> *Omoshiroi hon desu.*
> It's an interesting book.

> *Kore wa omoshiroi hon desu.*
> This is an interesting book.

> *Watashi no ja arimasen.*
> It isn't mine.

> *Kuruma wa watashi no ja arimasen.*
> The car isn't mine.

> *Ano furui kuruma wa watashi no ja arimasen.*
> That old car over there isn't mine.

See? Except for the added adjectives, all the sentence structures are just as you learned them previously. Students sometimes get into trouble when they learn new grammar points because they forget one important fact: everything you learned in previous lessons is still true. You do not have to reinvent the entire language to accommodate new forms.

In order to ask for a description of a thing, person, or place, ask:

> *NOUN wa dô desu ka.*
> (literally:) How is NOUN?
> "What is NOUN like?"

Vocabulary

soba	そば		buckwheat noodles
totemo	とても		very
oishii	おいしい		delicious
takai	たかい	高い	expensive, high
yasui	やすい	安い	cheap
ookii	おおきい	大きい	large
chiisai	ちいさい	小さい	small
akai	あかい	赤い	red
aoi	あおい	青い	blue, green
shiroi	しろい	白い	white
kuroi	くろい	黒い	black
kiiroi	きいろい	黄色い	yellow
suutsukeesu	スーツケース		suitcase
Bosuton baggu	ボストン・バッグ		totebag with two handles
nimotsu	にもつ	荷物	luggage

• By the way, some of the color words borrowed from English pattern as nouns, not as adjectives. These include *pinku, guriin, orenji-iro,* and *guree.* Thus *no* comes between the color word and the noun it describes: *pinku no uchi, guriin no kuruma.*

Examples:

1. Eric Jones walks into the university cafeteria and sees a Japanese acquaintance, Ikeda Masaru, eating a bowl of *soba* noodles.

Jones:	Ikeda-san!
Ikeda:	A, Joonzu-san!
Jones:	Sono soba wa dô desu ka?
Ikeda:	Oishii desu yo.
Jones:	Takai desu ka?
Ikeda:	Iie, totemo yasui desu.

Jones:	Mr. Ikeda!
Ikeda:	Oh, Mr. Jones.
Jones:	What's that *soba* like?
Ikeda:	It's delicious.
Jones:	Is it expensive?
Ikeda:	No, it's very cheap.

2. The students who have been placed by Intergaku are on a weekend trip to Nikkô, and they have just arrived at the train station. Ms. Hasegawa is trying to figure out whose luggage is whose.

Hasegawa:	Kono chiisai ryukku wa dare no desu ka?
Abdul:	Watashi no desu.
Hasegawa:	Jaa, kono chiisai suutsukeesu wa?
Wilson:	Boku no desu.
Hasegawa:	Kono akai Bosuton baggu wa Sumisu-san no desu ka?
Smith:	Chigaimasu. Watashi no wa aoi desu.
Hasegawa:	Sô desu ka? Saa. . .
Smith:	Watashi no nimotsu wa doko desu ka?

Hasegawa:	Whose is this small backpack?
Abdul:	It's mine.
Hasegawa:	Well, what about this big suitcase?
Wilson:	It's mine.
Hasegawa:	Is this red totebag yours, Ms. Smith?
Smith:	You're mistaken. Mine is blue.
Hasegawa:	Is that so? Hmm. . .
Smith:	Where's my luggage?

Practice 6.1

How would you say:

1. That is a small book.

2. This is a white notebook.

3. That over there is a red backpack.

4. This is a large desk.

5. That's an interesting letter.

6. This is a blue sweater.

7. Those are cheap shoes.

8. That book is small.

9. That notebook is white.

10. My backpack is red.

11. Mr. Ikeda's desk is large.

12. Ms. Suzuki's letter is interesting.

13. This sweater is blue.

14. Those shoes are cheap.

NEGATIVES

You may be wondering at this point how *-ku* adjectives got their name. The answer is that their adverbial (describing a verb) forms end in *-ku*. These adverbial forms in turn help make up the negative.

If you were to **guess** how to form the negative of a Japanese adjective, you would probably think, The negative of *hon desu* is *hon ja arimasen* or *hon ja nai desu,* so the negative of *takai desu* must be *takai ja arimasen* or *takai ja nai desu.*

That's a reasonable guess, but you'd be wrong. Here's how it really works.

taka-	*i*		*desu*	It is expensive.
taka-	*ku*	*nai*	*desu*	It is not expensive.
atarashi-	*i*		*desu*	It is new.
atarashi-	*ku*	*nai*	*desu*	It is not new.
furu-	*i*		*desu*	It is old.
furu-	*ku*	*nai*	*desu*	It is not old.
omoshiro-	*i*		*desu*	It is interesting.
omoshiro-	*ku*	*nai*	*desu*	It is not interesting.

In other words, the procedure is:

1. Drop the final *-i*
2. Replace it with *-ku*
3. Insert a *nai* in before the *desu.*
   OR
   Replace *desu* with *arimasen.*

This works with *-ku* adjectives 99.9999 percent of the time. The one, the one and only, sole, unique, rare exception to this rule is *ii* "good." Its old form is *yoi,* and the *-ku* form, *yoku,* is based on it, so the negative is *yoku nai desu.* There. You now know how to form the negative of every single *-ku* adjective. Just to make sure, let's practice with some common adjectives.

By the way, "very" and "not very" are two completely different words in Japanese. With a positive adjective, "very" is *totemo,* as in *Totemo oishii desu* "It's very tasty." With a negative adjective, use *amari,* as in *Amari oishiku nai desu* "It's not very tasty."

Practice 6.2a

Vocabulary

atatakai	あたたかい	暖かい	pleasantly warm
abunai	あぶない	危ない	dangerous
nagai	ながい	長い	long
mezurashii	めずらしい		unusual
suzushii	すずしい	涼しい	pleasantly cool
samui	さむい	寒い	cold (weather only)
osoi	おそい	遅い	late, slow
ii (-ku form: yoku)	いい（よく）		good
omoi	おもい	重い	heavy
muzukashii	むずかしい		difficult
tanoshii	たのしい	楽しい	enjoyable, fun

Form the negatives of each of these adjectives according to the examples given above. It doesn't matter whether you use *nai desu* or *arimasen.*

EXAMPLE:

Muzukashii desu. (It is difficult.) →
Muzukashiku nai desu. (It isn't difficult.)
Totemo tanoshii desu. (It is very enjoyable.) →
Amari tanoshiku arimasen. (It is not very enjoyable.)

1. Atatakai desu.

2. Totemo abunai desu.

3. Totemo nagai desu.

4. Mezurashii desu.

5. Suzushii desu.

6. Totemo yasui desu.

7. Samui desu.

8. Osoi desu.

9. Totemo ii desu.

Okay, that takes care of the *-ku* adjectives, and you already know how to negate a NOUN + *desu* sentence. That leaves the verbs: the negatives of their polite forms are equally simple and regular. One of the negatives should look familiar.

ari-	masu	[inanimate object] exists, is located, is here,
ari-	masen	[inanimate object] does not exist, is not located, is not here
i-	masu	[person or animal] exists, is located, is here
i-	masen	[person or animal] does not exist, is not located, is not here

(Yes, you've seen *arimasen* before in the negatives of *desu* and the adjectives.)

In other words, the procedure for forming the negative of the polite form of the verb is:

1. Remove the *-masu* ending.
2. Replace it with *-masen*.

That's all there is to it. That's really it. This procedure works for every Japanese verb except *desu*, which most grammarians believe isn't really a verb anyway, but a *copula*, or linking verb. Given any Japanese verb in the *masu* form, you should be able to form its negative. Let's try it.

Practice 6.2b

Polite Form	Plain Form	Kanji (If any)	Meaning
shimasu	suru		do, make
ikimasu	iku	行く	go
tabemasu	taberu	食べる	eat
nomimasu	nomu	飲む	drink
nemasu	neru	寝る	go to bed, sleep
mimasu	miru	見る	see, look, watch
kikimasu	kiku	聞く	listen, hear, ask
kaerimasu	kaeru	帰る	go home, return to one's usual place
yomimasu	yomu	読む	read
kimasu	kuru	来る	come
okimasu	okiru	起きる	get up

1. shimasu

2. ikimasu

3. tabemasu

4. nomimasu

5. nemasu

6. mimasu

7. kikimasu

8. kaerimasu

9. yomimasu

10. okimasu

(Are you bored yet? Maybe you are. But now you know everything there is to know about the negative of the polite form of the verb.)

By the way, the negative of the verb is used in invitations. Here's how Yamaguchi Mariko might invite Chan Ngan-fa to her party.

Yamaguchi: Watashi no paatii ni kimasen ka?
Chan: Ee, yorokonde.

Yamaguchi: Won't you come to my party?
Chan: Yes, gladly.

POINTING OUT WHERE THINGS ARE

Suppose that your textbook (*kyôkasho*) is in your briefcase (*kaban*), but the person you're talking to doesn't know that. Suppose also that this person wants to know where the textbook is. How would he or she phrase that question?

That's right:

Kyôkasho wa doko ni arimasu ka?

And your answer would be:

Kyôkasho wa kaban no naka ni arimasu.

You knew that, didn't you? Now let's take a slightly different look at the same situation. This time, your companion has no idea that you have a textbook anywhere and just wants to know what is inside the briefcase. Do you know how to ask that question? No, you don't, but you will if you continue reading.

Now, in that first question about where the textbook is, you already know that it exists somewhere, so your topic is the textbook, and the really important part of the sentence is the question about it.

In the question about what is inside the briefcase, the fact that there is something inside the briefcase is already known, and the important part of the question is **what** is inside there. So first take your sentence meaning "It's inside the briefcase":

Kaban no naka ni arimasu.

Now you need to add the "what." You've already learned *nan* as "what," but it has an alternate form, *nani,* and instead of *wa* you use the particle *ga,* so the question about what's inside the briefcase is phrased:

*Kaban no naka ni **nani ga** arimasu ka?*
What's inside the briefcase?

Since *nani* is the question word, you replace it with the answer while replying:

Kaban	no	naka	ni	**nani**	**ga**	arimasu	ka?
↓	↓	↓	↓	↓	↓	↓	
(Kaban	no	naka	ni)	**kyôkasho**	**ga**	arimasu	

There's a textbook (inside the briefcase).

You may be wondering about this *ga,* which is only natural, because every non-native speaker of Japanese has spent some time wondering about the difference between *wa* and *ga.* It's not a good idea to spend too much time worrying about this difference. Even so, there are a few general principles to keep in mind that will work much of the time.

1. If a topic is marked with *wa,* the comment is the most important part of the sentence. If a subject is marked with *ga,* it is the most important part of the sentence. Sometimes the difference is expressed in English as a difference in tone of voice.

   *Suzuki-san **wa** imasu.*—Ms. Suzuki **is here.**
   *Suzuki-san **ga** imasu.*—**Ms. Suzuki** is here.

   *Kono tatemono **wa** ginkô desu.*—This building is **the bank.**
   *Kono tatemono **ga** ginkô desu.*—**This building** is the bank.

2. If either *nani* "what" or *dare* "who" is the subject of a sentence, it is marked with *ga*, never, not in any circumstances, with *wa*.

> RIGHT: *Nani ga arimasu ka?* —What is there?
> WRONG: *Nani wa arimasu ka?*
>
> RIGHT: *Dare ga imasu ka?* —Who is there?
> WRONG: *Dare wa imasu ka?*

3. If the subject of the sentence is something that you have just noticed, it is marked with *ga*.

> *Asoko ni hebi ga imasu yo!*
> There's a snake over there!

4. When responding to a question, follow the same grammatical pattern in your reply, substituting the noun that is the answer for the question word.

> *Ano tatemono **wa** nan desu ka?* —<u>What</u> is that building over there?
>
> *Ano tatemono **wa** ginkô desu.* —That building over there is <u>the bank.</u>
>
> *Dono tatemono **ga** ginkô desu ka?* —<u>Which building</u> is the bank?
>
> *Ano tatemono **ga** ginkô desu.* —<u>That building over there</u> is the bank.

All in all, the best way to gain a feeling for *wa* and *ga* is to expose yourself to as much spoken and written Japanese as possible and to pay attention to how people express themselves. Don't ask native speakers without training in linguistics to explain these particles to you. They just use them instinctively without thinking about it. (Really now, what would you do if a Japanese friend asked you for a set of fool-proof rules concerning the use of "a" and "the"?)

Remember the phrase *Sumimasen ga* . . ."Excuse me, but. . ."? That's another use of *ga*, and it means "but," as in

> *Ookii desu ga, omoku nai desu.*
> It's big, but it isn't heavy.

So how do you tell the difference between the subject-marking *ga* and the *ga* that means "but"? It's actually quite easy. The subject-marking *ga* always follows a noun or pronoun, while the *ga* meaning "but" always follows a verb or an adjective.

Here are some examples of usage:

biru	ビル		Western-style building
tatemono	たてもの	建物	building
o-mawari-san	おまわりさん	お巡りさん	police officer on patrol
ne	ね		isn't it? isn't that right?
Sô desu ne.	そうですね。		Let me see now; hmm;
NOUN + dake	NOUN +だけ		only NOUN, just NOUN
ryôri	りょうり	料理	cuisine, cooking

Examples:

1. Ikeda Masaru is going for a job interview at Technopoly, and he doesn't know where it is. He stops at a *kôban* (neighborhood police booth) to ask for directions.

Ikeda:	Sumimasen ga, Tekunoporii Biru wa doko ni arimasu ka?
O-mawari-san:	Sô desu ne. Asoko ni ookii tatemono ga arimasu ne.
Ikeda:	Hai.
O-mawari-san:	Ano tatemono ga Tekunoporii Biru desu.

Ikeda:	Excuse me. Where is the Technopoly Building?
Policeman:	Let's see. There's a big building over there, right?
Ikeda:	Yes.
Policeman:	**That building** is the Technopoly Building.

2. Mr. Morimoto has phoned back to his office from a client's company, and he is talking to Ms. Shimizu.

Morimoto:	Tanaka-san wa imasu ka?
Shimizu:	Iie, kyô wa imasen.
Morimoto:	Saa, dare ga imasu ka?
Shimizu:	Watashi dake desu.

Morimoto:	Is Mr. Tanaka there?
Shimizu:	No, he isn't here today.
Morimoto:	Well, who is there?
Shimizu:	It's just me.

3. Mr. Nakagawa has been assigned to take some business contacts out to a fancy restaurant, so he asks his colleague Mr. Date, who is quite a gourmet, about one of the French restaurants he has in mind.

| Nakagawa: | Ra Kuronnu no ryôri wa dô desu ka? |
| Date: | Sô desu ne. Totemo takai desu ga, amari oishiku nai desu ne. |

| Nakagawa: | How is the food at La Couronne? |
| Date: | Let me see. It's very expensive, but it's not very tasty, you know. |

Practice 6.3

Look at the drawing of a student's room found in Chapter 5 on page 64. Describe what is located in each place indicated:

EXAMPLE:

(inside the wastebasket)
Kuzukago no naka ni tegami ga arimasu.

1. (under the bed)

2. (at the side of the desk)

3. (on top of the desk)

4. (in front of the window)

5. (on the floor)

6. (inside the aquarium)

7. (in front of the shelf)

8. (behind the chair)

9. (on top of the bed)

10. (inside the drawer)

11. (under the desk)

12. (on the wall)

NUMBERS ABOVE 10,000

When you learned about Japanese numbers in Chapter 4, the system seemed simple and straightforward, with only a few irregular pronunciations that could possibly trip you up. Actually, the higher numbers can cause problems at first, because they are based on units of 10,000.

All is well up to 9,999, which is *kyûsen kyûhyaku kyûjû kyû*. But there is no *jûsen* or anything else *-sen* above that. Instead, we start in on units of 10,000 (*man*), which will be the main unit all the way up to 100 million.

ichiman	10,000
jûman	100,000
hyakuman	1,000,000
senman	10,000,000
ichioku	100,000,000
jûoku	1,000,000,000

Thus "one million" is *hyakuman*, and "one billion" is *jûoku*. The Japanese version of a number such as "one billion two hundred thirty-four million five hundred sixty-seven thousand eight hundred ninety-one " (1,234,567,891), is

Jûnioku sanzen-yonhyaku-gojûroku-man nanasen happyaku kyûjûichi

(十二億三千四百五十六万七千八百九十一)

Numbers are such a basic part of everyone's vocabulary that it is sometimes difficult to re-think these large ones accurately, but here's a trick to help you out. Write the number down without commas and insert a comma every **four** places from the right instead of every three places from the right. (Note, however, that when Japanese people write out large numbers in real life, they insert the commas every three digits, just as people in Europe and North America do.)

12, 3456, 7891

The numerals in the first four places from the right are the old familiar thousands, hundreds, tens, and ones. The numerals in the next four places are expressed in terms of ten thousands or *man*. After that come four places expressed in terms of hundred millions or *oku*. The next four places are the trillions (*chô*), but you probably won't need them until you're well into your career in high finance or astronomy.

Practice 6.4

Read these numbers out loud in Japanese.

1. 10,000

2. 12,000

3. 20,000

4. 25,000

5. 48, 632

6. 50,005

7. 100,000

8. 234, 000

9. 1,000,000

10. 5,000,000

11. 10,000,000

12. 12, 345,678

13. 100,000,000

14. 250,000,000

15. 918,273,621

16. 1,000,000,000

SUMMING UP
MATOME
まとめ

1. Here is the rest of Mr. Nakagawa and Mr. Date's conversation about restaurants. Summarize what was said. You won't understand every word, but don't worry about that.

Nakagawa:	Ra Kuronnu wa oishiku nai desu ka? Jaa, doko no ryôri ga oishii desu ka?
Date:	Yappari Ra Furansu (La France) desu ne.
Nakagawa:	Ra Furansu desu ka? Soko no setto menyuu wa ikura desu ka?
Date:	Hassen en gurai da to omoimasu.

2. Complete the following dialogues based on the cues provided.

Nihonjin	にほんじん	日本人	Japanese person
tsumaranai	つまらない		boring
zeikanri	ぜいかんり	税関吏	customs officer
yôfuku	ようふく	洋服	(Western-style) clothing
enpitsu	えんぴつ	鉛筆	pencil

(a) You have told your Japanese acquaintance that you are going to fly home to Seattle for the summer.

Nihonjin:	Shiatoru made wa ikura desu ka?
You:	(Say that it's 75,000 yen.)

(b) You are reading a book in the university library, and you can barely keep awake. A Japanese acquaintance sitting across from you leans forward to whisper a question.

Nihonjin:	Sono hon wa tsumaranai desu ka?
You:	(Express the opinion that it's very boring.)

(c) You are returning to Japan from a brief visit to your home country, and the day before you arrived, some people were arrested at Tokyo's Narita Airport for attempting to smuggle drugs, so the customs officers (*zeikanri*) are interviewing international travelers very carefully.

Zeikanri: Sono suutsukeesu no naka ni nani ga arimasu ka?
You: (Tell him that there are clothes.)
Zeikanri: Jaa, sono Bosuton baggu no naka ni wa?
You: (Tell him that there are books and notebooks.)

(d) Mr. Tanaka sees you rummaging around in your desk drawer.

Tanaka: Sono hikidashi no naka ni nani ga arimasu ka?
You: (Tell him that there are pencils.)
Tanaka: Pen wa?
You: (There aren't any.)

Japanese inn (Taikanso, Atami)

Japan National Tourist Organization (JNTO)

CHAPTER 7

MAINICHI SHINBUN O YOMIMASU. (I READ THE NEWSPAPER EVERY DAY.)

In this chapter you will learn to:

1. talk about having things
2. describe your daily routine
3. tell time with greater accuracy

TALKING ABOUT HAVING THINGS

Remember the pattern NOUN *ga arimasu*? Well, it is also used to express the concept of having or possessing something:

NOUN$_1$ *wa* NOUN$_2$ *ga arimasu.*
NOUN$_1$ has NOUN$_2$.

The pattern literally means something like "As for NOUN$_1$, there is NOUN$_2$."

NOUN$_1$	wa	NOUN$_2$	ga	arimasu	
Watashi		kaban	ga	arimasu	I have a briefcase.
Tamura-san	wa	kuruma	ga	arimasu	Mr./Ms. Tamura has a car.
Chan-san	wa	terebi	ga	arimasu	Ms. Chan has a television set.

You may wonder whether it is possible to put *wa* in both particle slots, in other words, to say, NOUN$_1$ *wa* NOUN$_2$ *wa* arimasu. The answer is yes, but the sentence has a different shade of meaning.

If you say *Kaban ga arimasu,* that's either an announcement or the answer to the question *Nani ga arimasu ka?* "What do you have?" If you say *Kaban wa arimasu,* the connotation is something like, "You know you're talking about briefcases? Well, I have one," or "I do have a briefcase and other things as well," or "Compared to other things that I don't have, I do have a briefcase," or "I do have a briefcase, but I have more to say about that."

The difference is even clearer in the negative form. When you are telling someone that you *don't* have something, *wa* is the particle normally used: *Kaban wa arimasen* "I don't have a briefcase." If you use *ga* with the negative, it sounds as if you have just noticed that you don't have the item in question. *Kaban ga arimasen* "I don't have my briefcase (and I just realized it)."

When asking whether someone has something, the particle is often left out of the second slot in less formal conversation: *Kaban, arimasu ka?*

When talking about people or animals, the use of *imasu* is preferable to *arimasu,* as in *Joonzu-san wa Nihonjin no tomodachi ga imasu.* "Mr. Jones has Japanese friends."

By the way, a NOUN₁ *no* NOUN₂ expression such as *Nihonjin no tomodachi* can have two meanings. The first one is the one you've already learned, simple possession, so that *Nihonjin no tomodachi* can mean "the Japanese person's friend(s)." In this case, however, it means "friends who are Japanese." At times, only the second meaning makes sense. *Gakusei no Ikeda-san* can mean only "Mr. Ikeda, who is a student." Be aware of both possibilities when you see or hear a phrase in this form.

Remember that adjectives simply fit into the sentence in front of the noun that they describe: *Hasegawa-san wa atarashii sutereo ga arimasu.* "Ms. Hasegawa has a new stereo."

Here are some examples of usage:

tomodachi	ともだち	友達	friend
Nihon	にほん	日本	Japan
Nihonjin	にほんじん	日本人	Japanese person
Nihongo	にほんご	日本語	Japanese language
koora	コーラ		cola
petto	ペット		pet (animal)
jisho	じしょ	辞書	dictionary
gozaimasu	ございます		polite form of arimasu
de gozaimasu	でございます		polite form of desu
terebi	テレビ		television
rajio	ラジオ		radio
ke(re)do	け(れ)ど		but
Furansu	フランス		France
Supein	スペイン		Spain

Examples:

1. Eric Jones is at the train station on a hot day, and since he has a couple of minutes before his train comes in, he stops off at the newsstand to buy a cold drink.

Jones:	Koora, arimasu ka?
Ten'in:	Hai, gozaimasu kedo. . .
Jones:	Ikura desu ka?
Ten'in:	Hyaku en de gozaimasu.
Jones:	Jaa, sore o kudasai.

Jones:	Do you have cola?
Sales clerk:	Yes, we do.
Jones:	How much is it?
Sales clerk:	It's 100 yen.
Jones:	I'll take it.

•   As you learned in previous lessons, expressions with *gozaimasu* are more polite than expressions without it. Actually, *gozaimasu* is the polite form of *arimasu*. Since Japanese etiquette requires salespeople to be very polite to customers, you will probably hear *gozaimasu* if you do any shopping at all in Japan. NOUN +*de gozaimasu* is the polite equivalent of NOUN + *desu*.

2. Yamaguchi Mariko has noticed how fond Chan Ngan-fa is of the family cat, so she asks about the situation at her home in Hong Kong.

Mariko: Chan-san, petto, imasu ka?
Chan: Iie, petto wa imasen.

Mariko: Ms. Chan, do you have any pets?
Chan: No, I don't.

3. During her lunch hour, Ms. Suzuki practices English by reading popular novels. Today she has found some Spanish phrases in her current book, and she wants to know what they mean. She phones her colleague in the international division, Ms. Ishikawa.

Suzuki: Supeingo no jisho, arimasu ka?
Ishikawa: Supeingo no wa arimasen ne. Furansugo no wa arimasu kedo. . .

Suzuki: Do you have a Spanish dictionary?
Ishikawa: I'm afraid we don't have a Spanish one. We do have a French one, but. . .

• People sometimes put *ne* on the end of negative answers when they believe that the person asking the question will be disappointed to hear a negative reply. That's why Ms. Ishikawa puts a *ne* on the end of her negative answer, while Ms. Chan in the second example does not. Trailing off a sentence with *ga* or *ke(re)do* may indicate that the speaker is waiting for the listener's reaction.

As you may have inferred from that last dialogue, the names of languages are formed by adding *-go* to the name of the country or people who originated it: *Supeingo* "Spanish language," *Furansugo* "French language," *Nihongo* "Japanese language." The main exception is the English language, which is known as *eigo*, even though England itself is usually called *Igirisu* in modern Japanese.

Practice 7.1

Answer the following questions about yourself:

EXAMPLE:

Kimono, arimasu ka? →
Iie, kimono wa arimasen.
OR

Hai, kimono ga arimasu.
Do you have a kimono? →
No, I don't have a kimono.
OR
Yes, I have a kimono.

1. Kuruma, arimasu ka?

2. Terebi, arimasu ka?

3. Nihonjin no tomodachi, imasu ka?

4. Petto, imasu ka?

5. Rajio, arimasu ka?

6. Sutereo, arimasu ka?

7. Nihongo no jisho, arimasu ka?

8. Konpyuuta, arimasu ka?

DESCRIBING YOUR DAILY ROUTINE

In the previous chapter, you learned how to create the positive and negative forms of the polite form of the verb. Here are some of the verbs you saw in that lesson, along with a few others. The forms in parentheses are the dictionary forms.

> *okimasu (okiru)* wake up, get out of bed
> *abimasu (abiru)* take (a shower)
> *tabemasu (taberu)* eat
> *nomimasu (nomu)* drink
> *shimasu (suru)*   do
> *demasu (deru)* go out, appear, attend
> *kakimasu (kaku)* write
> *kaerimasu (kaeru)* return, go home
> *tsukurimasu (tsukuru)* make
> *mimasu (miru)* watch, look at, see
> *yomimasu (yomu)* read
> *nemasu (neru)* go to bed

This form of the verb has two possible meanings. *Shimasu* can mean "does habitually" or "will do," and *kakimasu* means "writes habitually" or "will write." None of these forms is equivalent to English forms such as "is doing" or "is writing," so you cannot use them to describe what a person or thing is doing currently or at this moment.

Any one of these verbs could be a complete sentence by itself, but you'd probably think that something was missing. You'd wonder "When does this person wake up?" "What does he or she eat?" and so on.

That's where our next two particles come in.

Some of the verbs in the preceding list are **transitive verbs.** That is, they describe doing an action to something or someone. In the English sentences "I wrote a letter" and "I ate lunch," both "wrote" and "ate" are transitive verbs, because "letter" receives the action of writing and "lunch" receives the action of eating. Grammarians refer to nouns like "letter" and "lunch" as **direct objects** when they receive the action of a verb. Can you find the direct objects of the following sentences?

(a) We bought a dog.
(b) Let's watch television.
(c) Can you fix my car?
(d) John and Susan ate the cookies.
(e) The car hit the wall.

(ANSWERS: 1. dog   2. television   3. car   4. cookies   5. wall)

In English, we determine the direct objects by their position in the sentence. If you heard a sentence such as "The cookies ate John and Susan," you would visualize a science fiction-like situation in which the cookies took their revenge on humanity!

In Japanese, the direct object of a verb is marked with the particle *o* . The normal word order is

$$\text{NOUN}_1 \, wa/ga \, \text{NOUN}_2 \, o \, \text{VERB}.$$
$$\text{NOUN}_1 \, \text{VERB(s)} \, \text{NOUN}_2.$$

NOUN₁	wa	NOUN₂	o	VERB	
Rie-san		sashimi		tabemasu	Rie-san eats raw fish.
Takashi-san		o-cha		nomimasu	Takashi-san will drink green tea.
Etsuko-san	wa	manga	o	yomimasu	Etsuko-san reads comic books.
Yôji-san		shawaa		abimasu	Yôji-san will take a shower.
Eri-san		nyuusu		mimasu	Eri-san watches the news.

Yes, you can substitute *ga* for *wa*, but there's a slight difference in emphasis. The two versions are the answers to different questions.

Etsuko-san	**wa**	nani	o	yomimasu ka?	**What** does Etsuko-san read?
↓	↓	↓	↓	↓	
Etsuko-san	**wa**	manga	o	yomimasu.	Etsuko-san reads **comic books.**
Dare	**ga**	manga	o	yomimasu ka?	**Who** reads comic books?
↓	↓	↓	↓	↓	
Etsuko-san	**ga**	manga	o	yomimasu.	**Etsuko-san** reads comic books.

So there is a slight difference in emphasis, but don't fret too much about which one to use. The difference you *should* fret about is the difference between *wa/ga* on the one hand and *o* on the other. SUBJECT-OBJECT-VERB is indeed the normal order for Japanese sentences, but the particles can override that rule. Take a sentence like

*Rie-san **wa** sashimi o tabemasu.*
Rie-san will eat raw fish.

If you put in a *ga* instead of an *o*, (a very common mistake, by the way) even if you keep exactly the same word order, you end up with a nasty-sounding situation in which some raw fish that perhaps isn't quite dead yet turns upon poor Rie:

*Rie-san **wa** sashimi **ga** tabemasu.*
As for Rie-san, the raw fish will eat her.

Using *ga* in place of *o* or vice versa is the type of mistake that can give Japanese people the giggles. Remember, these particles have specific functions within a sentence; you can't just throw in whichever one you feel like.

What confuses the issue a bit is that *wa* can substitute for *o* at times, particularly when the verb is negative.

Koohii o nomimasu ka?
*Iie, koohii **wa** nomimasen.*
Do you drink coffee?
No, I don't drink coffee.

The idea is that the questioner has brought up the topic of coffee, and the person answering is continuing with that topic. In addition, *wa* implies a comparison. The person doesn't drink coffee, but drinks something else or doesn't drink it but is willing to make it for other people.

The next particle you need is one that you've already seen: *ni*, as in *Asoko **ni** depaato ga arimasu* "There's a department store over there." The function of *ni* is to specify a point in space or time, so it usually corresponds to "at," "in," "to," "on," or sometimes "for." Thus *rokuji **ni*** means "at six o'clock," *Tôkyô **ni** imasu* means "is in Tokyo," *paatii **ni** ikimasu* means "will go to the party," *getsuyôbi **ni*** means "on Monday," and *asagohan **ni*** means "for breakfast."

Here, too, *wa* has a role to play. When you negate one of these phrases with *ni*, you need to add *wa* after the *ni*. If you're telling someone that your friend isn't in Japan, you say *Nihon ni wa imasen*. As with the replacement of *o*, the use of *wa* implies both continuation of the topic "You know this 'in Japan' business?" and comparison: "My friend is not in Japan but is somewhere else." After all, everyone has to be *somewhere*!

WATCH OUT

Discovering that *wa* is so versatile, you may be tempted to use it in every particle slot. You may get away with this tactic for a sentence or two, but eventually, you will start to sound very strange.

Vocabulary

mainichi	まいにち	毎日	every day
toosuto	トースト		toast
tamago	たまご	玉子	egg
miruku OR gyûnyû	ミルク OR ぎゅうにゅう	牛乳	milk
o-cha	おちゃ	お茶	Japanese-style tea, usually green tea
kôcha	こうちゃ	紅茶	Western-style tea, usually black tea
shinbun	しんぶん	新聞	newspaper
kaisha	かいしゃ	会社	[business] company, "the office"
dekakemasu (dekakeru)	でかけます (でかける)	出かけます	leave for, set out for, go out
shigoto	しごと	仕事	work (as a noun)
hirugohan	ひるごはん	昼御飯	lunch
mata	また	又	again
demasu (deru)	でます(でる)	出ます	leave
kaimono	かいもの	買い物	shopping
bangohan	ばんごはん	晩御飯	dinner (evening meal)
asagohan	あさごはん	朝御飯	breakfast
shawaa	シャワー		shower
abimasu (abiru)	あびます (あびる)	浴びます	to pour over one's self, used as equivalent to "take" when referring to showers
sore kara	それから		after that
yoru	よる	夜	evening, night

Vocabulary

gakkô	がっこう	学校	school (not used for colleges or universities)
manga	まんが	漫画	comic book, comic strip
sashimi	さしみ	刺身	raw fish slices

Practice 7.2a

Here's an account of a typical day in the life of Mr. Tanaka. See how much you understand; consult the vocabulary list.

Tanaka-san wa mainichi rokuji ni okimasu. Asagohan ni toosuto to tamago o tabemasu. Miruku o nomimasu. Shichiji ni kaisha ni dekakemasu. Hachiji kara jûniji made shigoto o shimasu. Jûniji ni hirugohan o tabemasu. Sore kara, mata shigoto o shimasu. Rokuji ni kaisha o demasu. Kaimono o shimasu. Uchi ni kaerimasu. Bangohan o tabemasu. Sore kara, joggingu o shimasu. Terebi o mimasu. Jûichiji ni shawaa o abimasu. Sore kara, nemasu.

Now answer these questions in English:

1. What time does Mr. Tanaka get up in the morning?

2. What does he eat for breakfast? What does he drink?

3. How many hours a day does he work, assuming that he gets an hour for lunch?

4. Do you think he usually cooks for himself or eats out? Why?

5. What two things does he do after dinner?

6. What does he do before going to bed?

You may have noticed that only the first sentence specifically mentioned Mr. Tanaka and that none of the other sentences had subjects or topics. That's because an individual Japanese sentence doesn't need a subject or topic if one has already been stated in a previous sentence. You just keep assuming the same topic or subject until another one is mentioned. Strictly speaking, you could restate the topic or subject in each sentence, but you would sound really *kudoi* (long-winded or tedious), not to mention unnatural, to a Japanese person.

For example, suppose we were talking about the Morimotos, Kiyoshi and Yumi.

> Kiyoshi-san to Yumi-san wa shichiji ni okimasu. Asagohan ni toosuto o tabemasu. Kiyoshi-san wa koohii o nomimasu. Yumi-san wa kôcha o nomimasu.

In the first sentence, Kiyoshi and Yumi are introduced as topics. Since no other topic is mentioned in the second sentence, both of them are still the topic of that sentence, that is, both of them eat toast. The third sentence starts with *Kiyoshi-san wa.* . ., so he is the topic of that sentence. The fourth sentence starts with *Yumi-san wa* . . ., so she is the topic of that sentence, and she will be the topic of all the following sentences until another topic is mentioned.

Practice 7.2b

Answer the following questions about your own daily routine. Remember that you do not have to begin each answer with *watashi wa.* In fact, you shouldn't, unless you're comparing yourself with someone else.

1. Nanji ni okimasu ka?

2. Asagohan ni nani o tabemasu ka? Nani o nomimasu ka? (If you don't eat breakfast, how would you say that?)

3. Nanji ni kaisha/daigaku/gakkô ni dekakemasu ka?

4. Nanji ni hirugohan o tabemasu ka?

5. Nanji ni kaerimasu ka?

6. Yoru wa, nani o shimasu ka? (Reminder: your answer may or may not contain *shimasu.*)

7. Nanji ni nemasu ka?

Practice 7.2c

Answer these questions negatively.

EXAMPLE:

Koohii o nomimasu ka? →
Iie, koohii wa nomimasen.

Do you drink coffee?
No, I don't drink coffee.
Sumisu-san wa Kanada ni imasu ka?
Iie, Kanada ni wa imasen.
Is Ms. Smith in Canada?
No, she isn't in Canada.

1. Jisho wa kaban no naka ni arimasu ka?

2. Terebi o mimasu ka?

3. Joggingu o shimasu ka?

4. Gozen rokuji ni okimasu ka?

5. Sashimi o tabemasu ka?

6. Nijô-jô wa Tôkyô ni arimasu ka?

7. Ras Begasu (Las Vegas) wa Kariforunia (California) ni arimasu
ka?

8. Tanaka-san wa kaisha ni imasu ka?

MORE ABOUT TELLING TIME

You have already learned how to tell time on the hour and half
hour, but in order to add more precision, you need to learn the
forms for counting minutes.

ippun	いっぷん	一分	one minute
nifun	にふん	二分	two minutes
sanpun	さんぷん	三分	three minutes
yonpun	よんぷん	四分	four minutes
gofun	ごふん	五分	five minutes
roppun	ろっぷん	六分	six minutes
nanafun	ななふん	七分	seven minutes
happun	はっぷん	八分	eight minutes
kyûfun	きゅうふん	九分	nine minutes
juppun	じゅっぷん	十分	ten minutes

The rest of the minutes are combinations of these forms.

jûippun	じゅういっぷん	十一分	eleven minutes
jûgo fun	じゅうごふん	十五分	fifteen minutes
nijuppun	にじゅっぷん	二十分	twenty minutes
nijû happun	にじゅうはっぷん	二十八分	twenty-eight minutes
sanjuppun	さんじゅっぷん	三十分	thirty minutes
yonjûni fun	よんじゅうにふん	四十二分	forty-two minutes

Times such as 9:15 or 10:50 are stated in the following format:

_____ ji_____ fun

kuji jûgo fun   = 9:15

jûji gojuppun = 10:50

yoji nijûippun = 4:21

There is no special word for quarter hours; people just say _jûgo fun_. For half hours, _-han_, as in _ichiji han_ (1:30), is most common in everyday conversation, but you will also hear forms such as _ichiji sanjuppun_, particularly in more formal situations.

Saying something like "1:55" sounds rather formal and stilted, both in English and in Japanese, and when you are talking about minutes before the hour, it is more common to use this form:

_____ ji____ fun mae_

_____ minutes to _____

niji gofun mae = five minutes to two

Practice 7.3

How would you say these times in Japanese? (You may need to review the correct ways to say "four o'clock," "seven o'clock," and "nine o'clock." [See page 46])

1. 2:20 A.M.

2. 4:16 P.M.

3. 5:40 A.M. (two ways)

4. 6:30 P.M. (two ways)

5. 3:57 A.M. (two ways)

6. 7:02 P.M.

7. 8:45 A.M. (two ways)

8. 9:29 P.M.

SUMMING UP
MATOME
まとめ

Vocabulary

eiga	えいが	映画	movie
VEHICLE ni norimasu	VEHICLEに のります(のる)	乗ります	to take, board, or ride a VEHICLE
densha	でんしゃ	電車	railroad or subway train
PLACE ni tsukimasu (tsuku)	PLACE につきます (つく)	着きます	arrive at PLACE
niku	にく	肉	meat
itsumo	いつも		always

Complete these dialogues according to the cues given.

1. Japanese television programs don't always start on the hour or half-hour. Ikeda Masaru has just heard that one of his favorite movies is playing on television tonight, so he asks you for details.

Ikeda: Sono eiga wa nanji kara desu ka?
You: (Tell him that it starts at 9:10 P.M.)
Ikeda: Nanji made desu ka?
You: (Tell him that it runs until 10:50.)

2. You and Mr. Sone are talking about your daily commutes.

Sone: Boku wa itsumo shichiji han no densha ni norimasu.
You: (Say that you always take the 7:45 train.)
Sone: Sono densha wa nanji ni Tôkyô eki ni tsukimasu ka?
You: (Say that it arrives at 8:15.)

3. Professor Koyanagi is planning to have some of the international students over for dinner, so she asks you about their eating habits.

Koyanagi: Uiruson-san to Sumisu-san wa sashimi o tabemasu ka?
You: (Say that they do. NOTE: Do **not** use *shimasu*.)
Koyanagi: Jaa, niku wa?
You: (Tell her that Ms. Smith eats meat, but Mr. Wilson doesn't.)

Sumo wrestling, one of the most traditional sports in Japan

Japan National Tourist Organization (JNTO)

CHAPTER 8

TOSHOKAN DE BENKYÔ SHIMASHITA.
(I STUDIED IN THE LIBRARY.)

In this chapter, you will learn to:

1. talk about events in the past
2. tell where actions take place
3. talk about the means by which actions are accomplished
4. express the idea of motion toward a place

EVENTS IN THE PAST

Talking about past events in the polite form is quite simple. To make a present-tense verb (one with a -*masu* ending) indicate a past action, simply change the -*masu* to -*mashita*. This will work with one hundred percent of these verbs:

shimasu	*shimashita*
does, will do	did
tabemasu	*tabemashita*
eats, will eat	ate
nomimasu	*nomimashita*
drinks, will drink	drank

Note that all the English verbs given as examples are irregular ("ate" instead of "eated"), so in this respect, Japanese is easier than English.

To change a negative present tense verb (one with a -*masen* ending) to the past tense, simply add *deshita*.

shimasen	*shimasen deshita*
doesn't do, won't do	didn't do
tabemasen	*tabemasen deshita*
doesn't eat, won't eat	didn't eat

The one exception to these regular verbs is *desu,* whose past tense is *deshita,* so the past tense of *gakusei desu* "is a student" is *gakusei deshita* "was a student."

The negative of *desu,* which is either *de wa arimasen* or *de wa nai desu,* has two possible past forms as well:

gakusei de wa arimasen	*gakusei de wa arimasen deshita*
is not a student	was not a student
gakusei de wa nai desu	*gakusei de wa nakatta desu*
is not a student	was not a student

Vocabulary

kakimasu (kaku)	かきます (かく)	書く	write
misemasu (miseru)	みせます (みせる)	見せる	show
kaimasu (kau)	かいます (かう)	買う	buy
shashin	しゃしん	写真	photograph
dekimasu (dekiru)	できます (できる)		to be able, to be possible, to finish
tsukurimasu (tsukuru)	つくります (つくる)	作る	make

Practice 8.1a

Change these sentences from statements about what Ms. Suzuki will do tomorrow or things that will be true tomorrow to statements about what Ms. Suzuki did yesterday or things that were true yesterday.

EXAMPLE:

Ashita shigoto o shimasu. →
Kinô shigoto o shimashita.
Tomorrow she will work. →
Yesterday she worked.

1. Ashita, tegami o kakimasu.

2. Ashita, atarashii rajio o kaimasu.

3. Ashita, Furansu ryôri o tabemasu.

4. Ashita, Kyôto ni dekakemasu.

5. Ashita, sushi o tsukurimasu.

6. Ashita, gozen goji ni okimasu.

7. Ashita, omoshiroi eiga o mimasu.

8. Ashita, tomodachi ni shashin o misemasu.

9. Ashita, dekimasu.

10. Ashita wa nichiyôbi desu.

Practice 8.1b

Answer the questions saying that you didn't do the things asked about.

EXAMPLE:

Dekimashita ka? →
Iie, dekimasen deshita.
Were you able to do it?
No, I wasn't.

Sandoitchi o tsukurimashita ka? →
Iie, tsukurimasen deshita.
Did you make sandwiches? →
No, I didn't.

1. Tegami o kakimashita ka?

2. Asagohan o tabemashita ka?

3. Ano kuruma o kaimashita ka?

4. Joggingu o shimashita ka?

5. Aisu tii (ice tea) o nomimashita ka?

6. Paatii ni ikimashita ka?

7. Kinô, imashita ka?

8. Kinô, shinbun o yomimashita ka?

If you were asked how adjectives form their past tense, you would probably guess: Just change the *desu* to *deshita* so that *takai desu* becomes *takai deshita*.

Well, that's a good guess, but it's not correct. Actually, a clue to the past tense of the adjective is found in the past tense of *de wa nai desu*, which is *de wa nakatta desu*. Note what happens here. The *-i* of *nai* is changed to *-katta*, and everything else stays the same. This is precisely the pattern for the past tenses of adjectives.

taka-	i	desu	is expensive
taka-	katta	desu	was expensive
atarashi-	i	desu	is new
atarashi-	katta	desu	was new

The major exception is *ii*, "good," which, as you remember, has an irregular negative, *yoku nai desu* or *yoku arimasen*. Its past tense is also irregular: *yokatta desu*. This form *yokatta* is very common in conversational Japanese, because people say *yokatta!* in situations where English-speakers would say "Oh, good!"

Practice 8.1c

Change the following adjectives to their past tense forms.

EXAMPLE:

Oishii desu. →
Oishikatta desu.
It is delicious. →
It was delicious.

1. Samui desu.

2. Atsui desu.

3. Nagai desu. (It is long.)

4. Mijikai desu. (It is short.)

5. Yasui desu. (It is cheap.)

6. Muzukashii desu. (It is difficult.)

7. Omoi desu. (It is heavy.)

8. Akarui desu. (It is bright.)

The past negatives of adjectives are fairly simple as long as you can remember that the past tense of *de wa nai desu/de wa arimasen* is *de wa nakatta desu/de wa arimasen deshita.*

oishiku nai desu It isn't delicious.	*oishiku nakatta desu* It wasn't delicious.
oishiku arimasen It isn't delicious.	*oishiku arimasen deshita* It wasn't delicious.

Practice 8.1d

Take all the adjectives in Practice 8.1c and change them to the past negative form. It doesn't matter which negative you use.

EXAMPLE:

Oishii desu. →
Oishiku nakatta desu OR
Oishiku arimasen deshita.
It's delicious. →
It wasn't delicious.

Now you know all the forms that the adjective can take in the polite style of speaking. Here are some examples of usage:

mô sukoshi de	もうすこしで	もう少しで	in a little while
dôshite	どうして		why
zenbu	ぜんぶ	全部	the whole thing, all of it
dansu paatii	ダンス・パーティー		a dance

1. Mr. Tanaka and Mr. Morimoto have to present a report at a four o'clock meeting. At 3:50, Mr. Tanaka is hurrying to put together the handouts, because for a long time, he couldn't get the presentation software to work correctly.

Morimoto:	Dô desu ka?
Tanaka:	Mô sukoshi de. . . Hai, zenbu dekimashita!
Morimoto:	A, yokatta!
Morimoto:	How is it?
Tanaka:	It won't be long. . . Yes, the whole thing's done.
Morimoto:	Oh, good!

2. Thomas Wilson, Ikeda Masaru, and Chan Ngan-fa are talking about what they did over the weekend.

Ikeda:	Doyôbi no dansu paatii ni ikimashita ka?
Chan:	Watashi wa ikimashita. Tanoshikatta desu yo.
Wilson:	Boku wa ikimasen deshita.
Ikeda:	Sô desu ka? Dôshite?

Ikeda:	Did you go to Saturday's dance?
Chan:	I went. It was fun.
Wilson:	I didn't go.
Ikeda:	Really? Why [not]?

• Chan Ngan-fa says *watashi wa ikimashita* instead of just *ikimashita*, because she is comparing herself to Thomas Wilson, who didn't go. If this were a two-way conversation between Ikeda Masaru and Chan Ngan-fa, she probably would not include the *watashi wa*, because it would be obvious who the subject was.

WHERE ACTIONS TAKE PLACE

You have already learned that the versatile particle *ni* can indicate where something or someone is located, as in

Uiruson-san wa Nihon ni imasu.
Mr. Wilson is in Japan.

It can also indicate appearance in a place or getting into position.

Ano isu ni suwarimashita.
She sat down on that chair.

Gozen kuji ni eki no mae ni atsumarimashita.
We gathered in front of the station at 9:00 A.M.

However, once you've arrived at the right place and started doing things, the place is marked with *de*.

Hoomu de densha o machimashita.
I waited for the train on the platform.

Shokudô de hirugohan o tabemashita.
I ate lunch in the dining hall.

Nihon de shodô o naraimashita.
I took lessons in calligraphy in Japan.

Abuduuru-san wa itsumo toshokan de benkyô shimasu.
Ms. Abdul always studies in the library.

Here are some examples of usage.

suwarimasu (suwaru)	すわります (すわる)	座わる	sit
atsumarimasu (atsumaru)	あつまります (あつまる)	集まる	gather
hoomu	ホーム		train station platform
machimasu (matsu)	まちます (まつ)	待つ	wait
shokudô	しょくどう	食堂	dining hall
naraimasu (narau)	ならいます (ならう)	習う	learn, take lessons in
shodô	しょどう	書道	artistic calligraphy
benkyô shimasu (suru)	べんきょう します(する)	勉強	study
taitei	たいてい		usually
ya	や		and things like that
tokidoki	ときどき	時々	sometimes
supootsu kurabu	スポーツ・クラブ		health club
puuru	プール		swimming pool
oyogimasu (oyogu)	およぎます (およぐ)	泳ぐ	swim

tenisu	テニス		tennis
haikingu	ハイキング		hiking
erai	えらい	偉い	impressive, distinguished (in reference to people)
nagisa	なぎさ	渚	beach
ongaku	おんがく	音楽	music
gorogoro shimasu (suru)	ごろごろ します (する)		lie around and do nothing
undô	うんどう	運動	exercise
heya	へや	部屋	room

Examples:

1. Eric Jones and Teramura Chieko are talking about their study habits.

Jones:	Teramura-san wa doko de benkyô shimasu ka?
Teramura:	Watashi wa taitei toshokan de benkyô shimasu. Joonzu-san wa?
Jones:	Boku wa taitei heya de benkyô shimasu.

Jones:	Where do you study?
Teramura:	I usually study in the library. What about you?
Jones:	I usually study in my room.

• Note that Eric Jones says just *heya* instead of *boku no heya* Repeating *boku* would sound repetitious, and it is unnecessary, because there has been no change of subject.

2. Mr. Sone and Ms. Suzuki are talking about what they usually do on weekends.

Sone:	Nichiyôbi wa taitei nani o shimasu ka?
Suzuki:	Taitei supootsu kurabu de undô shimasu ga. . .
Sone:	Hee?
Suzuki:	Tokidoki haikingu ya tenisu o shimasu.
Sone:	Sô desu ka?
Suzuki:	Demo, kinô wa kurabu no puuru de oyogimashita.
Sone:	Erai desu ne. Boku wa taitei terebi no mae de gorogoro shimasu yo.

Sone:	What do you usually do on Sundays?
Suzuki:	I usually exercise at the health club. . .
Sone:	Oh?
Suzuki:	. . .but sometimes I hike or play tennis.
Sone:	Is that right?
Suzuki:	However, yesterday, I swam in the club's pool.
Sone:	That's impressive. I usually lie around in front of the TV.

• It may seem as if Mr. Sone is interrupting, but actually, he is throwing in what the Japanese call *aizuchi*, little remarks that listeners make to let the speaker know that they are following along. This is such a deeply ingrained habit in Japanese culture that if you don't use *aizuchi* in a one-on-one conversation, especially on the telephone, the speaker may assume that you aren't listening.

Practice 8.2

Say that you did the following things in the places indicated.

EXAMPLE:

(study) (library) →
Toshokan de benkyô shimashita.
I studied in the library.

1. (eat lunch) (dining hall)

2. (play tennis) (park)

3. (read book) (beach)

4. (buy meat) (supermarket)

5. (listen to music) (inside the car)

6. (take lessons in karate) (Japan)

7. (see movie) (on television) (Yes, you use *de* here.)

8. (work from 9:00 to 3:00) (bank)

9. (drink tea) (hotel)

10. (make sushi) (home)

HOW ACTIONS ARE ACCOMPLISHED

Another use of *de* is to indicate that the noun marked with it is the means by which an action was accomplished.

> *Pen de kakimashita.*
> I wrote with a pen.

> *Taitei hashi de tabemasu.*
> I usually eat with chopsticks.

> *Itsumo sekken de araimasu.*
> I always wash it with soap.

> *Hikōki de ikimashita.*
> I went by plane.

Here are some examples.

hashi	はし	箸	chopsticks
karee raisu	カレーライス		rice with a curry-flavored sauce
gohan	ごはん	御飯	cooked rice
sekken	せっけん	石鹸	soap
araimasu (arau)	あらいます (あらう)	洗う	wash
hikôki	ひこうき	飛行機	airplane
supuun	スプーン		spoon
sentakuki	せんたくき	洗濯機	washing machine
minasan	みなさん	皆さん	all of you, you people
te	て	手	hand
fune	ふね	船	ship, boat

1. Ms. King still isn't quite accustomed to life in Japan. She and Ms. Ishida go out to lunch together, and they stop in at a restaurant that specializes in curry rice, which Ms. King has never eaten. When the waitress brings it, she sets spoons down next to the plates.

King:	Hashi wa doko desu ka?
Ishida:	Hashi desu ka?
King:	Ee, Nihonjin wa hashi de gohan o tabemasu ne?
Ishida:	A, karee raisu wa chigaimasu yo. Supuun de tabemasu.

King:	Where are the chopsticks?
Ishida:	Chopsticks?
King:	Yes. Japanese people eat rice with chopsticks, right?
Ishida:	Oh, curry rice is different. You eat it with a spoon.

2. Coming from a tropical country, Zaini Abdul has never had to take care of wool clothes, but when winter rolls around, she buys some sweaters. She asks Amanda Smith for advice on how to take care of them.

Abdul:	Sentakuki de araimasu ne?
Smith:	Iie, iie. Te de araimasu yo.

Abdul:	You wash them in the washing machine, right?
Smith:	No, no. You wash them by hand.

3. The international students are talking about how they came to Japan.

Wilson:	Minasan wa hikôki de kimashita ne?
Kim:	Iie, boku wa fune de kimashita.

Wilson:	All of you came by plane, right?
Kim:	No, I came by ship.

MOTION TOWARD A PLACE

Okay. One more particle for this chapter. You've already learned how to say PLACE *ni ikimasu/kimasu/kaerimasu*. This is fine, but there's another particle used with these verbs of motion. It's *e*, and in fact, it is used exclusively with verbs of motion to indicate movement toward a destination.

> *Uchi e kaerimashita.*
> I returned home.

> *Suiyôbi ni Nihon e kimashita.*
> I came to Japan on Wednesday.

> *Mainichi asoko e ikimasu.*
> I go there every day.

The difference between the two particles is that *e* emphasizes the process of motion while *ni* emphasizes arrival at the destination. *Ni* is the more versatile particle: it can be used both for verbs of motion and verbs of position, while *e* can be used only, solely, just, exclusively for verbs of motion. In addition, *ni* is preferred when speaking of going to an event, such as a party or a festival. So why can't you just use *ni* all the time and just forget about *e* ? Well, sometimes you need to use *e*, as when asking a fragmentary question about a verb of motion:

> *–Dekakemasu yo.*
> *–Doko e?*
> (NOT *doko ni*)
> I'm heading out.
> Where to?

Practice 8.3

Tell whether these sentences are true (T) or false (F). Some of them are based on dialogues in this chapter, while others are based on real life.

1. Nihonjin wa itsumo hashi de tabemasu.

2. Amerikajin wa supuun de sandoitchi o tabemasu.

3. Kimu-san wa fune de Nihon e kimashita.

4. Uiruson-san wa hikôki de Nihon e kimashita.

5. Sone-san wa terebi no mae de undô shimasu.

6. Nichiyôbi ni wa, Suzuki-san wa taitei puuru de oyogimasu.

7. Sumisu-san wa te de seetaa o araimasu.

8. Kingu-san wa supuun o tabemashita.

SUMMING UP
MATOME
まとめ

Okay, now you have a lot of different particles, and maybe it's time to list and review them. (Don't worry. There will be more.)

wa	marks the topic
ga	emphasizes the subject
o	marks the direct object of a verb
ni	indicates location in time or space
de	indicates 1) where action takes place or 2) the means by which an action is performed
e	indicates motion towards a destination
no	indicates possession or other connections
kara	indicates source "from"
made	indicates the endpoint "until"

1. Fill in the blanks with the proper particles. Read the whole sentence through first, figure out what it most likely means, and then put in the particles that will make that meaning plain by clarifying the relationships among the words. Remember that there is a reason for each particle. Then read the sentence over again. Does it make sense, or have you created a nonsensical sentence, like the one in Chapter 6 about the *sashimi* eating Rie?

a. Chan-san____ Honkon (Hong Kong) ___ imasu.
   Doyôbi____ dekakemashita.

b. Ikeda-san___ watashi____ tomodachi desu.

c. Dare___ kono sarada (salad)___ tsukurimashita ka?

d. Tanaka-san____ niku ___ tabemasu ka?

e. Kaigi____ jûji _____ jûichiji _____ desu.

f. Uchi____ mae___ kuruma__ arimasu yo. Dare__ kuruma desu
   ka?

g. Are_____ nan desu ka?

h. Watashi_____ maiasa, rokuji_____ okimasu ga, ruumumeeto
   (roommate) ___ taitei shichiji _____ okimasu.

i. Joonzu-san____ kaban____ tsukue____ shita____ arimasu.

2. Complete the dialogues:

a. Teramura Chieko is asking you about your vacation (*yasumi*).

    Teramura: Yasumi ni doko e ikimashita ka?
    You: (Tell her that you went to Okinawa.)
    Teramura: Sô desu ka? Dô deshita ka?
    You: (Tell her that it was very enjoyable. You swam every day.)
    Teramura: Sore wa yokatta desu ne. Okinawa no ongaku o kikimashita ka?
    You: (You didn't.)

b. You and Ikeda Masaru are talking about what you did on Saturday.

    Ikeda: Doyôbi ni nani o shimashita ka?
    You: (Tell him that you saw a movie in Shinjuku [a neighborhood in Tokyo].)
    Ikeda: Sô desu ka? Omoshirokatta desu ka?
    You: (It wasn't very interesting.)
    Ikeda: Sô desu ka? Sore kara wa?
    You: (Tell him that you returned home.)

A LAND OF FESTIVALS

Hahrii Festival, Okinawa

Ose-Myoojin Festival, Shizuoka

Snow Festival, Sapporo

Hakata-Fukuoka Dontaku Festival

YASUKATTA DESU KARA, MITTSU KAIMASHITA. (BECAUSE THEY WERE CHEAP, I BOUGHT THREE.)

In this chapter you will learn to:

1. say "also"
2. talk about the months and days of the month
3. talk about quantities
4. give the reasons for something
5. say "with"

HOW TO SAY "ALSO"

The Japanese particle corresponding to the English words "too" or "also" is *mo*, but it is used quite differently from its English counterparts. Take, for example, the following English sentence:

I taught English conversation in Japan, too.

Without a context you don't know whether this means

(a) I (as well as someone else) taught English conversation in Japan.
(b) I taught English conversation (as well as something else) in Japan.
(c) I taught English conversation in Japan (as well as somewhere else).

In real life, English speakers distinguish these three meanings by their tone of voice:

(a) **I** taught English conversation in Japan, too.
(b) I taught **English conversation** in Japan, too.
(c) I taught English conversation **in Japan**, too.

In Japanese, on the other hand, these three meanings would be expressed by different word orders. The basic sentence, without "too," would translate as

Watashi wa Nihon de eikaiwa o oshiemashita.
I taught English conversation in Japan.

The three meanings of "I taught English conversation in Japan, too" would be expressed as follows:

(a) *Watashi **mo** Nihon de eikaiwa o oshiemashita.*
(b) *Watashi wa Nihon de eikaiwa **mo** oshiemashita.*
(c) *Watashi wa Nihon de **mo** eikaiwa o oshiemashita.*

In other words, *mo* comes after the noun phrase that would be emphasized if you were expressing that meaning in English.

You may be wondering what has happened to *wa, ga,* and *o.* The answer is that they disappear, because *mo* always replaces them.

(d) *Hon **ga** arimasu.*
There's a book.

*Hon **mo** arimasu.*
There's a book, also.

(e) *Teepu **o** kikimashita.*
I listened to tapes.

*Teepu **mo** kikimashita.*
I listened to tapes, too.

(f) *Tanaka-san **wa** sûgaku o senkô shimashita.*
Mr. Tanaka majored in mathematics.

*Date-san **mo** sûgaku o senkô shimashita.*
Mr. Date also majored in mathematics.

The other particles just let *mo* tag along behind them.

(g) *Eki no mae **ni** basu no teiryûjo ga arimasu.*
There's a bus stop in front of the station.

*Ginkô no mae **ni mo** arimasu.*
There's [one] in front of the bank, too.

(h) Nihon de Eikaiwa o oshiemashita.
I taught English conversation in Japan.

*Kankoku **de** mo eikaiwa o oshiemashita.*
I taught English conversation in South Korea, too.

(i) *Kyôto e ikimashita.*
I went to Kyôto.

Nara e mo ikimashita.
I went to Nara, too.

A pair of *mo*'s usually corresponds to the English "both. . . and."

Karate mo shodô mo naraimashita.
I took lessons in both karate and calligraphy.

Kyôto e mo Nara e mo ikimashita.
I went to both Kyôto and Nara.

Practice 9.1

Vocabulary

eikaiwa	えいかいわ	英会話	English conversation
oshiemasu (oshieru)	おしえます (おしえる)	教える	teach
sûgaku	すうがく	数学	mathematics
NOUN o senkô shimasu (suru)	NOUN を せんこうします (する)	専攻する	to major in NOUN
Kankoku	かんこく	韓国	South Korea
nomimono	のみもの	飲み物	beverage
kippu	きっぷ	切符	ticket
urimasu (uru)	うります(うる)	売る	sell
Doitsugo	ドイツご	ドイツ語	German (language)
Suisu	スイス		Switzerland
kudamono	くだもの	果物	fruit
eiga	えいが	映画	movie
eigakan	えいがかん	映画館	movie theater
basu no teiryûjo	バスの ていりゅうじょ	バスの 停留所	bus stop

Read each of the following statements. Then make up a question or statement based on the cues.

EXAMPLE:

Amanda Sumisu wa Kanadajin desu.
Amanda Smith is Canadian.
(Ask if Thomas Wilson [Tomasu Uiruson] is also Canadian.) →
Tomasu Uiruson mo Kanadajin desu ka?

1. Hoteru no mae ni basu no teiryûjo ga arimasu.
   (Ask if there is a taxi stand [*takushii noriba*] too.)

2. Hoteru no mae ni basu no teiryûjo ga arimasu.
   (Ask if there is one in front of the station, too.)

3. Kinô, Shinjuku de kaimono o shimashita.
   (Ask if the person shopped in Shibuya [another neighborhood in Tokyo], too.)

4. Ikeda-san wa eiga no kippu o urimashita.
   (Ask if he sold beverages,too.)

5. Teramura-san wa Suisu de Furansugo o benkyô shimashita.
   (Ask if she studied German, too.)

6. Teramura-san wa Suisu de Furansugo o benkyô shimashita.
   (Ask if she also studied in France.)

7. Teramura-san wa Suisu de Furansugo o benkyô shimashita.
   (Ask if Ms. Ishida also studied French in Switzerland.)

8. Kyôto to Nara e ikimashita.
   (Ask if both Kyôto and Nara were interesting.)

THE MONTHS AND DAYS OF THE MONTH

Naming the months in Japanese is easy, because they are simply numbered from one to twelve. Pay attention to the forms in bold type, however, because *yongatsu, nanagatsu,* and *kyûgatsu* are not used.

ichigatsu	いちがつ	一月	January
nigatsu	にがつ	二月	February
sangatsu	さんがつ	三月	March
shigatsu	しがつ	四月	April
gogatsu	ごがつ	五月	May
rokugatsu	ろくがつ	六月	June
shichigatsu	しちがつ	七月	July
hachigatsu	はちがつ	八月	August
kugatsu	くがつ	九月	September
jûgatsu	じゅうがつ	十月	October
jûichigatsu	じゅういちがつ	十一月	November
jûnigatsu	じゅうにがつ	十二月	December

The days of the month are a little more complicated, because the first ten days are irregular, being based on the ancient Japanese calendar system. The rest are more regular, although there are a couple of tricky spots, marked with bold type in the list.

tsuitachi	ついたち	一日	first [day]
futsuka	ふつか	二日	second
mikka	みっか	三日	third
yokka	よっか	四日	fourth
itsuka	いつか	五日	fifth
muika	むいか	六日	sixth
nanoka	なのか	七日	seventh
yôka	ようか	八日	eighth
kokonoka	ここのか	九日	ninth
tooka	とおか	十日	tenth
jûichinichi	じゅういちにち	十一日	eleventh
jûninichi	じゅうににち	十二日	twelfth
jûyokka	じゅうよっか	十四日	fourteenth
jûgonichi	じゅうごにち	十五日	fifteenth
jûkunichi	じゅうくにち	十九日	nineteenth
hatsuka	はつか	二十日	twentieth
nijûichinichi	にじゅういちにち	二十一日	twenty-first
nijûyokka	にじゅうよっか	二十四日	twenty-fourth
nijûgonichi	にじゅうごにち	二十五日	twenty-fifth
nijûkunichi	にじゅうくにち	二十九日	twenty-ninth
sanjûnichi	さんじゅうにち	三十日	thirtieth
sanjûichinichi	さんじゅういちにち	三十一日	thirty-first

To ask about the date and month of an event, ask: EVENT *wa nangatsu nannichi desu ka?*

> *Kurisumasu wa nangatsu nannichi desu ka?*
> *Jûnigatsu nijûgonichi desu.*
> What month and day is Christmas?
> It's December 25.

Note that the day comes directly after the month without any particles in between. However, when you have an expression such as "the first of this month," *no* is inserted between the month and the day: *kongetsu no tsuitachi* "the first of this month."

"Birthday" is *tanjôbi*, and its honorific form, used to refer to someone else's birthday, is *o-tanjôbi*, so when asking when someone's birthday is, ask *O-tanjôbi wa nangatsu nannichi desu ka?* When answering, however, take off the *o-*, because you are never supposed to use honorifics in reference to anything connected with yourself.

O-tanjôbi wa nangatsu nannichi desu ka?
Tanjôbi desu ka? Rokugatsu muika desu.
What is the date of your birthday?
My birthday? It's June 6.

Practice 9.2

Vocabulary

kotoshi	ことし	今年	this year
nan'yôbi	なんようび	何曜日	what day of the week?
o-shôgatsu	おしょうがつ	お正月	New Year's Day
raishû	らいしゅう	来週	next week
senshû	せんしゅう	先週	last week
konshû	こんしゅう	今週	this week
sengetsu	せんげつ	先月	last month
raigetsu	らいげつ	来月	next month
kongetsu	こんげつ	今月	this month

Here are some Japanese holidays with their dates written in Japanese. Write their dates in English.

1. bunka no hi (Culture Day): jûichigatsu mikka

2. kodomo no hi (Children's Day): gogatsu itsuka

3. midori no hi (Greenery Day): shigatsu nijûkunichi

4. keirô no hi (Respect for the Aged Day): kugatsu jûgonichi

What are these dates in Japanese? You may have to consult a calendar.

5. O-shôgatsu wa nangatsu nannichi desu ka?

6. Barentain Dee wa? (HINT: That's the holiday with all the hearts and flowers.)

7. O-tanjôbi wa nangatsu nannichi desu ka?

8. Fourth of July wa nangatsu nannichi desu ka?

9. Harouiin wa nangatsu nannichi desu ka? (HINT: That's the holiday when people dress up in costume.)

10. Raigetsu no tsuitachi wa nangatsu nannichi desu ka?

11. Kongetsu no jûhachinichi wa nan'yôbi desu ka?

12. Konshû no nichiyôbi wa nannichi desu ka?

13. Senshû no kayôbi wa nannichi deshita ka?

14. Raishû no suiyôbi wa nannichi desu ka?

QUANTITIES

In English we count most objects or events simply by placing a number in front of the noun: "one child," "two dogs," "three shirts," "four pencils," "five books," "six apples." In Japanese, each of these nouns—children, dogs, shirts, pencils, books, and apples —is counted differently.

This sounds terribly complicated until you remember that English has special ways of counting certain things. If you say "two papers," that means two newspapers or two research papers. To refer to two of those flat things made of wood pulp, you have to say "two sheets of paper." Restaurant personnel may talk of "two breads," but most people say "two loaves of bread" or "two slices of bread."

Japanese just carries this further. Here are the most common *counters*. (There are others, but some of them are so obscure that most Japanese people don't use them in ordinary conversation.) We will introduce the specifics of each one in later chapters, but this is a brief overview:

-nin	-にん	(人)	people
-mai	-まい	(枚)	flat objects, such as paper, clothing, leaves, CDs, etc.
-hon	-ほん	(本)	long, slender objects, such as pencils, fingers, trees, bottles, and even cassette tapes (if you unwind them)
-satsu	-さつ	(冊)	bound volumes, such as books, magazines, and notebooks
-hiki	-ひき	(匹)	small animals
-tô	-とう	(頭)	large animals
-dai	-だい	(台)	appliances and vehicles

You've already learned the basic counting numbers, which are based on the Chinese number system, but the language also contains a remnant of the old native Japanese number system. These numbers are used in counting objects or events that have no other specific counter, and they run only from one through ten.

hitotsu	ひとつ	一つ	one
futatsu	ふたつ	二つ	two
mittsu	みっつ	三つ	three
yottsu	よっつ	四つ	four
itsutsu	いつつ	五つ	five
muttsu	むっつ	六つ	six
nanatsu	ななつ	七つ	seven
yattsu	やっつ	八つ	eight
kokonotsu	ここのつ	九つ	nine
too	とお	十	ten
ikutsu?	いくつ？		how many?

Do these look vaguely familiar? If not, compare them with the names of the first ten days of the month. Yes, both sets come from the same ancient Japanese numbers. So now that you have them, what do you do with them? And what do you do if you have more than ten of whatever it is you're counting?

That last question is the easiest to answer: you just use the normal Chinese-derived numbers: *Hako no naka ni peepaa kurippu ga gojû arimasu.* "There are fifty paper clips in the box," etc. As for what you do with these and other expressions of quantity, you need to pay attention to the word order. There are two normal word orders:

NOUN	particle	QUANTITY	VERB	
Ringo	ga	hitotsu	arimasu.	There is one apple.
Isu	o	futatsu	kaimashita.	I bought two chairs.

You could also express these ideas using this pattern:

QUANTITY	no	NOUN	particle	VERB
Hitotsu	no	ringo	ga	arimasu.
Futatsu	no	isu	o	kaimashita.

There is a slight difference between the two patterns. The second pattern is used when referring to some specific or previously mentioned objects, and it is often preceded by *kono, sono,* or *ano.*

> *Isu o futatsu kaimashita.*
> I bought two chairs.
>
> *Kono futatsu no isu o kaimashita.*
> I bought these two chairs.

Don't worry too much about this distinction. Just avoid using English word order and engrave the phrases *NOUN-particle-QUANTITY-VERB* and *QUANTITY-no-NOUN-particle-VERB* on your brain. The same word order is used with non-numerical expressions of quantity, such as *zenbu* "all of it, the whole thing," *takusan* "a lot, much," and *mina* "all, everyone."

Here are some examples.

ringo	りんご		apple
takusan	たくさん		a lot, much
hotchikisu	ホッチキス		stapler
keshigomu	けしゴム	消しゴム	eraser
rooru pan	ロールパン		roll (bread)
booru	ボール		ball
kamibukuro	かみぶくろ	紙袋	paper bag
tsukaimasu (tsukau)	つかいます (つかう)	使う	use
o-sara	おさら	お皿	dishes (literally, "plates")
kokonattsu	ココナッツ		coconut
koohii jawan	コーヒー ぢゃわん	コーヒー 茶碗	coffee cup

Examples:

1. The international students are having a tropical-theme party, and Ikeda Masaru and Amanda Smith are working on the refreshments and decor.

Sumisu: Kokonattsu wa ikutsu arimasu ka?
Ikeda: Kokonattsu wa. . .kokonotsu arimasu yo. Jaa, orenji wa?
Sumisu: Orenji wa takusan kaimashita.

Smith: How many coconuts are there?
Ikeda: There are nine coconuts. Well, what about oranges?
Smith: I bought a lot of oranges.

2. Chan Ngan-fa has taken it upon herself to tidy up the Yamaguchis' kitchen, when Mrs. Yamaguchi walks in.

Yamaguchi: Ara! O-sara o zenbu araimashita ka?
Chan: Iie, kono mittsu no koohii jawan dake desu.

Yamaguchi: Oh, my! Did you wash all the dishes?
Chan: No, just these three coffee cups.

Practice 9.3

Complete the following exchanges according to the cues given.

EXAMPLE:

Ringo wa ikutsu arimasu ka?
(There are eight apples.) →
Ringo wa yattsu arimasu.

1. Hotchikisu wa ikutsu arimasu ka?
   (There are three staplers.)

2. Nani o kaimashita ka?
   (I bought six rolls.)

3. Sono kamibukuro no naka ni nani ga arimasu ka?
   (There are seven balls.)

4. Nani o tsukaimashita ka?
   (I used these two coffee cups.]

5. Ringo wa takusan tabemashita ka?
   (No, I ate one.) (Could you say, "I ate just one"? Think about
   it.)

6. Ano bideo (video) o mimashita ka?
   (Yes, I saw the whole thing.)

7. A: Irasshaimase.
   B: (Please give me four sandwiches.)

8. Nihongo no teepu o kikimashita ka?
   (Yes, I listened to a lot of them.)

GIVING REASONS

When we give reasons in English, we put "because" or "since" in
front of the **reason**. The **result** of the reason may come either
before or after the reason.

> I ate a lot, because it was delicious.
> result   reason

Since it was cheap, I bought it.
reason   result

In Japanese, however, the equivalent to "because" or "since" always comes after the reason:

oishikatta desu kara. . . because it was tasty

yasukatta desu kara. . . because it was cheap

Nihonjin desu kara. . . because they are Japanese

Teepu o kikimasen deshita kara. . . because I didn't listen to the tapes

Then the result comes after the reason in normal word order.

Oishikatta desu kara, takusan tabemashita.
Because it was delicious, I ate a lot.

Yasukatta desu kara, mittsu kaimashita.
Because they were cheap, I bought three.

Nihonjin desu kara, hashi de gohan o tabemasu.
Because they're Japanese, they eat rice with chopsticks.

Teepu o kikimasen deshita kara, kikitori no shiken ni shippai shimashita.
Since I didn't listen to the tapes, I failed the listening test.

If you put the reason after the result, it sounds like an afterthought:

Kikitori no shiken ni shippai shimashita—teepu o kikimasen deshita kara.
I failed the listening test, uh,—because I didn't listen to the tapes.

In ordinary conversation, you may hear fragmentary answers ending in *kara,* particularly as answers to questions. If you have trouble remembering where to put *kara,* think of it as meaning "and so." Then you'll know that you need to put it after the reason.

Vocabulary

shiken ni gôkaku shimasu (suru)	しけんに ごうかくします (する)	試験に 合格する	to pass a test
shiken ni shippai shimasu (suru)	しけんに しっぱいします (する)	試験に 失敗する	to fail a test
kikitori no shiken	ききとりの しけん	聞き取り の試験	a listening test (in a language class)
hanashimasu (hanasu)	はなします (はなす)	詰す	speak, talk
Mareeshia	マレーシア		Malaysia
oboemasu (oboeru)	おぼえます (おぼえる)	覚える	to memorize, to acquire a skill
Marayago	マラヤご	マラヤ語	Malay (language)
Chûgokujin	ちゅうごくじん	中国人	Chinese person
Kantongo	カントンご	カントン語	Cantonese (language)
minna	みんな		all, everyone (quantity word)
yorokobimasu (yorokobu)	よろこびます (よろこぶ)	喜ぶ	to be pleased or delighted
okorimasu (okoru)	おこります (おこる)	怒る	get angry
shukudai	しゅくだい	宿題	homework
komarimasu (komaru)	こまります (こまる)	困る	to be a problem, to be a hassle, to be upset
dashimasu (dasu)	だします (だす)	出す	to send out, to hand in
soshite	そして		and then, in addition

Ikeda Masaru has noticed that Zaini Abdul is very good at languages. He asks her about it.

Ikeda: Abuduuru-san wa eigo o hanashimasu ne.
Abuduuru: Ee, sô desu. Mareeshia no gakkô de wa, eigo mo
            Marayago mo tsukaimasu kara, minna oboemasu.
            Soshite, Chûgokujin no tomodachi mo imasu kara,
            Kantongo mo sukoshi oboemashita.

Ikeda: Ms. Abdul, you speak English, don't you?
Abdul: Yes, that's right. In Malaysian schools they use both
            English and Malay, so everyone picks it up. And
            then I've acquired a little Cantonese, too, because I
            have Chinese friends.

Practice 9.4

Write reasons for each result, as indicated in the cues.

EXAMPLE:

_____ *mittsu kaimashita.*
(because they were cheap)
Yasukatta desu kara, mittsu kaimashita.
Because they were cheap, I bought three.

1. _____komarimasu.
   (Because I don't have money)

2. _____kaimasen deshita.
   (Because it was expensive)

3. _____watashi mo ikimashita.
   (Because Ms. Hasegawa went)

4. _____sensei wa okorimashita.
   (Because everyone failed the test)

5. _____sensei wa yorokobimashita.
   (Because everyone passed the test)

6. _____ shukudai mo dashimasen deshita.
   (Because that student didn't go to the university today)

HOW TO SAY "WITH"

You have already learned that *de* can mean "with" in sentences such as *Pen de kakimasu.* However, this works only when you mean "with" in the sense of "by means of." When you mean "with" in the sense of "in the company of someone else," you need to use the particle *to,* and yes, it's the same *to* that means "and." Sometimes it is expanded into *to issho ni . . . ,* which cannot mean anything other than "with."

> *Tomodachi to (issho ni) kaimono o shimashita.*
> I went shopping with a friend.

> *Chan-san to (issho ni) Chûgoku ryôri o tsukurimashita.*
> I made Chinese food together with Ms. Chan.

When you are talking about two people doing the same activity mutually or against each other, then it is more common to use *to* by itself.

> *Ikeda-san to hanashimashita.*
> I spoke with Mr. Ikeda.

> *Morimoto-san to tenisu o shimashita.*
> I played tennis with Mr. Morimoto.

Vocabulary

mochiron	もちろん	of course
yappari	やっぱり	in the end, after all, now that I think about it
dekiru dake	できるだけ	as much as possible
katakoto gurai	かたことぐらい	just a few words (of a language)

Teramura Chieko has heard from Ikeda Masaru that Zaini Abdul speaks four languages, so she asks her about it.

Teramura: Abuduuru-san wa mochiron, Nihonjin to wa Nihongo o hanashimasu ga, Amerikajin ya Kanadajin to wa?

Abuduuru: Maa, tokidoki Sumisu-san ya Uiruson-san to wa eigo o hanashimasu ga, yappari Nihon ni imasu kara, dekiru dake Nihongo o tsukaimasu.

Teramura: Chan-san to wa Kantongo o hanashimasu ka?

Abuduuru: Kantongo wa katakoto gurai desu kara, amari tsukaimasen.

Teramura: Ms. Abdul, of course you speak Japanese with Japanese people, but what about with Americans or Canadians?

Abdul: Hmm, sometimes I speak English with Ms. Smith or Mr. Wilson, but since I'm in Japan, I use Japanese as much as possible.

Teramura: Do you speak Cantonese with Ms. Chan?

Abdul: My Cantonese is only a few words, so I don't use it much.

- The *wa* after *to* is the *wa* of comparison.

SUMMING UP
MATOME
まとめ

Complete the dialogues according to the cues provided.

mô sugu	もうすぐ		pretty soon
modorimasu (modoru)	もどります (もどる)	戻ります	return [to a place that isn't your permanent home]
shutchô	しゅつちょう	出張	business travel
ryokô	りょこう	旅行	trip, journey

1. Ms. Ishida has heard that you are being sent on a business trip to New Zealand.

Ishida: Itsu shutchô ni dekakemasu ka?

You: (Tell her that you'll depart on the second of next month.)

Ishida: Sô desu ka? Dare to issho ni ikimasu ka?

You: (Tell her that you are going with Mr. Nogata.)

2. Lucky you! You're going back to your home country for a visit, and you've planned it so that you will return to Japan by going around the world. Of course, Yamaguchi Mariko wants to hear all about it.

Mariko: Itsu dekakemasu ka?

You: (Tell her that you're leaving on June 10.)

Mariko: Sô desu ka? Itsu Nihon ni modorimasu ka?
You: (Tell her that you'll return on September 24.)
Mariko: Hee? Nagai ryokô desu nee! Nan de ikimasu ka?
You: (Tell her that, of course, you'll go by plane.)

3. You walk into a bakery.

Ten'in: Irasshaimase.
You: (Get the clerk's attention and ask how much those rolls are.)
Ten'in: Hitotsu hyaku en de gozaimasu.
You: (Think it over and ask for five.)
Ten'in: Hai, zenbu de gohyaku en de gozaimasu.

Kinkakuji Temple *(Golden Pavilion)*, Kyoto

Japan National Tourist Organization (JNTO)

CHAPTER 10

TEGAMI O KAITE, YÛBIN DE DASHIMASHITA. (I WROTE A LETTER AND MAILED IT.)

In this chapter, you will learn:

1. another class of adjectives
2. about expressing likes and dislikes
3. the all-important -te form
4. how to give commands and make requests

ANOTHER CLASS OF ADJECTIVES

You have already learned about the class of adjectives that end in -ai, -ii, -ui, or -oi, but there's another class of adjectives, commonly referred to as the na- adjectives. These usually end in something other than vowel + i, and some of the most common ones are:

kirei	きれい		clean and neat, pretty
benri	べんり	便利	convenient
genki	げんき	元気	healthy, in good spirits
taisetsu	たいせつ	大切	important
kantan	かんたん	簡単	simple
fukuzatsu	ふくざつ	複雑	complicated

At first glance, they pattern like nouns.

kantan desu is simple	*kantan deshita* was simple
kantan de wa nai desu or *kantan de wa arimasen* is not simple	*kantan de wa nakatta desu* or *kantan de wa arimasen deshita* was not simple

The major difference between *na-* adjectives and other adjectives, and between *na-* adjectives and nouns, is what happens when they come before a noun. This is where the *na* part comes in:

kirei na uchi	a pretty (or clean and neat) house
benri na basu	a convenient bus
genki na kodomo	a healthy child
taisetsu na tegami	an important letter
kantan na hôhô	a simple method
fukuzatsu na mondai	a complicated problem

These *na-* adjective + noun phrases fit into sentences just like any other adjective + noun phrases:

> *Benri na basu wa arimasen ka?*
> Isn't there a convenient bus?

> *Kantan na hôhô de ano fukuzatsu na mondai o kaiketsu shimashita.*
> I solved that complicated problem by a simple method.

Example:

The Yamaguchi family has moved to a new house, and they have invited Chan Ngan-fa to see it. She is talking to them on the phone to find out how to get there.

Vocabulary

tooi	とおい	遠い	far
jitensha	じてんしゃ	自転車	bicycle
tokoro	ところ	所	place

Chan: Eki kara tooi desu ka?
Yamaguchi: Iie, jitensha de go fun desu.
Chan: Benri na tokoro desu ne.
Yamaguchi: Ee, sore ni kaimono mo totemo benri desu.
Chan: A, sore mo taisetsu desu ne.

Chan: Is it far from the station?
Yamaguchi: No. It's five minutes by bicycle.
Chan: It's a convenient place, isn't it?
Yamaguchi: Yes. Besides, shopping is convenient, too.
Chan: Oh, that's important, too, isn't it?

Practice 10.1

Vocabulary

kikai	きかい	機械	machine
doresu	ドレス		dress
shorui	しょるい	書類	document
kanpeki (na)	かんぺき (な)	完璧	perfect
chakuriku	ちゃくりく	着陸	landing (of an airplane)

How would you say:

1. This is a complicated machine.

2. This is a simple problem.

3. This is a pretty dress.

4. This is an important document.

5. This was a perfect landing.

6. This machine is complicated.

7. This problem is simple.

8. This dress is pretty.

9. This document is important.

10. This landing was perfect.

LIKES AND DISLIKES, SKILLS AND WEAKNESSES

In English, we express likes and dislikes with a SUBJECT-VERB-OBJECT combination:

I like ice cream.
I dislike liver.

In Japanese, the pattern is NOUN₁ *wa* NOUN₂ *ga* (*or wa*) *NA-ADJECTIVE desu*.   The two *na-* adjectives in question are *suki* "liked" and *kirai* "disliked." By the way, *kirai* is one of the very few exceptions to the rule that adjectives ending in *-ai* are *ku-* adjectives.

NOUN₁	wa	NOUN₂	ga or wa	NA-ADJ.	desu
Watashi	wa	aisu kuriimu	ga	suki	desu
I like ice cream.					
Watashi	wa	rebaa	ga	kirai	desu
I dislike liver.					

WATCH OUT

Do not confuse *kirei* "clean, pretty" and *kirai* "disliked." You can see how confusing these two could get you into trouble: *Suzuki-san wa kirei desu* "Ms. Suzuki is pretty" and *Suzuki-san wa kirai desu* "I dislike Ms. Suzuki" will have quite different effects on Ms. Suzuki when she hears about them.

When asking about what another person likes, you may say *o-suki* instead of just *suki*. Since *o-* is an honorific; however, it is omitted in the reply, in keeping with the rule that people never use honorifics with anything connected with themselves.

> *Shabu-shabu, o-suki desu ka?*
> Do you like *shabu-shabu?* (a kind of do-it-yourself beef stew cooked at the table)
> *Hai, suki desu.*
> Yes, I like it.

So why are *suki* and *kirai* considered *na-* adjectives? Well, just look at what happens when they precede a noun:

> *Kore ga o-suki **na** aisu kuriimu desu ne?*
> This is the ice cream that you like, isn't it?

> *Kirai **na** shigoto deshita.*
> It was work that I disliked.

Another NOUN₁ *wa* NOUN₂ *ga* NA-ADJECTIVE *desu* pattern has to do with being skilled (*jôzu*) or unskilled (*heta*).

> *Teramura-san wa bareebooru ga jôzu desu.*
> Ms. Teramura is good at volleyball.

> *Ano hito wa tenisu ga heta desu ne.*
> That person over there is bad at tennis, isn't he?

The honorific form of *jôzu* is *o-jôzu,* and if you spend time in Japan, you will undoubtedly run into someone who tells you:

> *Nihongo ga o-jôzu desu nee.*
> You're good at Japanese, aren't you?

Don't believe anyone who tells you that. The comment is intended as an encouragement to keep studying, and you'll know that you've really arrived when people **stop** saying it to you.

WATCH OUT

Both *kirai* and *heta* are fairly strong words, so if you only mildly dislike something or think that someone's skills are mediocre, it's better to say *amari suki ja nai desu* "I don't like it very much" instead of *kirai desu,* or *amari jôzu ja arimasen* "isn't very skilled" or *amari dekimasen* "can't do very much" instead of *heta desu.*

When referring to your own skills or abilities, *tokui* is preferable to *jôzu* and *nigate* is preferable to *heta. Tokui* and *nigate* not only refer to your skill in the activity but also indicate whether you enjoy it.

> *Ongaku ga tokui desu.*
> I'm good at music, and I enjoy it.

> *Tenisu ga nigate desu.*
> I'm bad at tennis, and I don't enjoy it.

Vocabulary

shumi (honorific: go-shumi)	しゅみ (honorific ごしゅみ)	趣味 (御趣味)	hobby, pastime
supootsu	スポーツ		sport
yakyû	やきゅう	野球	baseball
suiei	すいえい	水泳	swimming
sukii	スキー		skiing
dokusho	どくしょ	読書	reading (as a leisure activity)
engeki	えんげき	演劇	acting
e	え	絵	drawn or painted picture
kitte	きって	切手	postage stamp
chiisai toki	ちいさいとき	小さい時	during childhood (literally: "small time")
natsu	なつ	夏	summer
fuyu	ふゆ	冬	winter
shûshû	しゅうしゅう	収集	collecting

Examples:

Ms. Hasegawa is looking for someone to make the poster for the international students' year-end party, and Thomas Wilson just happens to be in the office.

Hasegawa: Uiruson-san, e, o-jôzu desu ka?
Wilson: Boku desu ka? Nigate desu yo.
Hasegawa: Saa, dare ga jôzu desu ka?
Wilson: Sô desu ne. Joonzu-san ga jôzu desu ne.
Hasegawa: Sô desu ka? Jaa, Uiruson-san no go-shumi wa nan desu ka?
Uiruson: Natsu wa suiei o shimasu ga, fuyu wa sukii o shimasu. Chiisai toki wa kitte o shûshû shimashita ga. . .

Hasegawa: Mr. Wilson, are you good at drawing?
Wilson: Me? I'm terrible at it.
Hasegawa: Hmm, who's good at it?
Wilson: Let me see. Mr. Jones is.
Hasegawa: Is that so? Well, what are your hobbies?
Wilson: I swim in the summer and ski in the winter. When I was a kid I collected stamps, but. . .

Practice 10.2

Mark the following sentences about your skills, likes, and dislikes either true (T) or false (F).

1. Aisu kuriimu ga kirai desu.

2. E ga jôzu desu.

3. Suiei ga tokui desu.

4. Dokusho ga suki desu.

5. Engeki ga nigate desu.

6. Yakyû ga kirai desu.

7. Nihongo ga suki desu.

8. Supootsu ga heta desu.

THE ALL-IMPORTANT -*TE* FORM

Now you are going to meet one of the most important and versatile forms of the verbs, the -*te* form. This form has little meaning by itself, but it is used in combination with other elements to perform all sorts of linguistic functions.

Many students struggle with -*te* forms because they look as if they come out of nowhere, but in fact, they are completely predictable for each class of verb.

First you need to understand that all Japanese verbs fit into one of three classes: one-step (*ichidan*), five-step (*godan*) and irregular. We can take care of that last category first. It has only two members:

Polite Form	Dictionary Form	*-te* Form	Meaning
shimasu	suru	shite	do
kimasu	kuru	kite	come

The dictionary forms of one-step verbs all end in *-iru* or *-eru*. Most verbs ending in *-eru* are one-step, as are about half of the verbs ending in *-iru,* but if the dictionary form of a verb ends in *-aru, -oru, -uru,* or anything except *-iru* or *-eru,* it cannot possibly be one-step. If you can grasp this principle, you will cut down on the number of times you have to ask your instructor for the *-te* form of a verb.

One-step verbs get their name from the fact that all endings are attached to the same stem. Look at this chart of the one-step verbs that you have seen before and see if you can figure out the principle. The hyphens are included to make the boundaries between the stems and the endings clear.

Polite Form	Dictionary Form	*-te* Form	Meaning
i-masu	i-ru	i-te	be located
ne-masu	ne-ru	ne-te	lie down, sleep
tabe-masu	tabe-ru	tabe-te	eat
abi-masu	abi-ru	abi-te	pour over, take [a shower]
oki-masu	oki-ru	oki-te	wake up
de-masu	de-ru	de-te	leave, appear
mi-masu	mi-ru	mi-te	see, watch, look
mise-masu	mise-ru	mise-te	show
deki-masu	deki-ru	deki-te	be able, finish
oshie-masu	oshie-ru	oshie-te	teach, inform

As you can see, the principle is that each of these verbs has a single stem, such as *i-, ne-,* or *tabe-,* and all endings are added directly to that stem.

```
ne-masu          tabe-masu
ne-ru            tabe-ru
ne-te            tabe-te
```

Practice 10.3a

Here are six one-step verbs that you've never seen before. Fill in their dictionary forms and -*te* forms. (You do not have to memorize the individual verbs at this point.)

Polite Form	Dictionary Form	-*te* Form	Meaning
iremasu			put in, include
shimemasu			close
akemasu			open
tarimasu			be sufficient
kimasu			wear
karimasu			borrow, rent

The five-step verbs are more complicated, because the -*te* form depends on the consonant of the last syllable. The basic underlying pattern is most clearly seen in the verbs whose dictionary form ends in -*su*.

Polite Form	Dictionary Form	-*te* Form	Meaning
-imasu	-u	-ite	–
dashimasu	dasu	dashite	send out, hand in

Practice 10.3b

Here are some -*su* verbs to practice the regular pattern with.

Polite Form	Dictionary Form	-*te* Form	Meaning
keshimasu			extinguish, turn off
naoshimasu			fix, repair
otoshimasu			drop
kashimasu			lend, rent out
sagashimasu			look for

Twelve hundred years ago, all Japanese verbs were this regular, but over the centuries, sound changes have crept into the language. Verbs ending in *-ku,* for example, lose their *-k-* in the *-te* form.

Polite Form	Dictionary Form	*-te* Form	Meaning
kakimasu	kaku	kaite	write
tsukimasu	tsuku	tsukimasu	arrive
kikimasu	kiku	kiite	hear, listen

Practice 10.3c

Try these verbs.

Polite Form	Dictionary Form	*-te* Form	Meaning
nakimasu			cry
manekimasu			beckon
arukimasu			walk
ugokimasu			move around
nozokimasu			omit

There is one semi-exception to this pattern. Go is *ikimasu/iku,* but its *-te* form is *itte.* Otherwise, it's a normal five-step verb.

Verbs ending in *-gu* follow nearly the same pattern, except that their *-te* form is actually a *-de* form. See if you can complete the rest of the table.

Practice 10.3d

Polite Form	Dictionary Form	*-te* Form	Meaning
oyogimasu	oyogu	oyoide	swim
isogimasu			hurry
kogimasu			row
kasegimasu			earn
nugimasu			take off shoes or clothing

Verbs ending in *-mu, -bu,* or *-nu* also have what amounts to a *-de* form. See if you can complete the table.

Practice 10.3e

Polite Form	Dictionary Form	*-te* Form	Meaning
yomimasu	yomu	yonde	read
yorokobimasu	yorokobu	yorokonde	be happy
shinimasu	shinu	shinde	die (This is the only *-nu* verb in modern Japanese)
nomimasu			drink
hagemimasu			make an effort
fumimasu			step on
narabimasu			get in line
musubimasu			bind
asobimasu			play, goof off

All verbs ending in *-aru, -uru, -oru,* or *-tu,* some verbs ending in *-iru,* and a couple of verbs ending in *-eru* have a *-te* form with a doubled *-t-.* See if you can complete this table.

Practice 10.3f

Polite Form	Dictionary Form	-te Form	Meaning
arimasu	aru	atte	be located
urimasu	uru	utte	sell
norimasu	noru	notte	ride, board
hashirimasu	hashiru	hashitte	run
kaerimasu	kaeru	kaette	return home
machimasu	matsu	matte	wait
narimasu			become
magarimasu			turn (a corner)
mekurimasu			turn [pages]
kezurimasu			sharpen
orimasu			break, bend
toorimasu			pass through
okorimasu			get angry
tachimasu			stand up
kirimasu			cut
majirimasu			be mixed
kerimasu			kick
shaberimasu			talk

Practice 10.3g

The final group consists of verbs whose dictionary forms end in *-au, -iu, -uu,* or *-ou.* (There are no verbs ending in *-eu.*) They, too, have a *-tte* form instead of a *-te* form. Complete the table.

Polite Form	Dictionary Form	*-te* Form	Meaning
araimasu	arau	aratte	wash
iimasu	iu	itte	say
nuguimasu	nuguu	nugutte	wipe
omoimasu	omou	omotte	think, have an opinion
aimasu			meet
waraimasu			laugh
tsukaimasu			use
chigaimasu			be different
suimasu			sip
nuimasu			sew
hiroimasu			pick up
sasoimasu			invite
mayoimasu			wander

You may have noticed that a few polite forms and dictionary forms are found under both the one-step and five-step verbs. The important point to note is that there are no completely overlapping forms.

Polite Form	Dictionary Form	*-te* Form	Meaning
kimasu	kiru	kite	wear (one-step)
kirimasu	kiru	kitte	cut (five-step)
kimasu	kuru	kite	come (irregular)
okimasu	okiru	okite	wake up (one-step)
okimasu	oku	oite	put (five-step)
karimasu	kariru	karite	borrow, rent (one-step)
karimasu	karu	katte	clip (five-step)

Thus, if you know any two forms of a verb, you know whether it's one-step or five-step. Remember:

1. If the stem is the same on both forms, then you have a one-step verb.

> *kimasu/kiru/kite* "wear"
> *okimasu/okiru/okite* "wake up"
> *karimasu/kariru/karite* "borrow"

2. If the two stems are different, then you have a five-step verb.

> *okimasu/oku/oite* "put"
> *karimasu/karu/katte* "clip"

3. *Shimasu/suru/shite* and *kimasu/kuru/kite* are irregular, and *ikimasu/iku/itte* is partly irregular, as are a few honorific verbs that you haven't met yet.

From now on, newly introduced one-step verbs will be marked with (1), and new irregulars will be marked with (irr). Assume that all other new verbs are five-steps. Whatever the case, you should know how to produce their *-te* forms.

SEQUENCES, COMMANDS, AND REQUESTS

All right, now that you have all these wonderful *-te* forms, what will you do with them?

One of the handiest uses is in polite commands and requests. The form is:

> VERB-*te kudasai*
>
> *Mite kudasai*
> Please look.
>
> *Matte kudasai*
> Please wait.

This is the normal polite command and request form, but it is not used when offering someone food or drink, because it sounds as if you're ordering the person to accept. For example, a hospital nurse could say, *Kore o nonde kudasai* "Please drink this," but someone offering a beverage to a guest would say, *Nomi masen ka?*

These command and request forms are verbs, and so they take the same position in the sentence as any other verb.

Yonde kudasai.
Please read.
Toshokan de kono hon o yonde kudasai.
Please read this book in the library.

Practice 10.4a

Vocabulary

VEHICLE o oriru (1)	VEHICLE をおりる (1)	降りる	get off a VEHICLE
namae (honorific: o-namae)	なまえ (honorific: おなまえ)	名前	name
pasupooto	パスポート		passport
hayaku	はやく	早く	early, quickly

Imagine that you are guiding a group of Japanese tourists around your city. Tell them to:

EXAMPLE:

Wait here.
Koko de matte kudasai.

1. Board the bus.

2. Get off the bus.

3. Buy tickets.

4. Look at that building over there.

5. Listen to this tape.

6. Write their names.

7. Show their passports.

8. Go to bed early.

9. Wake up at 6:00 A.M.

In order to tell a person to do first one thing and then another, put both -te forms in front of *kudasai.*

> *Tegami o kaite, yûbin de dashite kudasai.*
> Please write a letter and mail it.

> *Shawaa o abite, atama mo aratte kudasai.*
> Please take a shower and also wash your hair.

You can use a similar construction to describe a sequence of actions carried out by one person. Whether you are speaking of past, future, or present events, only the last verb in the sequence needs to have an indication of tense.

> *Tegami o kaite yûbin de dashimashita.*
> I wrote a letter and mailed it.

> *Shawaa o abite atama mo araimashita.*
> I took a shower and also washed my hair.

To emphasize that the second activity took place after the first, put *kara* after the first -te form.

> *Nihon kara kaette kara, daigakuin ni hairimashita.*
> After returning home from Japan, I entered graduate school.

WATCH OUT

It's possible to confuse the *kara* meaning "because" and the *kara* meaning "after," but not if you watch for one all-important clue. That is, the *kara* meaning "after" is **always** preceded by a -te form:

> *Kaette kara* . . "After returning home. . ."
> *Kaerimashita kara*. . . "Because I returned home. . . "

If a -te form is followed by a form of *kuru* "come," this means that the subject of the verb did the action and came back. This is the origin of the expression *Itte kimasu* "I'll go and come back." When a form of *itte kuru* is used with a place name, it means that the subject took a short trip there and back.

> *Yokohama e itte kimashita.*
> I took a short trip to Yokohama.
> (I went to Yokohama and came right back.)

Shinbun o katte kimashita.
I went and bought a newspaper.
(I bought a newspaper and came back.)

Practice 10.4b

Vocabulary

PLACE ni hairu	PLACE にはいる	入る	enter PLACE
daigakuin	だいがくいん	大学院	graduate school
PLACE ni shûshoku suru	PLACE に しゅうしょく する	就職する	get a job at PLACE
NOUN o yûbin de dasu	NOUN を ゆうびんで だす	郵便で 出す	mail NOUN
SCHOOL o sotsugyô suru	SCHOOL を そつぎょう する	卒業する	graduate from SCHOOL
jugyô ni deru (1)	じゅぎょうに でる (1)	授業に出る	attend class
nooto	ノート		notebook
atama o arau	あたまを あらう	頭を 洗う	wash one's hair (*Atama* is literally head)
enpitsu	えんぴつ	鉛筆	pencil
mizu	みず	水	water
sugu	すぐ		soon, right away

Each item lists two activities. Say that one happened after the other. The two activities may not be listed in chronological order, so you may have to figure out which one would logically happen first.

EXAMPLE:

(*sugu asagohan o taberu*) (*okiru*) →
Okite kara, sugu asagohan o tabemashita.
After getting up, I ate breakfast right away.

1. (enpitsu ya nooto o kau) (jugyô ni deru)

2. (Nihon no kaisha ni shûshoku suru) (daigaku o sotsugyô suru)

3. (kitte o kau) (tegami o yûbin de dasu)

4. (kitte o takusan shûshû suru) (uru)

5. (benkyô suru) (toshokan e iku)

6. (terebi o miru) (neru)

7. (atama o arau) (puuru de oyogu)

8. (hikôki o oriru) (tomodachi ni denwa suru)

SUMMING UP
MATOME
まとめ

Complete these dialogues according to the cues given.

1. Ms. Ishida is helping you straighten up your desk.

Ishida: Kore wa taisetsu na shorui desu ka?
You: (Tell her that they're not very important.)

2. You are at a swimming pool with some Japanese friends, including Teramura Chieko.

Teramura: Suiei ga o-jôzu desu ne.
You: (Tell her that no, you like swimming, but you are not very good at it.)

3. Ms. Yamaguchi is asking you about your weekend.

Yamaguchi: Nichiyôbi ni nani o shimashita ka?
You: (Say that you took a short trip to Kamakura by train.)
Yamaguchi: Sô desu ka? Daibutsu (Great Buddha) o mimashita ka?
You: (Yes, and after seeing the Great Buddha you ate lunch at a small restaurant.)
Yamaguchi: Sore kara wa?

You: (Tell her that you saw a lot of pretty temples and shrines.)

4. What are the *-te* forms of these verbs? You have never seen them before, but they follow the rules.

a. oyobu (extend) (5)

b. mogu (pick) (5)

c. yaku (bake, burn) (5)

d. tasu (add) (5)

e. kikoeru (be audible) (1)

f. agaru (rise) (5)

g. How would you know that all these verbs except (e) are five-step verbs if they weren't numbered?

REVIEW
CHAPTERS 6–10

Study the following calendar, which belongs to a student. Then answer the questions. (It doesn't matter which month these things happened in.)

SUN.	MON.	TUES.	WED.	THURS.	FRI.	SAT.
				1 Orchestra practice	2 Video night	3 Party 9:00
4	5 Research paper due	6 Orchestra practice	7	8 Orchestra practice	9 Dance	10 Softball game 1:00
11 Picnic 2:00	12	13 Orchestra practice	14 Japanese test	15 Orchestra practice	16 One-act plays	17 Shopping in the city
18 My birthday!	19 Math test!	20 Orchestra practice	21	22 Orchestra practice	23 Lecture series	24 Hiking
25	26	27 Orchestra practice	28 Watch TV at student union	29 Orchestra practice	30 Orchestra concert	

ronbun	ろんぶん	論文	research paper
renshû suru	れんしゅうする	練習 する	practice
hontô	ほんとう	本当	true
uso	うそ	嘘	false
shibai	しばい	芝居	(theatrical) play
kôen	こうえん	講演	lecture
nan'yôbi	なんようび	何曜日	what day of the week?
yôfuku	ようふく	洋服	[Western-style] clothing
kyôshitsu	きょうしつ	教室	classroom
suteki (na)	すてき (な)		wonderful, great
buutsu	ブーツ		boots
shatsu	シャツ		shirt
ookesutora	オーケストラ		orchestra
shiai	しあい	試合	game (athletic), match
pikunikku	ピクニック		picnic

1. Ookesutora no renshû wa nan'yôbi deshita ka?

2. Kono gakusei wa nannichi ni ronbun o dashimashita ka?

3. Kono gakusei no tanjôbi wa nannichi deshita ka? Nan'yôbi deshita ka?

4. Sûgaku no shiken wa nannichi deshita ka? Nan'yôbi deshita ka?

5. Kono gakusei wa nannichi ni haikingu ni ikimashita ka? Sore wa nan'yôbi deshita ka?

6. Nihongo no shiken wa nannichi deshita ka?

7. Paatii wa nannichi deshita ka?

8. Ookesutora no konsaato wa nannichi deshita ka? Nan'yôbi deshita ka?

9. Hontô desu ka? Uso desu ka?

   (a) Kono gakusei wa mainichi terebi o mimashita.
   (b) Kono gakusei wa ongaku ga heta desu.
   (c) Kono gakusei wa supootsu o shimasen.
   (d) Kono gakusei wa jûroku nichi ni shibai o mimashita.
   (e) Kono gakusei wa nijûni nichi ni kôen o kikimashita.
   (f) Dansu paatii mo sofutobooru no shiai mo doyôbi deshita.

Complete the following dialogues based on the cues given.

10. You are talking with Ikeda Masaru.

    Ikeda: Doyôbi ni nani o shimashita ka?
    You: (Tell him that you went shopping.)
    Ikeda: Nani o kaimashita ka?
    You: (Tell him that you bought a lot of shirts.)
    Ikeda: Sô desu ka?
    You: (At Marui [the name of a department store] you also saw some great boots, but. . .)
    Ikeda: Buutsu desu ka?
    You: (However, you didn't buy those, because they were very expensive.)
    Ikeda: Sô desu ka? Ikura deshita ka?
    You: (Tell him that they were 25,000 yen.)
    Ikeda: Hee? Takakatta desu nee. Ja, dare to issho ni kaimono ni ikimashita ka?
    You: (Tell him that you went with Mr. Kim.)

11. You are helping Ms. Hasegawa and some of the international students get ready for the year-end party.

Hasegawa: Isu wa ikutsu arimasu ka?
You: (Tell her that there are eight.)
Hasegawa: Sore dake desu ka? Komarimashita ne.
You: (Tell her that there are chairs in the neighboring classroom, too.)
Hasegawa: A, yokatta!

CHAPTER 11

GINKÔ NO KADO O MIGI E MAGARIMASU. (TURN RIGHT AT THE CORNER WHERE THE BANK IS.)

In this chapter you will learn to:

1. ask and give directions on the street
2. talk about ongoing actions
3. use some verbs whose direct objects take *ga*
4. talk about what will probably happen

ASKING AND GIVING DIRECTIONS ON THE STREET

Japanese streets have no names. Instead, addresses are a matter of narrowing down a location from municipality (*to, shi,* or *fu*) to ward (*ku*) to neighborhood (*machi or chô*), to area (*chôme*) to block (*banch*) to lot (*shikich*). For example, the address

> Tôkyô-to
> Nakano-ku
> Nogata 2-1-5

indicates a building located in the metropolis of Tokyo, Nakano ward, Nogata neighborhood, second area, first block, fifth lot. Thus, unless you have a detailed neighborhood-by-neighborhood map of the kind that taxi drivers use, you can't pinpoint the location of a building by its address. Advertisements for businesses typically contain inset maps showing directions from the nearest public transportation stop. Another option is to find the general area and ask at the local police booth (*kôban*), where neighborhood maps and directories of residents are kept.

Students sometimes have difficulty with the routines for asking and giving directions, because the sentences involved may turn out to be rather long, but you already have the necessary basic ingredients, namely:

(a) asking where something is

(b) telling where something is located

(c) describing sequences of actions with -*te* forms

It's best to begin your question with an equivalent of "Excuse me, but..." Here are a couple of them:

Sumimasen ga. . .	すみんせんが . . .	Excuse me, but...
Chotto ukagai-masu ga...	ちょっとうかがいますが . . .	I'm [humbly] making a little bit of an inquiry, but...

Suppose you are asking where the Yamato Hotel is. As you already know, one way to frame that question is

Yamato Hoteru wa doko ni arimasu ka?

The answer may be very simple, as in the previous chapters: *Asoko desu* or *Ano tatemono desu.* On the other hand, you may have to travel far and turn a lot of corners, since the streets in most Japanese cities are not laid out in a grid pattern. Then you need these expressions:

michi o massugu iku	みちを まっすぐ いく	道を まっすぐ 行く	go straight along the street
kado o magaru	かどを まがる	角を 曲がる	turn the corner
migi e magaru	みぎへ まがる	右へ 曲がる	turn right
hidari e magaru	ひだりへ まがる	左へ 曲がる	turn left
tomaru	とまる	止まる	stop
kôsaten	こうさてん	交差点	intersection
shingô	しんごう	信号	traffic light
tsukiatari	つきあたり	突き当たり	T-shaped intersection
yokomichi	よこみち	横道	side street
tsugi (no)	つぎ(の)	次	next
hashi	はし	橋	bridge
wataru	わたる	渡る	go across
chikai	ちかい	近い	near, close
sugu soba	すぐそば		close vicinity, right near
aruite	あるいて (from あるく)	歩いて	walking
meetoru	メートル		meter
gasorin sutando	ガソリン・ スタンド		gas station
wakarimashita	わかりました		I see. (I have understood.)
ichiban	いちばん	一番	number one
ichibanme, nibanme, etc.	いちばんめ, にばんめ,etc.,	一番目 二番目	first, second, etc.

Amanda Smith has been invited to a wedding at a hotel in the suburbs of Tokyo. Since the nearest commuter train station is about a kilometer away from the hotel, she stops to ask directions at the police booth outside the station.

Smith:	Sumimasen ga, Shin Yamato Hoteru wa doko ni arimasu ka?
O-mawari-san:	Shin Yamato Hoteru desu ka? Chotto tooi desu ne.
Smith:	Sô desu ka?
O-mawari-san:	Ee. Jaa, asoko ni hasi arimasu ne.
Smith:	Ee.
O-mawari-san:	Ano hashi o watatte, gohyaku meetoru massugu itte. . .
Smith:	Hai.
O mawari-san:	Ginkô no kado o migi e magarimasu.
Smith:	Migi desu ne? Hai.
O-mawari-san:	Sore kara, tsugi no shingô o hidari e magarimasu.
Smith:	Tsugi no shingô desu ne? Hai.
O-mawari-san:	Sono sugu soba no ookii biru ga Shin Yamato Hoteru desu.
Smith:	Wakarimashita. Dômo arigatô gozaimasu.

Smith:	Excuse me, but where's the Shin-Yamato Hotel?
Police Officer:	The Shin-Yamato Hotel? It's a little bit far.
Smith:	Really?
Police Officer:	Yes. Well, there's a bridge over there, right?
Smith:	Yes.
Police Officer:	Cross that bridge and go straight ahead for five hundred meters. . .
Smith:	Yes.
Police Officer:	Turn right at the corner where the bank is.
Smith:	Right, yes? Okay.
Police Officer:	After that, turn left at the next traffic light.
Smith:	The next traffic light, yes?
Police Officer:	The building right near there is the Shin-Yamato Hotel.
Smith:	I see. Thank you very much.

Practice 11.1a

How would you say this? (The sentence patterns you need are all in the dialogue.)

1. Nijô Castle? It's very close.

2. There's a traffic light over there, right?

3. You cross this street and go 100 meters straight ahead.

4. You turn left at the intersection where the station is.

5.   The building next to the gas station is the bookstore.

Practice 11.1b

You work at a tourist information booth downtown in the large city nearest you, and you frequently have to answer questions from Japanese tourists. Here are some of the things you tell some of these tourists.

1. You turn left at the next corner.

2. You turn right at the traffic light and go 200 meters.

3. You turn left at the T-shaped intersection and go straight for 800 meters.

4. You turn right at the second traffic light and enter the next little side street.

5. There's a hotel over there, right? Yumyum Restaurant is inside that hotel.

Practice 11.1c

Vocabulary

PLACE o deru (1)	PLACE を でる (1)	出る	leave PLACE, go out from PLACE
PLACE no mukaigawa	PLACE の むかいがわ	向かい側	across from PLACE
denkiseihin	でんきせいひん	電気製品	electronic products
rekoodo-ya	レコ-ドや	レコード屋	record store
kaikan	かいかん	会館	a hall that rents rooms for meetings and events
pan-ya	パンや	パン屋	bakery
Sekijûji Byôin	せきじゅうじ びょういん	赤十字病院	Red Cross Hospital
eigakan	えいがかん	映画館	movie theater
kutsu-ya	くつや	靴屋	shoe store
biyôin	びようおん	美容院	hair salon
butiiku	ブティーク		boutique
karuchaa sentaa	カルチャー・ センター		culture center
hidarigawa	ひだりがわ	左側	left side
migigawa	みぎがわ	右側	right side
gofukuten	ごふくてん	呉服店	store selling traditional Japanese clothing

Ms. Blake (from Chapter 3) has been sent to a small city in northern Japan to help set up Widgetronics' new sales office there. On the day before the office opens, she decides to go on a massive shopping expedition in the main commercial district so that she can furnish her apartment more comfortably. Since she has never been here before, she needs directions, starting from the train station. Study the map below and give her directions for each segment of the shopping trip. The bare outline of each set of directions is provided. All you have to do is fill in the blanks.

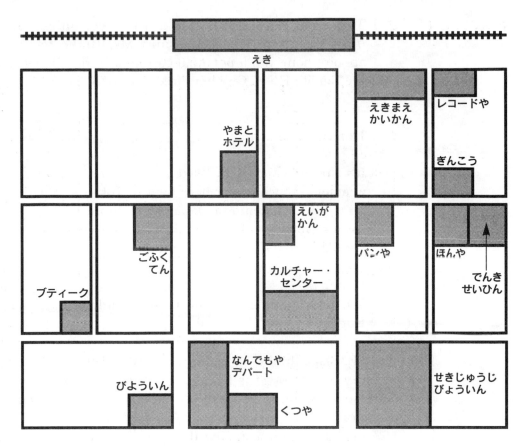

EXAMPLE:

First she needs to go to the bank to cash travelers' checks and open an account. She asks a station employee where the nearest bank is.

<u>Eki</u> o dete, <u>hidari</u> e magarimasu. Nibanme no <u>kado</u> o migi e <u>magarimasu.</u> Ginkô wa tsugi no <u>kôsaten</u> no sugu soba ni arimasu.

1. Now she wants to buy a local guidebook so she can learn about the history and natural surroundings of the city, so she asks a bank employee where a bookstore is. The bank employee tells her that there's a bookstore across from this bank.

   _____ ginkô no _____ni hon'ya ga arimasu yo.

2. Ms. Blake's apartment feels rather quiet and empty, so she decides to see if she can find a reasonably priced portable stereo. She asks a bookstore employee if there's an electronics store nearby. The bookstore employee answers.

   _____no mise wa kono hon'ya no _____ ni arimasu.

3. There was nothing suitable at the electronics store, and besides, it's nearly noon, and Ms. Blake has a lunch appointment with a potential customer in the dining room of the Yamato Hotel. Give her directions to the hotel.

_____o dete, _____ e magarimasu. Yamato Hoteru wa sanbanme no _____ni arimasu.

4. It's November, and Ms. Blake is beginning to realize that the weather is much colder here than in Tokyo, so she decides to go to the Nandemo-ya Department Store to look for some winter clothes. Give her directions, assuming that she is leaving from the hotel's east entrance.

Hoteru o_____, migi _____magarimasu. Tsukiatari ___migi e magarimasu. Nandemo-ya Depaato wa tsugi no_____ ni _____.

5. Ms. Blake thinks that a short kimono jacket (*hanten*) might be just the thing for lounging around at home on winter evenings, but she doesn't like the selection at the department store, so she asks where a traditional clothing store is. Give her directions, assuming that she is leaving from the store's west entrance.

Depaato o dete, _____e magarimasu. Gofukuten wa ____banme no kado no _____ gawa ni arimasu.

DESCRIBING ONGOING ACTIONS

As you remember from Chapter 7, the form of the verb that ends in -*masu* describes either habitual or future actions. In order to describe a continuous, ongoing action, you need a new construction:

VERB-*te iru/imasu*

Much of the time it corresponds to the English *is VERB-ing*. Even though *iru /imasu* used by itself refers only to animate subjects, a -*te iru* form can refer to either animate or inanimate subjects.

Tomasu Uiruson wa tegami o kaite imasu.
Thomas Wilson is writing a letter.

Watashi no tokei wa susunde imasu.
My watch is running fast ("advancing").

Sometimes the *-te iru* form refers to ongoing states or repeated actions.

> *Kono goro chikatetsu de kayotte imasu.*
> I'm commuting by subway these days.

> *Mado o shimete imasu.*
> I'm closing the windows.

> *Suzuki-san wa okotte imasu.*
> Ms. Suzuki is angry.

> *Ikeda Masaru wa Mitaka ni sunde imasu.*
> Ikeda Masaru lives in Mitaka. (Mitaka is a suburb of Tokyo.)

But not all *-te iru* forms correspond to English *-ing* forms. This correspondence holds true only for the so-called **continuous** (*keizokuteki*) verbs, verbs describing actions that can theoretically be continued indefinitely: writing, eating, drinking, walking, swimming, playing, speaking, and so on.

Japanese has another class of verbs, the so-called **instantaneous** (*shunkanteki*) verbs. These verbs are treated as "either-or" situations with no possibility of a transitional state. The verbs of motion are included in this class, and so *itte iru* does **not** mean "is going," *kite iru* does not mean "is coming," and *kaette iru* does not mean "is returning." Instead, they mean "has gone," "has come," and "has returned."

> *Morimoto-san wa Oosaka e itte imasu.*
> Mr. Morimoto has gone to Osaka.

> *Chan-san no tomodachi wa Nihon ni kite imasu.*
> Ms. Chan's friend has come to Japan.

> *Abuduuru-san wa Mareeshia ni kaette imasu.*
> Ms. Abdul has returned to Malaysia.

From the Japanese point of view, if you've set out from your starting point at all, you're gone, and if you're here, you've come. Thus you can't use *itte iru* or *kite iru* in the sense of "is on the way."

Two other common punctual verbs are *dekiru*, in the sense of "be finished," and *hairu* "enter, be inside, be included."

> *Uchi ga dekite imasu.*
> The house is finished.

> *Sore wa ookii shoppingu baggu desu ne. Nani ga haitte imasu ka?*
> That's a big shopping bag. What's inside it?

Practice 11.2

Vocabulary

sakkaa o suru	サッカー を する		play soccer
gitaa	ギター		guitar
susumu	すすむ	進む	advance, run fast (clocks, watches, etc.)
chikatetsu	ちかてつ	地下鉄	subway
kayou	かよう	通う	commute
shimeru	しめる (1)	閉める	close, shut
shoppingu baggu	ショッピング・ バッグ		shopping bag
sumu	すむ	住む	live, dwell
Mekishiko	メキシコ		Mexico
Takao	たかお	高尾	a popular hiking area west of Tokyo
hiku	ひく	弾く	play a stringed or keyboard instrument

It's a warm, sunny spring day, and the students are relaxing on the roof of the international students' dormitory or on the lawn in front. Chan Ngan-fa is talking to Yamaguchi Mariko on her cellular phone and telling what everyone is doing. What will she say about the following people?

EXAMPLE:

Thomas Wilson is writing letters.
Tomasu Uiruson wa tegami o kaite imasu.

1. Amanda Smith is listening to tapes.

2. Zaini Abdul is reading a book.

3. The Mexican students are playing soccer.

4. Kim Byong-il is drinking cola.

5. Paul duPont is playing the guitar.

6. Wang Peijin is talking with Nguyen My Lam.

7. Kurt Schmidt is studying.

8. Tove Hansen is sleeping.

9. George Masaela is watching the soccer game.

Then Mariko asks about a couple of students that Chan Ngan-fa hasn't mentioned, so she tells her that:

10. Teramura Chieko has gone to Takao.

11. Ikeda Masaru has gone home to Mitaka.

VERBS WHOSE DIRECT OBJECTS TAKE *GA*

You've been warned not to mix up your subject and object particles, but in fact, certain verbs and expressions that take direct objects in English take *ga* in Japanese. You've already met two types of expressions that fall into this catergory.

> *Tanaka-san wa konpyuuta **ga** arimasu.*
> Mr. Tanaka has a computer.

> *Watashi wa aisu kuriimu **ga** suki desu.*
> I like ice cream.

Thinking of *konpyuuta* and *aisu kuriimu* as direct objects marked with *ga* is one approach, but you can also think of these constructions more literally, so that these words aren't direct objects at all.

> As for Mr. Tanaka, there is a computer.

> As for me, ice cream is liked.

It is also possible to think of the five most common *ga* verbs in the same way.

Watashi wa Supeingo ga wakarimasu.
I understand Spanish.
(As for me, Spanish is understandable.)

Watashi wa chizu ga irimasu.
I need a map.
(As for me, a map is necessary.)

Ishida-san wa sukeeto ga dekimasu.
Ms. Ishida can skate.
(As for Ms. Ishida, skating is possible.)

Koko kara Fujisan ga miemasu.
You can see Mt. Fuji from here.
(From here Mt. Fuji is visible.)

Watashi wa ongaku ga kikoemasu.
I can hear music.
(As for me, music is audible.)

Even though *wakaru* is usually translated as "understand," its meaning is broader than that. For example, *wakarimashita* (not plain old *wakarimasu*) is the most common response to an explanation or command: "I have understood what you said."

When talking about needing specific numbers of things, you follow the word order **NOUN particle QUANTITY VERB** or **QUANTITY *no* NOUN particle VERB.**

Kono nimai no seetaa ga irimasu.
I need these two sweaters.

Kono nooto wa sansatsu irimasu.
I need three of these notebooks.

Vocabulary

chizu	ちず	地図	map
-mai	-まい	枚	counter for flat objects and clothing
Nani ka goyô desu ka?	なにか ごよう ですか。	何か 御用 ですか。	Is there something you want me to do?
kami	かみ	紙	paper
-satsu	-さつ	冊	counter for bound volumes such as books, magazines, and notebooks
fûtô	ふうとう	封筒	envelope
mô + QUANTITY	もう+ QUANTITY		QUANTITY more (e.g. *mô hitotsu* = "one more")
Fujisan	ふじさん	富士山	Mt. Fuji
mieru (1)	みえる (1)	見える	can see, be visible
kikoeru (1)	きこえる (1)	聞える	can hear, be audible

Ms. Murayama hasn't worked at the company as long as Ms. Suzuki has, so she ranks lower on the Japanese social scale, and Ms. Suzuki sometimes sends her on errands.

Suzuki: Murayama-san!
Murayama: Hai. Nani ka goyô desu ka?
Suzuki: Ee, kono ookii fûtô ga mô nihyaku mai irimasu kara, katte kite kudasai.
Murayama: Hai, wakarimashita.

Suzuki: Ms. Murayama!
Murayama: Yes, is there something you want?
Suzuki: Yes, we need two hundred more of these large envelopes, so please go buy some.
Murayama: Yes, all right.

• To count flat objects, simply add *mai* to the number in question: *ichi mai, ni mai, san mai,* etc. The counter for books, magazines, and notebooks, *satsu,* goes through some variations:

issatsu	いっさつ	一冊	one volume
nisatsu	にさつ	二冊	two volumes
sansatsu	さんさつ	三冊	three volumes
yonsatsu	よんさつ	四冊	four volumes
gosatsu	ごさつ	五冊	five volumes
rokusatsu	ろくさつ	六冊	six volumes
nanasatsu	ななさつ	七冊	seven volumes
hassatsu	はっさつ	八冊	eight volumes
kyûsatsu	きゅうさつ	九冊	nine volumes
jussatsu	じゅっさつ	十冊	ten volumes

Practice 11.3

Vocabulary

めがね	眼鏡	eyeglasses
こわす	壊す	break [something]
ふべん(な)	不便	inconvenient
し		and furthermore
ちかく	近く	vicinity
はしる	走る	run
よく		often, well
いつも		always
しょうせつ	小説	novel
がいこくご	外国語	foreign language
じしょ	辞書	dictionary

Match the beginnings of these sentences with the verbs that best complete them.

EXAMPLE:

Muzukashii Nihongo no shôseetsu o yonde imasu kara, ii jisho ga _d_ .
(irimasu)
Because I'm reading a difficult Japanese-language novel, I <u>need</u> a good dictionary.

1. Megane o kowashimashita kara,
   atarashii megane ga____.   a. wakarimasu

2. Tonari no hito no rajio ga__.   b. miemasu

3. Sugu Nihon e ikimasu kara, pasupooto ga___.   c kikoemasu

4. Koko kara Kamakura no Daibutsu ga_____.   d. irimasu

5. Kono Doitsugo no shôsetsu, _____ ka?   e. arimasu

6. Tanaka-san wa karate ga_____.   f. dekimasu

7. Koko wa fuben desu shi, suupaa mo arimasen shi, kono chikaku ni wa densha mo basu mo hashirimasen kara, kuruma ga_____.

8. Yamaguchi Mariko wa pinku no doresu ga_____.

TALKING ABOUT PROBABILITY

Suppose that Mr. Morimoto is making an extended trip to various branch offices, and you are asked where he will go tomorrow. You already know how to frame that answer if you are sure that he will be going to Sapporo.

> *Ashita wa Sapporo e ikimasu.*
> Tomorrow he's going to Sapporo.

But suppose you aren't sure. He has urgent business at the Sapporo office, and so you think that he will *probably* go there, but you wouldn't swear to it. In that case, your answer would be:

> *Ashita wa Sapporo e iku deshô.*
> Tomorrow he'll probably go to Sapporo.

Imagine now that your neighbor is talking about buying a new stereo system. When he mentions the configuration he has in mind, you know for certain that it's very expensive, so you say:

> *Sore wa takai desu yo!*
> That's expensive!

However, if you don't know for sure, you can say:

> *Sore wa takai deshô!*
> That's probably expensive.

The pattern is:

> PLAIN VERB + *deshô*
> PLAIN ADJECTIVE + *deshô*
> NOUN + *deshô*

Yes, *deshô* replaces *desu,* at least when used in conjunction with all the verbal and adjectival forms that you've had so far. (You don't know the plain negative or the plain past forms yet, but you will.)

Practice 11.4

Vocabulary

ame	あめ	雨	rain
furu	ふる	降る	to fall (precipitation) *Ame ga futte iru* "It's raining."
yama	やま	山	mountain
toru	とる	取る or 撮る	take, get

Answer these questions in the *deshô* form to indicate that you think your answer is probably true.

EXAMPLE:

Morimoto-san wa hikôki de Sapporo e ikimasu ka? →
Hai, hikôki de iku deshô.
Will Mr. Morimoto go to Sapporo by plane? →
Yes, he'll probably go by plane.

1. Kyô wa ame ga furimasu ka?

2. Sumisu-san wa Furansugo ga wakarimasu ka?

3. Uiruson-san wa shiken ni gôkaku shimasu ka?

4. Kimu-san wa nete imasu ka?

5. Hansen-san wa sukii ga dekimasu ka?

6. Raishû no shiken wa muzukashii desu ka?

7. Kore wa benri ja nai desu ka?

8. Ano kata wa Takahashi sensei desu ka?

9. Chan-san wa Nara de shashin o torimasu ka?

SUMMING UP
MATOME
まとめ

1. You're back in that downtown information booth, answering the questions of Japanese tourists. Tell them to:
   (a) please board that bus over there and get off in front of the Nightcap Hotel
   (b) please go into the hotel and turn left
   (c) please cross the street and wait ("be waiting") over there

2. You and Teramura Chieko are having an afternoon snack in the campus coffee shop, and you spot Ikeda Masaru and Kim Byong-il at a nearby table, having a conversation.

Teramura: Sono hanashi, kikoemasu ka?
You: (Say that you can hear, but you don't understand it. Ask if they are speaking Korean.)
Teramura: Sô desu ne. Kankokugo o renshû shite iru no deshô ne.
You: (Say that Mr. Ikeda is impressive.)

CHAPTER 12

GO-KYÔDAI WA NANNIN DESU KA? (HOW MANY BROTHERS AND SISTERS DO YOU HAVE?)

In this chapter, you will learn:

1. to describe your family and count people
2. to talk about ages
3. to describe what you want
4. to make suggestions

DESCRIBING YOUR FAMILY

The tricky part about describing your family in Japanese is distinguishing the terms that are used to name your own relatives from the terms that are used to name other people's relatives and the terms used to address these relatives.

And there are separate words for "older brother," "younger brother," "older sister," and "younger sister," but no generic words for "brother" or "sister."

English Term	My Relative	Other Person's Relative	Form of Address
family	kazoku	go-kazoku	—
father	chichi	o-tôsan	o-tôsan papa
mother	haha	o-kaasan	o-kaasan mama
parents	ryôshin	go-ryôshin	—
older brother	ani	o-niisan	o-niisan
older sister	ane	o-neesan	o-neesan
younger	otôto	otôtosan	given name
brother			without -san

English Term	My Relative	Other Person's Relative	Form of Address
younger sister	imôto	imôtosan	given name without -san
siblings	kyôdai	go-kyôdai	—
grandfather	sofu	o-jiisan	o-jiisan
grandmother	sobo	o-baasan	o-baasan
uncle	oji	ojisan	ojisan
aunt	oba	obasan	obasan
grandchild	mago	o-magosan	given name without -san/ given name + -chan
nephew	oi	oigosan	given name without -san/ given name + -chan
niece	mei	meigosan	given name without -san/ given name + -chan
husband	shujin otto	go-shujin	anata (literally "you")
wife	kanai tsuma	okusan	given name without -san
child	kodomo	o-kosan	given name without -san / given name with -chan
son	musuko	musuko-san o-botchan	
daughter	musume	o-jôsan	

• *Chan* is used instead of *san* when addressing children, especially girls. (People outside the family, such as teachers, address boys with their given name + *kun* and boys talking among themselves may address one another with their family name + *kun*.)

• Children are taught to address teenagers and people in their twenties as *o-niisan* or *o-neesan*. People of their parents' generation are addressed as *ojisan* or *obasan*, and people of their grandparents' generation or older are addressed as *o-jiisan* or *o-baasan*. If you go to Japan, don't be surprised if a child you've never seen before suddenly addresses you as if you were a relative.

In order to describe your family fully, you need to be able to state how many siblings, cousins, and other relatives you have, and counting people in Japanese is a bit complicated, because the words for "one person" and "two people" have been retained from the ancient number system.

hitori	ひとり	一人	one person
futari	ふたり	二人	two people
sannin	さんにん	三人	three people
yonin	よにん	四人	four people
gonin	ごにん	五人	five people
rokunin	ろくにん	六人	six people
shichinin	しちにん	七人	seven people
hachinin	はちにん	八人	eight people
kunin	くにん	九人	nine people
jûnin	じゅうにん	十人	ten people
hitori zutsu	ひとりずつ	一人ずつ	one person each, one person at a time
nannin	なんにん	何人	how many people?

To ask how many brothers and sisters a person has, say:

Go-kyôdai wa nannin desu ka?
How many brothers and sisters do you have?
(How many people are your siblings?)

Examples:

1. Zaini Abdul is going back to Malaysia for her brother's wedding, and Teramura Chieko asks about her family.

Teramura: Go-kyôdai wa nannin desu ka?
Abdul: Yonin desu. Ani to ane to otôto to imôto ga hitori zutsu imasu.
Teramura: Ookii go-kazoku desu ne!

Teramura: How many brothers and sisters do you have?
Abdul: Four: an older brother, an older sister, a younger brother, and a younger sister, one of each.
Teramura: It's a big family, isn't it?

When talking to adults you don't know well, it is a good idea to preface any personal questions with

> *Shitsurei desu ga...*
> It's rude of me to ask, but. . .

2. James Green is the director of the Tokyo branch of an American company, and he has been told to select a Japanese employee to go to the home office in San Francisco for a year of training. He has chosen Mr. Aoki, and now he is asking him some personal questions to find out what accommodations, if any, need to be made for his family.

Vocabulary

shitsurei (na)	しつれい (な)	失礼 (な)	rude, impolite
kekkon suru	けっこん する	結婚 する	get married
(o)-shigoto	(お)しごと	(お)仕事	work
honyakuka	ほんやくか	翻訳家	translator
orimasu	おります		humble form of *imasu*

Green:	Aoki-san wa kekkon shite imasu ka?
Aoki:	Hai, kekkon shite orimasu.
Green:	Okusan no o-shigoto wa?
Aoki:	Hai, honyakuka de gozaimasu.
Green:	Jaa, o-kosan wa?
Aoki:	Hai, chiisai musume ga hitori orimasu.

Green:	Are you married, Mr. Aoki?
Aoki:	Yes, I am.
Green:	What's your wife's occupation?
Aoki:	She's a translator.
Green:	What about children?
Aoki:	We have one small daughter.

• *Kekkon suru* is a punctual verb, so *kekkon shite iru* does **not** mean "is in the process of getting married." Instead, it means "is married." The verb phrases *rikon suru* "get divorced" and *ninshin suru* "become pregnant" are also punctual.

• Mr. Aoki uses *de gozaimasu* instead of *desu* and *orimasu* instead of *imasu* because Mr. Green is his supervisor, and therefore Japanese etiquette requires that he use extra-polite language with him.

Kei (70)   Ichirô (75)

Kenji (47) Michiko (45)   Yoshimasa (40)   Etsuko (35)

Yôichi (18)   Emi (15)   Mika (11)

Look at the drawing of the Sasakis' family tree. Here is Sasaki Yoshimasa's description of his family.

Haha no Kei to chichi no Ichirô wa futari to mo kenzai desu. Ane no Michiko wa nijû nen mae ni Yamada Kenji to kekkon shite, kodomo ga futari imasu. Ue no ko wa otoko no ko de, Yôichi to iimasu. Shita no ko wa onna no ko de, Emi to iimasu. Oi no Yôichi wa mô sugu daigaku ni hairimasu ga, mei no Emi wa mada kôkôskei desu. Boku wa kanai no Etsuko to musume no Mika to sannin de, Yokohama no manshon ni sunde imasu.

• The *de* of *otoko no ko de, Yôichi to iimasu* is the *-te* form of *desu*. As you will remember from Chapter 9, a verb in the *-te* form followed by a verb in the sentence-final form usually means $VERB_1$ and $VERB_2$, so the sentence means "is a boy and is named Yôichi." Similarly, *onna no ko de, Emi to iimasu means* "is a girl and is named Emi."

Vocabulary

haha no Kei to chichi no Ichirô	ははの ケイと ちちの いちろう	母の ケイと 父の 一郎	my mother Kei and my father Ichirô (note similar constructions throughout)
kenzai (na)	けんざい(な)	健在(な)	alive and well
futari to mo	ふたりとも	二人とも	both people, both of them
nijûnen mae ni	にじゅうねん まえに	20年前に	twenty years ago
kôkôsei	こうこうせい	高校生	high school student
mada	まだ		still (with a positive adjective or verb)
NAME to iimasu	NAME といいます		is called NAME
otoko	おとこ	男	male
onna	おんな	女	female
otoko no ko	おとこのこ	男の子	boy
onna no ko	おんなのこ	女の子	girl
ue no . . .	うえの...	上の...	older (referring to relatives)
shita no . . .	したの...	下の...	younger (referring to relatives)
sannin de	さんにんで	三人で	in a group of three, the three of us
manshon	マンション		condominium apartment

Practice 12.1

Now imagine that instead of Sasaki Yoshimasa describing his own family, we have Mr. Morimoto, who has known the family a long time, telling someone else about them. What would he say?

EXAMPLE:

He could begin by saying:
Sasaki Yoshimasa-san no o-kaasan no Kei-san to o-tôsan no Ichirô-san wa (o-)futari to mo (go-)kenzai desu.
Sasaki Yoshimasa's mother Kei and father Ichirô are both alive and well.

Complete the paragraph on a separate piece of paper.

TALKING ABOUT AGES

To ask how old someone is, ask either

> *O-ikutsu desu ka?*
> or
> *Nansai desu ka?*

The ages of children ten and under can be described with the *-tsu* numerals: *hitotsu, futatsu, mittsu,* etc. The other possibility is the counter *-sai,* which can be used to describe any age.

issai	いっさい	一歳	one year old
nisai	にさい	二歳	two years old
sansai	さんさい	三歳	three years old
yonsai	よんさい	四歳	four years old
gosai	ごさい	五歳	five years old
rokusai	ろくさい	六歳	six years old
nanasai	ななさい	七歳	seven years old
hassai	はっさい	八歳	eight years old
kyûsai	きゅうさい	九歳	nine years old
jussai	じゅっさい	十歳	ten years old
hatachi	はたち	二十歳	twenty years old

With the exception of *hatachi,* "twenty years old," all other ages are combinations of the same ten elements: *jûissai* "eleven years old," *nijûhassai* "twenty-eight years old," *gojussai* "fifty years old."

For the ages of infants less than a year old, use *seigo* "after birth" plus the following expressions for counting months:

ikkagetsu	いっかげつ	一ヶ月	one month
nikagetsu	にかげつ	二ヶ月	two months
sankagetsu	さんかげつ	三ヶ月	three months
yonkagetsu	よんかげつ	四ヶ月	four months
gokagetsu	ごかげつ	五ヶ月	five months
rokkagetsu	ろっかげつ	六ヶ月	six months
nanakagetsu	ななかげつ	七ヶ月	seven months
hakkagetsu	はっかげつ	八ヶ月	eight months
kyûkagetsu	きゅうかげつ	九ヶ月	nine months
jukkagetsu	じゅっかげつ	十ヶ月	ten months
jûikkagetsu	じゅういっかげつ	十一ヶ月	eleven months
jûnikagetsu	じゅうにかげつ	十二ヶ月	twelve months

These terms can also be used to express lengths of time:

Sankagetsu Nihon ni imashita.
I was in Japan for three months.

Ikkagetsu no koosu desu.
It's a one-month course.

WATCH OUT

There is a distinction between the names of the months and the words for numbers of months. A common mistake is to confuse words like *ichigatsu, nigatsu* "January," " February," with words like *ikkagetsu, nikagetsu* "one month," "two months."

Vocabulary

da kara	だから		therefore
akachan	あかちゃん	赤ちゃん	baby

Mr. Green continues interviewing Mr. Aoki about his family.

Green:	O-jôsan wa o-ikutsu desu ka?
Aoki:	Seigo jukkagetsu desu.
Green:	A, sô desu ka? Da kara, mada akachan desu ne?
Green:	How old is your daughter?
Aoki:	She's ten months old.
Green:	Oh, really? Then, she's still a baby, isn't she?

Practice 12.2

Vocabulary

umareru (1)	うまれる (1)	生まれる	be born
nansai de	なんさいで	何歳で	at what age
hajimete	はじめて	初めて	for the first time
nakunaru	なくなる	亡くなる	die (polite form)

Look at the Sasaki family tree on page 180 and tell how old each person is.

EXAMPLE:

Ichirô-san wa nanajûgo sai desu.

1.

2.

3.

4.

5.

6.

7.

8.

Figure out how old each person was at the time of the events described. The numbers representing the years are written out in words instead of in numerals.

9. Aoki-san wa sen kyûhyaku rokujû go nen ni umaremashita. Sen kyûhyaku kyûjû ni nen ni kekkon shimashita. Nansai de kekkon shimashita ka?

10. Tomasu Uiruson wa sen kyûhyaku nanajû roku nen ni umaremashita. Sen kyûhyaku kyûjû roku nen ni hajimete Nihon ni kimashita. Nansai de kimashita ka?

11. Tanbara-san wa sen happyaku kyûjû san nen ni umarete, sen kyûhyaku kyûjû ni nen ni nakunarimashita. Nansai de nakunarimashita ka?

EXPRESSING WHAT YOU WANT

In English and most other European languages, saying that you want to do something is fairly simple. You just use a form of the verb corresponding to "want" with the infinitive of the verb describing the action you would like to carry out. Saying that you want a certain item is even easier: you just use the same verb "want" with a direct object.

I want to buy a bicycle.
I want a bicycle.

The Japanese equivalents of these two sentences, however, do not much resemble each other.

Jitensha o kaitai desu.
I want to buy a bicycle.

Jitensha ga hoshii desu.
I want a bicycle.

It is very easy to form the verbal construction. Simply take the *-masu* form of the verb, drop the *-masu,* and replace it with *-tai desu.*

shimasu do	*shitai desu* I want to do	*shitaku nai desu* I don't want to do
kaimasu buy	*kaitai desu* I want to buy	*kaitaku nai desu* I don't want to buy
tabemasu eat	*tabetai desu* I want to eat	*tabetaku nai desu* I don't want to eat

This *-ai desu/-aku nai desu* pattern should look familiar to you, because it's exactly the same as the pattern used in conjugating adjectives. That's right: even these *-tai* forms come from verbs; they act like adjectives.

These *-tai* forms are usually used 1) in statements about what the speaker wants to do, or 2) in direct questions about what the listener wants to do. The idea behind this is that you can't really know what is going on in another person's mind, so you can't really have direct knowledge of what he or she wants.

In order to talk about what a third person wants, you may use roundabout constructions corresponding to "My friend appears to want to see this video" or "My friend is talking about wanting to see this video" or "My cousin acts as if he or she wants to see this video." The third option is the easiest. The suffix *-tagaru* goes onto the *-masu* stem:

mi-masu
see (polite form)

mi-tai desu
[I] want to see

mi-tagaru
[some other person] acts as if s/he wants to see

Even though the *-tai* forms act like adjectives, the *-tagaru* forms act like verbs, and they are most often used in their *-te iru* forms.

Tomodachi mo kono bideo o mitagatte imasu.
My friend [is acting as if s/he] wants to see this video, too.

It is not considered polite to use these *-tagaru* forms when referring to people who rank above you in the Japanese social system, such as teachers or supervisors.

In addition, invitations are often phrased as negative questions:

Watashitachi to issho ni ikimasen ka?
Won't you go along with us?

None of these forms can be used to talk about wanting objects. For this you need the adjective *hoshii.* Like *suki,* it occurs in a *wa. . . ga* pattern:

NOUN₁ *wa* NOUN₂ *ga hoshii desu.*

Watashi wa kamera ga hoshii desu.
I want a camera.

Taipuraitaa wa hoshiku nai desu.
I don't want a typewriter.

Hoshii cannot refer to what a third person wants. Instead, you have to use the verb *hoshigaru.*

Imôto wa atarashii oobaa o hoshigatte imasu.
My younger sister wants a new overcoat.

Note that the "object" of *hoshii* is marked with *ga* while the object of *hoshigaru* is marked with *o.*

Practice 12.3

Vocabulary

yukata	ゆかた	浴衣	*yukata*, cotton kimono worn on informal occasions in warm weather
keitai denwa	けいたい でんわ	携帯 電話	cellular phone
dentaku	でんたく	電卓	electronic calculator
oobaa	オーバー		overcoat
shamisen	しゃみせん	三味線	*shamisen*, a traditional stringed instrument similar to a banjo
Yooroppa	ヨーロッパ		Europe

How would you say it?

1. I want to go to Japan.

2. I don't want to go to the hospital.

3. My friend wants to go to Europe.

4. I don't want to drink cola.

5. Do you want to take lessons in *shamisen?*

6. The students want to go home.

7. I want a *yukata.*

8. I don't want a cellular phone.

9. My younger sister wants a bicycle.

10. I want a calculator.

MAKING SUGGESTIONS AND OFFERS

To express the idea of "let's do. . ." (or sometimes "I will do"), simply change the *-masu* ending to *-mashô*.

> *Sa, tabemashô.*
> Well then, let's eat.
>
> *Sensei ni sôdan shimashô.*
> Let's consult the teacher.

When followed by the question particle *ka*, *-mashô* means "should I?" or "shall we?"

> *Dekakemashô ka?*
> Shall we set off?
>
> *Shashin o torimashô ka?*
> Should I take a picture?

Practice 12.4

How would you say it?

1.   Let's buy a map.

2.   Let's go by subway.

3.   Let's listen to the radio.

4.   Let's go into this store.

5.   Let's swim a hundred meters.

6.   Should I write a letter?

7.   Should I study this textbook?

8.   Should I practice calligraphy?

9.   Shall we watch this video?

10.   Shall we get on this train?

SUMMING UP
MATOME
まとめ

Complete the dialogues according to the cues given.

Vocabulary

isha	いしゃ	医者	medical doctor
kyôshi	きょうし	教師	non-honorific word for *teacher*, used in reference to one's self or one's own relatives
irassharu (irasshaimasu)	いらっしゃる (いらっしゃいます)		honorific equivalent of *imasu*
bengoshi	べんごし	弁護士	lawyer

1. It will soon be your birthday, and Teramura Chieko is trying to figure out what to get you.

Teramura: Nani ga hoshii desu ka?
You: (Think about it and say that you want a stereo.)
Teramura: Sore dake desu ka?
You: (Tell her that you also want to see that new movie.)

2. A Japanese acquaintance is asking you about your family.

Nihonjin: Go-ryôshin mo Nihon ni irasshaimasu ka?
You: (Say that they're in America—and don't use honorifics!)
Nihonjin: Go-ryôshin no o-shigoto wa nan desu ka?
You: (Say that your father is a medical doctor and your mother is a schoolteacher.)
Nihonjin: Go-kyôdai wa nannin desu ka?
You: (You have one older brother and one younger sister.)
Nihonjin: O-niisan mo gakusei desu ka?
You: (Say that he isn't; he's a lawyer.)
Nihonjin: Sô desu ka? O-neesan wa?
You: (Say that she's still a high school student.)

Takayama Festival

CHAPTER 13

SONO MIZU O NONDE WA IKEMASEN. (YOU MUSTN'T DRINK THAT WATER.)

In this chapter you will learn to:

1. talk about something becoming something else
2. ask, give, and deny permission
3. express the concepts of "no one," "nowhere," "nothing," "anyone," "anywhere," "anything"
4. compare one item with another

TALKING ABOUT SOMETHING BECOMING SOMETHING ELSE

The concept of "becoming" or "turning into" is usually expressed with the verb *naru*, but the pattern within the sentence is determined by whether you are talking about a noun or an adjective.

(a) *ku*-adjective (in the *-ku* form) + *naru*

> *yasuku naru*
> become cheap

> *akaku naru*
> become red, turn red

(b) Noun / *na*-adjective + *naru*

> *benri ni naru*
> become convenient

> *isha ni naru*
> become a physician

These forms cannot be used for certain phrases that are "become" phrases in English. For example, "become angry" is a phrase in English, but it is a single verb, *okoru* in Japanese, as is "become tired," which is *tsukareru*.

okorimashita
became angry, got angry

tsukaremashita
became tired, got tired

Similarly, "become old, grow old" is indeed *furuku naru* when you are talking about inanimate objects, but it is *toshi o toru* when you are talking about people.

All of these expressions, whether with or without *naru*, are *punctual*. That is, their *-te iru* forms do not mean "is becoming" but "has become" or "is in that state."

isogashiku natte imasu
has become busy

okotte imasu
has become angry, is angry

toshi o totte imasu
has become old, is old

tsukarete imasu
has become tired, is tired

In case you're wondering how to say "is in the process of becoming," the answer is that there are many ways, depending on the vocabulary item in question, and they are too numerous to discuss at this point.

It is possible to put *naru* into the *-tai* form:

isha ni naritai
I want to become a doctor.

Vocabulary

isogashii	いそがしい	忙しい	busy
tsukareru (1)	つかれる (1)	疲れる	become tired, get tired
toshi o toru	としをとる	年をとる	grow old (referring to people)
kaeru	かえる	蛙	frog

Example:

Chan Ngan-fa is visiting the Yamaguchis on a very hot day.

Yamaguchi: Atsuku narimashita ne.
Chan: Sô desu ne. Eki kara aruite kite, tsukaremashita.

Yamaguchi: It's gotten hot, hasn't it?
Chan: It certainly has. I got tired walking here from the station.

Practice 13.1

How would you say it?

1. became expensive

2. has become interesting

3. becomes difficult

4. became a lawyer

5. has become **angry**

6. has become a teacher

7. is tired

8. has become rude

9. becomes complicated

10. turned into a frog

ASKING, GIVING, AND DENYING PERMISSION

The versatile -*te* form (which you learned in Chapter 10) is used in asking, giving, and denying persmission. The form for asking permission is:

VERB-*te mo ii desu ka?*
Is it all right to VERB?

Kore o tsukatte mo ii desu ka?
Is it all right to use this?

Koko de bentô o tabete mo ii desu ka?
Is it all right to eat box lunches here?

If you need to be more polite, you can substitute *yoroshii* for *ii.* In order to grant someone permission, you can say:

Hai, dôzo.
Yes, please do.

Hai, ii desu yo.
Yes, it's fine.

You need to be a bit careful when denying someone permission. The most direct way is

VERB-*te wa ikemasen*

Koko de bentô o tabete wa ikemasen.
It's forbidden to eat box lunches here.

This form should be reserved for situations in which something really is literally officially forbidden, dangerous, or taboo. In order to deny a request politely, as when someone has asked for permission to smoke, you should use a more indirect phrase:

Maa, chotto. . . (spoken in a trailing off voice)
Well, it's a little bit. . .

Maa, chotto muzukashii desu ne.
Well, it's a little bit difficult.

Môshiwake arimasen ga, go-enryo kudasai.
I'm sorry to have to say this, but please don't.
(I have no excuse, but please refrain.)

In general, Japanese people do not like to deny requests directly (except in the case of parents dealing with children, etc.), so if you make a request of a Japanese person and you get what sounds like a vague answer or an attempt to change the subject, you should interpret that as "no."

By the way, if you offend someone or break some rule, even if you think it's a silly rule, don't try to argue your way out of any trouble you may get into as a result. Apologize with *môshiwake arimasen or môshiwake gozaimasen* (if you need to be extra humble) and promise *Nido to shimasen* "I won't do it again." Arguing for your "rights" will only get you into further trouble.

Vocabulary

kitanai	きたない		dirty
niwa	にわ	庭	garden
tabako o suu	タバコを すう	タバコを 吸う	smoke (especially cigarettes)
go-enryo kudasai	ごえんりょ ください	御遠慮 ください	Please refrain from. . .
moshiwake arimasen or moshiwake gozaimasen	もうしわけ ありません/ もうしわけ ございません	/申し訳 ありません /申し訳 ございません	I'm sorry (used when politely turning down a request or when apologizing for something when you are in the wrong.) The form with *gozaimasen* is even more polite.
o-miyage	おみやげ		souvenirs, presents brought back from a trip
kariru (1)	かりる (1)	借りる	borrow
PERSON ni tanomu	PERSON に たのむ	頼む	make a request of PERSON

Examples:

1. The international students are visiting Kamakura on a very hot day. As they are walking around in a temple garden with a guide, Amanda Smith spots an outdoor faucet and rushes to refill her water bottle.

Guide: Sono mizu o nonde wa ikemasen yo!
Smith: Sô desu ka?
Guide: Ee, kitanai mizu desu kara, niwa de tsukatte mo ii desu kedo, nonde wa ikemasen.

Guide: You mustn't drink that water.
Smith: Really?

Guide: Yes. It's dirty water, so it's all right to use it in the garden, but you mustn't drink it.

2. It's a pleasant afternoon, and Thomas Wilson feels like going on a bike ride, but he doesn't own a bicycle. He asks Ikeda Masaru if he may borrow his.

Wilson: Jitensha o karite mo ii?
Ikeda: Boku no jitensha? Saa, boku mo. . .
Wilson: Ii yo. Kimu-san ni tanomu kara.

Wilson: May I borrow your bicycle?
Ikeda: My bicycle? Hmm. . . I, too,. . .
Wilson: Oh, it's all right. Because I'll ask Mr. Kim.

• By this time, Thomas Wilson and Masaru Ikeda have become very good friends, and so they speak to each other in the dictionary form.

3. Mr. Tanabe is in the hospital, and Mr. Konishi, his colleague from work, comes to visit him. After a while, Mr. Konishi asks the nurse if he may smoke.

Konishi: Kangofu-san, koko de tabako o sutte mo ii desu ka?
Kangofu: Môshiwake gozaimasen ga, tabako wa go- enryo kudasai.

Konishi: Nurse, may I smoke here?
Nurse: I'm sorry, but please refrain from smoking.

• People on the job are sometimes addressed by their job title plus -san: *Kangofu-san* "Nurse," *Hon-ya-san* "Mr./Ms. Bookstore Owner, " etc. The exceptions are teachers and physicians, who are addressed as *Sensei*.

Practice 13.2

Ask for permission to do the following things:

EXAMPLE:

come tomorrow →
Ashita kite mo ii desu ka?

1. take photographs

2. borrow a pencil

3. eat these sandwiches

4. study in this room

5. play soccer in the park

6. read this newspaper

7. write with a pencil

8. wash the car

9. use the telephone

10. consult a lawyer

THE CONCEPTS OF "NO ONE," "NOWHERE," AND "NOTHING"

You already know how to answer an informational question positively:

Nani o kaimashita ka?
What did you buy?

Yôfuku o kaimashita.
I bought clothes.

What if you have to answer that you didn't buy anything? Or if some other situation came up zero? Well, of course, you have to make the verbs negative, but that's not enough. You have to change the particles, too.

Nani	**o**	kaimashita ka?
↓	↓	↓
Nani	**mo**	kaimasen deshita.
I didn't buy anything.		
Dare	**ga**	imashita ka?
↓	↓	↓
Dare	**mo**	imasen deshita.
No one was there.		
Doko	**e**	ikimashita ka?
↓	↓	↓
Doko	**e mo**	ikimasen deshita.
I didn't go anywhere.		

As in other contexts, *mo* replaces *wa, ga,* and *o,* but it is added to the other particles, such as *ni* and *e.*

> *Nani mo wakarimasen.*
> I don't understand anything.
>
> *Dare mo dekimasen.*
> Nobody can do it.
>
> *Doko ni mo arimasen.*
> It isn't anywhere.
>
> *Dore mo kaimasen deshita.*
> I didn't buy any of them.

For some reason, *itsu mo* means *always,* not *never.* There are several ways to say *never,* and you will learn some of them in later chapters.

Vocabulary

denwa o kakeru (1)	でんわを かける (1)	電話を かける	make a phone call
denwa ni deru (1)	でんわに でる (1)	電話に 出る	answer the phone
ka (between nouns)	か		or
kissaten	きっさてん	喫茶店	coffee shop, coffeehouse
taiikukan	たいいくかん	体育館	gymnasium
hen (na)	へん(な)	変(な)	odd, strange
sagasu	さがす	探す	look for
sakki	さっき		just now, just a little while ago

Example:

Eric Jones is having trouble finding Kim Byong-il, so he asks Teramura Chieko where he is.

Jones: Sakki Kimu-san no heya e denwa o kakemashita ga, dare mo demasen deshita.

Teramura: Hen desu nee. Toshokan ka kissaten ni iru deshô ne.

Jones: Iie, toshokan de mo kissaten de mo taiikukan de mo sagashite kimashita ga, doko ni mo imasen yo.

Jones: Just now I phoned Mr. Kim's room, but nobody answered.

Teramura: That's strange, isn't it? Maybe he's at the library or in the coffee shop.

Jones: No, I went and looked in the library and in the coffee shop and in the gym, but he isn't anywhere.

Practice 13.3a

Answer these questions using *nani mo, dare mo, doko ni/e mo*, **etc.**

EXAMPLE:

Hikidashi no naka ni nani ga arimasu ka?
Nani mo arimasen.
What's inside the drawer?
There isn't anything.

1. Emi-chan wa doko ni imasu ka?

2. Dare ga kono konpyuuta o tsukatte imasu ka?

3. Asagohan ni nani o tabemashita ka?

4. Dore o mimashita ka?

5. Dare ga o-sara o araimashita ka?

6. Nani o kiite imasu ka?

Practice 13.3b

How would you say these?

1. I didn't see anything.

2. They aren't selling it anywhere.

3. No one speaks English. (As for English, no one speaks it.)

4. I won't buy anything.

5. I didn't write anything.

COMPARISONS

Comparisons between two nouns can be stated either positively or negatively:

> Tôkyô is larger than Kyôto.
> Kyôto is not as large as Tôkyô.

Both types of comparisons also exist in Japanese. One pattern for positive comparisons is:

> NOUN₁ *wa* NOUN₂ *yori* ADJECTIVE *desu.*
>
> *Nara wa Kyôto yori furui desu.*
> Nara is older than Kyôto.
>
> *Nihon no bukka wa Amerika no bukka yori takai desu.*
> Japan's consumer prices are higher than America's consumer prices.

Hirano-san wa Noguchi-san yori atama ga ii desu.
Mr. Hirano is smarter than Mr. Noguchi.

The above pattern is used when making a statement about an already established topic. Another pattern is

NOUN$_2$ *yori* NOUN$_1$ *(no hô) ga* ADJECTIVE *desu.*

Kyôto yori Nara no hô ga furui desu.
Nara is older than Kyôto.

Udon yori soba ga suki desu.
I like *soba* better than *udon.*

Hoka no densha yori Shinkansen no hô ga hayai desu.
The Bullet Train is faster than other trains.

This structure is used when answering the question:

NOUN$_1$ *to* NOUN$_2$ *to, dochira no hô ga* ADJECTIVE *desu ka?*
Which is more ADJECTIVE, NOUN$_1$ or NOUN$_2$?

Nara to Kyôto to, dochira no hô ga furui desu ka?
Which is older, Nara or Kyôto?

Soba to udon to, dochira no hô ga o-suki desu ka?
Which do you like better, *soba* or *udon* ?

If there isn't much difference between the two nouns being asked about, you can answer:

Onaji gurai desu.
They're about the same.

In these particular constructions, there is nothing corresponding to the English "-er" comparative ending or the "more" used in the comparative forms of longer verbs. However, when no direct comparison occurs within a single sentence, the adjective may be preceded by *motto* "more."

Amerika e kaette kara, motto ii konpyuuta o kaimashita.
After returning to America, I bought a better computer.

There are no irregular forms, like the English "good," "better" or "bad," "worse."

Vocabulary

bukka	ぶっか	物価	consumer prices
NOUN wa atama ga ii	NOUN は あたまがいい	頭がいい	NOUN is smart
Shinkansen	しんかんせん	新幹線	the Shinkansen ("Bullet Train")
hoka no NOUN	ほかの NOUN	他の	other NOUN(s)
onaji gurai	おなじ ぐらい	同じ ぐらい	approximately the same
ryokan	りょかん	旅館	traditional inn
ooi	おおい	多い	numerous
motto	もっと		more

Practice 13.4a

How would you say this?

1. Which is better, this textbook or that textbook?

2. Which do you like better, *sukiyaki* or *tempura?*

3. What are you more skilled at, French or Spanish?

4. Which is faster, the bus or the subway?

5. Sapporo is colder than Tokyo.

6. The subway is faster than the bus.

7. Traditional inns are more interesting than hotels.

8. Kanji are more complicated than hiragana.

9. The Japanese [person] teachers are more numerous than the American [person] teachers.

Negative comparisons follow the pattern:

NOUN₁ *wa* NOUN₂ *hodo* NEGATIVE PHRASE

Basu wa chikatetsu hodo hayaku nai desu.
The bus isn't as fast as the subway.

Tôkyô wa Okinawa hodo atsuku arimasen.
Tôkyô is not as hot as Okinawa.

Inu wa uma hodo ookiku nai desu.
Dogs are not as large as horses.

Practice 13.4b

Vocabulary

uma	うま	馬	horse
inu	いぬ	犬	dog
shukudai	しゅくだい	宿題	homework
nezumi	ねずみ	鼠	rat, mouse
kowai	こわい	怖い	fearsome, scary
raion	ライオン		lion

Each item contains two nouns and two verbal or adjectival phrases. State the relation between the two nouns both positively and negatively.

EXAMPLE:

Amerika/ Nihon/ ookii
Amerika wa Nihon yori ookii desu.
Nihon wa Amerika hodo ookiku arimasen

1. Kanji/hiragana/muzukashii

2. Paatii/shukudai/tanoshii

3. Hawai/Nihon/chikai

4. Raion/nezumi/kowai

5. Kono shashin/hoka no shashin/kirei

SUMMING UP
MATOME
まとめ

A. Look at the following drawings and make up a comparative sentence for each one, using the words given. Your sentence may be either a positive or a negative comparison.

1. shiroi inu/kuroi inu/chiisai

2. Sumisu-san no uchi/Joonzu-san no uchi/furui

3. kono nezumi/sono nezumi/atama ga ii

4. kono uma/ hoka no uma/ hayai

5. Okinawa/Hokkaidô/samui

B. Complete the following dialogues according to the cues given.
1. It is your first day at a Japanese university, and you walk into your first class carrying a cup of coffee.

Sensei:	Koko de koohii o nonde wa ikemasen yo.
You:	(Ask if that's so.)
Sensei:	Ee, kissaten de nonde mo ii n desu ga, kyôshitsu no naka de nonde wa ikemasen.

You: (Apologize, implying that you were in the wrong, and say that you won't do it again.)

2. You are from Minnesota, and you are visiting Tôkyô on business in January. You meet with Mr. Tanaka at a coffee shop.

Tanaka: Samuku narimashita nee.
You: (Agree.)
Tanaka: Minesota mo samui deshô ne.
You: (Say that Minnesota is colder than Tôkyô.)
Tanaka: Shiberia to onaji gurai desu ka?
You: (Tell him that it's not as cold as Siberia.)

SENSEI NI KAIGAI RYÔKO NO OMIYAGE O SASHIAGEMASHITA. (I GAVE MY INSTRUCTOR A SOUVENIR FROM MY OVERSEAS TRIP.)

In this chapter, you will learn to:

1. say "anything," "something," "anyone," "someone," "anywhere," "somewhere"
2. make the dictionary form negative
3. talk about giving
4. talk about going somewhere for a purpose

"ANYTHING," "SOMETHING," "ANYONE," "SOMEONE," "ANYWHERE," "SOMEWHERE"

In the previous chapter, you learned how to say "nothing," "no one," and "nowhere." The terms for "anything," "anyone," and "anywhere" are superficially similar, but they pattern differently. They are formed as follows:

nan de mo anything	nan de mo dekiru can do anything
dare de mo anyone	dare de mo dekiru anyone can do it
doko de mo anywhere	doko de mo dekiru can do it anywhere
itsu de mo anytime	itsu de mo dekiru can do it anytime
dore de mo Any one of several	dore de mo dekiru can do any one of them
Dono NOUN de mo any one of several NOUNS	dono supootsu de mo dekiru can play any sport
dochira de mo either one of two	dochira de mo dekiru can do either one

Note that these forms are **not** equivalent to the "anything," "anyone," "anywhere" of "Did you buy anything?" or "Is anyone home?" or "Is there a good restaurant anywhere?" In these sentences, the any- forms are equivalent in meaning to "something," "someone," and "somewhere," the forms for which are described later in this section. The *de mo* forms presented here mean "anything and everything," "anyone and everyone," "anywhere and everywhere," or "anytime and every time."

> Dare de mo shitte imasu.
> Anyone and everyone knows.

> Nan de mo shûri shimasu.
> They repair anything and everything.

> Onsen wa doko ni de mo arimasu.
> Hot spring resorts are anywhere and everywhere.

> Itsu de mo ii desu.
> Anytime is fine.

> Nihon no densha wa doko e de mo ikimasu.
> Japanese trains go anywhere and everywhere.

Vocabulary

shiru	しる	知る	find out
shitte iru	しっている	知っている	knows, is familiar with
shûri suru	しゅうりする	修理する	repair
onsen	おんせん	温泉	hot spring resort

Practice 14.1a

How would you say it?

1. Everyone understands.

2. They go on foot (walking) anywhere and everywhere.

3. They're selling anything and everything.

4. They're using any of several.

5. Please come to my house anytime.

6. I like either one.

7. I like any of them.

8. Any Japanese person knows it.

• The dictionary form of the verb *shiru* means "find out, realize," but its *-te iru* form means "know," so in order to say that you are acquainted with a person or place or know a fact, you say *shitte imasu*. The pattern is not entirely symmetrical, however, because the form *shitte imasen* is not used. Instead, "I don't know" is *shirimasen*.

The some- words, such as "something," "someone," "somewhere," "sometime" are formed by adding *ka* to the corresponding pronouns.

nani ka something	*Fukuro no naka ni nani ka arimasu.* There's something inside the bag.
doko ka somewhere	*Yasumi ni doko ka e ikimasu ka?* Are you going somewhere for your vacation?
itsu ka sometime	*Itsu ka asobi ni kimasen ka?* Won't you come over to visit sometime?
dare ka someone	*Dare ka kono mado kara haitte kimashita.* Someone come in through this window.

• *kara* is used to indicate the means of entering a place: *Doa no shita kara iremashita;* "I put it in under the door."

These *ka* and *de mo* forms are often *not* followed by *wa, ga,* or *o.*

When talking about something indefinite, the *-ka* forms are placed before the indefinite noun.

> *Dare ka jôzu na hito wa imasen ka?*
> Isn't there some skilled person or other here?

> *Nani ka tsumetai mono ga nomitai desu nee.*
> I want to drink something cold.

> *Doko ka anzen na tokoro wa arimasen ka?*
> Isn't there some safe place?

Practice 14.1b

Vocabulary

atatakai	あたたかい	暖かい	pleasantly warm
tsumetai	つめたい	冷たい	cold to the touch
asobi ni iku/kuru	あそびに いく /くる	遊びに 行く /来る	go/come to a person's house for an informal social visit
shinsetsu (na)	しんせつ(な)	親切	kind, nice
fukuro	ふくろ	袋	bag, sack
mingeihin	みんげいひん	民芸品	folk craft objects
anzen (na)	あんぜん(な)	安全	safe

Fill in the blanks with either *nani ka, dare ka,* or *doko ka.*

1. _____ atatakai tokoro e ikitai desu.

2. _____ kirei na yôfuku o kaitai desu.

3. _____ shinsetsu na hito to kekkon shitai desu.

4. Hoteru no _____ ni tanonde kudasai.

5. _____ mingeihin o katte kaerimashô.

6. _____ koko no gakusei ni kiite kudasai.

THE PLAIN NEGATIVE FORM

Forming the negative of the dictionary forms of one-step verbs is simple. Just take the -*masu* stem and add -*nai*. This form is the plain equivalent of the -*masen* form.

> tabe-masen
> tabe-nai
>
> mi-nai
> mi-masen
>
> i-nai
> i-masen

The five-step verbs require a change of vowels. First, take the -*masu* stem, which ends in -*i*, and replace it with -*a*. Then add -*nai*. You need to watch out for a couple of tricky pronunciation changes involved with these forms, but fortunately, they are the same for all verbs with the same endings.

Dictionary Form	-*masu* Stem	Plain Negative	Meaning of Plain Negative
kaku	kakimasu	kakanai	not write
dasu	dashimasu	dasanai	not send out
matsu	machimasu	matanai	not wait
shinu	shinimasu	shinanai	not die
yomu	yomimasu	yomanai	not read
asobu	asobimasu	asobanai	not play around
wakaru	wakarimasu	wakaranai	not be clear
kau	kaimasu	kawanai	not buy
iu	iimasu	iwanai	not say
suu	suimasu	suwanai	not sip, smoke
omou	omoimasu	omowanai	not have an opinion

Note that the verbs with dictionary forms ending in -*su* or -*tsu* and -*masu* stems ending in -*shi* or -*chi* have plain negatives ending in -*sanai* and -*tanai*, not -*shanai*, -*tsanai*, or -*chanai*. In other words, you simply replace the -*u* or -*i* syllable with its corresponding -*a* syllable. Note also that the verbs whose dictionary forms end in -*au*, -*iu*, -*uu*, or -*ou* insert a -*w*- into their plain negatives.

There are three exceptions to the rules given above.

1. The plain negative of *aru* is just plain *nai*, not *aranai*.

> *O-kane ga arimasen.*
> *O-kane ga nai.*
> I don't have any money.

2. The plain negative of *suru* "do" is *shinai*.
3. The plain negative of *kuru* "come" is *konai*. (A common mistake is to give the plain negative of *kuru* as *kinai*, but that's the negative of *kiru* "wear.")

Practice 14.2a

Using the last chart as a model, give the plain negatives of the verbs whose dictionary forms are listed below.

1. yaku (bake, burn)

2. ugoku (move around)

3. kasu (lend)

4. sagasu (look for)

5. tatsu (stand)

6. nomu (drink)

7. erabu (choose)

8. yobu (summon)

9. naru (become)

10. noru (ride, board)

11. kaeru (5) (return)

12. uru (sell)

13. au (meet)

14. hirou (pick up)

15. nuguu (wipe)

16. miseru (1) (show)

17. akiru (1) (get tired of)

18. hashiru (5) (run)

So now that we have this plain negative form, what do we do with it? Well, there's always good old *deshô,* which you studied in Chapter 11, and a number of forms you haven't seen yet. Remember?

> *Iku deshô*
> probably will go

The way to say "probably will not go" is

> *Ikanai deshô*

Practice 14.2b

Vocabulary

Hirune o suru	ひるね をする	昼寝 をする	take a nap
katazukeru(1)	かたづける (1)	片付ける	tidy up, straighten up

Mr. Tanaka has been seriously ill, and the doctor has ordered complete rest and a restricted diet. In fact, his mother will be moving in for the time being to take care of him, screen his phone calls, and keep him company. The following is a list of activities. Tell whether he probably will or will not do them during his convalescence.

EXAMPLE:

tenisu o suru →
Tenisu wa shinai deshô

1. Mainichi, hirune o suru

2. Piza o taberu

3. Kaisha ni iku

4. Denwa ni deru

5. Rajio o kiku

6. Sake o nomu

7. Apaato o katazukeru

8. Oyogu

9. O-kaasan to issho ni terebi o miru

10. Hon o yomu

Now that you know about the negative of the dictionary form, you can also handle the negative counterparts of some forms that you already know from other contexts.

The first of these is the negative imperative (command/request) form. Simply add -*de* to the -*nai* form and follow it with *kudasai*.

> *Sore ni sawaranaide kudasai.*
> Don't touch that.
>
> *Enpitsu wa tsukawanaide kudasai.*
> Please don't use a pencil.

This form is completely regular, assuming that you know the negative of the dictionary form.

Practice 14.2c

Vocabulary

NOUN ni sawaru	NOUN に さわる	触る	touch NOUN
ANIMAL ni esa o yaru	ANIMAL に えさをやる	餌をやる	give feed to an animal
kenka suru	けんかする	喧嘩	have an argument
e	え	絵	painted or drawn picture
kamera	カメラ		camera
wasureru (1)	わすれる (1)	忘れる	forget
EVENT ni okureru (1)	EVENT に おくれる (1)	遅れる	be late to EVENT

You are showing some Japanese tourists around your state. How would you tell them not to do the following things?

1. not to touch the picture

2. not to feed the horse

3. not to argue

4. not to forget their cameras

5. not to be late to breakfast

6. not to ride in that taxi

GIVING

English essentially has only one verb meaning "give." Of course, we have some fancy equivalents, such as "grant," "bestow," and "donate," but all of them can be used in reference to any person. Not so with Japanese verbs of giving. Yes, **verbs.** The Japanese language has five verbs corresponding to the English word "give."

But before we get into that, here's the pattern for sentences about giving:

$$PERSON_1 \; wa \; (PERSON_2) \; ni \; OBJECT \; o \; GIVE$$

Note that PERSON$_2$, the recipient, can be omitted in some cases. The reason is that the verb itself may contain an indication of who the recipient is.

The first verb of giving is *ageru* (1), which refers to the speaker or someone else giving to some third person who is an approximate equal. The recipient is never I or we.

> *Yamaguchi-san wa Chan-san ni yukata o agemashita.*
> Ms. Yamaguchi gave Ms. Chan a *yukata*.

> *Tomodachi ni tii-shatsu o agemashita.*
> I gave my friend a T-shirt.

The second verb is *sashiageru,* which is like *ageru,* except that the recipient ranks higher than the giver. Thus, it is used for talking about giving things to teachers, supervisors, and other people who deserve extra politeness under the Japanese social system.

>*Sensei ni kaigai ryokô no o-miyage o sashiagemashita.*
>I gave the teacher a souvenir of my trip overseas.

>*O-seibo ni shachô ni o-cha o sashiagemashita.*
>I gave the company president some green tea as a year-end present.

• When Japanese people travel, they bring back souvenirs for just about everyone they deal with from day to day.

• *O-seibo* is the year-end gift. The Japanese give gifts to all the people to whom they feel some sort of obligation. The corresponding summer gift is called *o-chûgen*.

The third verb is *yaru,* which is like *ageru* and *sashiageru,* except that it is used for talking about giving things to lower-ranking people or to animals and plants. Traditionally, people used it in reference to younger family members or to their subordinates at work, but some younger people think it sounds rude to equate a person with an animal or plant, so they use *ageru* in reference to younger family members or subordinates.

>*Hana ni mizu o yarimashô.*
>Let's give the flowers some water.

>*Maiasa, neko ni esa o yarimasu.*
>I feed the cat every morning.

The fourth verb is *kureru* (1), which refers to someone else giving something to the speaker or a member of the speaker's group. As such, it often means "give to me" or "give to us." Because *kureru* includes this meaning, it is often not necessary to add "me" or "us" to the sentence.

>*Chichi to haha wa suteki na sutereo o kuremashita.*
>My father and mother gave me a great stereo.

>*Teramura-san wa kirei na sensu o kuremashita.*
>Ms. Teramura gave me a pretty folding fan.

The final verb of giving is *kudasaru.* Like *kureru,* it means "give to me" or "give to us," but the giver always ranks above the recipient and is not a family member. If this verb sounds vaguely familiar, it is because it is the source of *kudasai.*

>*Nihongo no sensei wa watashitachi ryûgakusei ni chiisai jisho o kudasaimashita.*
>The Japanese-language instructor gave us international students little dictionaries.

As you can see from the example, *kudasaru* is partly irregular. The negative of the dictionary form is *kudasaranai*, which is regular, and the *-te* form is *kudasatte*, which is also regular, but the *-masu* form is *kudasaimasu*.

Practice 14.3

Vocabulary

kaigai ryokô	かいがい りょこう	海外旅行	overseas travel
o-seibo	おせいぼ	お歳暮	year-end gift
hana	はな	花	flower
suteki (na)	すてき (な)		great, fantastic
sensu	せんす	扇子	folding fan
ryûgakusei	りゅうがくせい	留学生	student studying abroad
shachô	しゃちょう	社長	company president
iyaringu	イヤリング		earring
sôri daijin	そうり だいじん	総理大臣	prime minister

And here are the forms for the counter *-hon,* which is used to count long, narrow objects such as pens, pencils, bottles, chopsticks, ropes, and casette tapes (think of what they look like if you unwind them).

ippon	いっぽん	一本	one long narrow object
nihon	にほん	二本	two long, narrow objects
sanbon	さんぽん	三本	three long, narrow objects
yonhon	よんほん	四本	four long, narrow objects
gohon	ごほん	五本	five long, narrow objects
roppon	ろっぽん	六本	six long, narrow objects
nanahon	ななほん	七本	seven long, narrow objects
happon	はっぽん	八本	eight long, narrow objects
kyûhon	きゅうほん	九本	nine long, narrow objects
juppon	じゅっぽん	十本	ten long, narrow objects

Fill in the blanks with the past tense of the most appropriate verb of giving: *ageru, sashiageru, yaru, kureru,* **or** *kudasaru.*

EXAMPLE:

Neko ni sakana o yarimashita.
I gave the cat some fish.

1. Ishida-san wa Tanaka-san ni chokoreeto o _____.

2. Watashi wa ane ni seetaa o _____.

3. Ane wa (watashi ni) iyaringu o _____.

4. Takahashi sensei wa sôri daijin ni hon o _____.

5. Inu ni mizu o _____.

6. Sensei wa (watashi ni) Nihon no chizu o _____.

7. Ani wa (watashi ni) pen o sanbon _____.

8. Mei to oi ni nooto o issatsu zutsu_____.

GOING SOMEWHERE FOR A PURPOSE

When you talk about going somewhere in order to do something, the pattern is

PLACE *e* (NOUN) *o -masu* STEM *ni* MOTION VERB

Depaato e yôfuku o kai ni ikimashita.
I went to the department store in order to buy clothes.

Kono resutoran e Chûgoku ryôri o tabe ni kimashita.
I came to this restaurant in order to eat Chinese food.

If the verb in question is a compound with *suru* (such as *benkyô suru* or *renshû suru*), then you have two possibilities:

Nihongo o benkyô shi ni kimashita.
or
Nihongo no benkyô ni kimashita.
I came in order to study Japanese.

Practice 14.4

Vocabulary

kenbutsu suru	けんぶつ する	見物 する	do sight seeing
hakubutsukan	はくぶつかん	博物館	museum (scientifc or historical)
tenrankai	てんらんかい	展覧会	exhibition
boroichi	ぼろいち	ぼろ市	flea market
odoru	おどる	踊る	dance
uta o utau	うた を うたう	歌を歌う	sing a song
zasshi	ざっし	雑誌	magazine

Make up sentences about what people came or went or returned to do, using the cues listed below.

EXAMPLE:

Amerika/kenbutsu suru/kuru →
Amerika e kenbutsu ni kimashita
or
Amerika e kenbutsu shi ni kimashita.

1. Hakubutsukan/ tenrankai o miru/ iku

2. Boroichi/furui hon o uru/iku

3. Puuru/oyogu/kuru

4. Kurabu/odoru/kuru

5. Kankoku/eigo o oshieru/iku

6. Karaoke kurabu/uta o utau/iku

7. Hawai/shôsetsu o kaku/kaeru

8. Toshokan/atarashii zasshi o yomu/kuru

SUMMING UP
MATOME
まとめ

Each of the following sentences contains one error of grammar or usage. Rewrite the sentences in their correct forms.

EXAMPLE:

Pen ni kakitai desu. →
Pen de kakitai desu.
"I want to write with a pen."

1. Dare mo wakarimasu.

2. Eigakan e eiga o miru ni ikimasen ka?

3. Neko ni sakana o sashiagemashita.

4. Ame ga futte imasu kara, dare mo ikunai deshô.

5. Otôto wa watashi ni suteki na shatsu o kudasaimashita.

6. Ishida-san wa Tanaka-san o chokoreeto ni agemashita.

7. Asoko de wa nani ka tsukurimasen.

8. Dare ka oishii resutoran wa arimasen ka?

9. Dare mo shitte imasen.

10. Takahashi sensei wa watashitachi ryûgakusei ni kirei na sensu o agemashita.

11. Abunai desu kara, tsukaimasen kudasai.

12. Abuduuru-san wa hamu o tabanai deshô.

Traditional Sagi Dance

CHAPTER 15

DÔ IU IMI DESU KA? (WHAT DOES IT MEAN?)

In this chapter you will learn:

1. the past tense of the dictionary form
2. how to talk about what you can and cannot do
3. another set of *ko-so-a-do* words
4. the *no da* construction

THE PAST TENSE OF THE DICTIONARY FORM

Here is another reason to be glad that you studied Chapter 10 so thoroughly: the past tense of the dictionary form (the plain past) is completely predictable and derivable from the *-te* form.

All you have to do is take the *-te* form, whatever it is, and change the *-te* or *-de* ending to *-ta* or *-da*.

Dictionary Form	-te Form	Plain Past	Meaning of Plain Past
kaku	kaite	kaita	wrote
oyogu	oyoide	oyoida	swam
dasu	dashite	dashita	sent out
matsu	matte	matta	waited
shinu	shinde	shinda	died
yomu	yonde	yonda	read
asobu	asonde	asonda	played around
wakaru	wakatte	wakatta	was clear, understood
kau	katte	katta	bought
iu	itte	itta	said
suu	sutte	sutta	sipped, smoked
omou	omotte	omotta	thought
taberu	tabete	tabeta	ate
miru	mite	mita	saw
kuru	kite	kita	came
suru	shite	shita	did
iku	itte	itta	went

There is one exception to all this beautiful symmetry. The *-te* form of the copula *da/desu* is the irregular *de,* and its past tense is *datta.*

> *Kinô, Nikkô e itte kita yo.*
> *Kirei datta deshô?*
> Yesterday I took a short trip to Nikkô.
> It was pretty, wasn't it?

The negative plain past is just as easy and regular as the positive. All you do is take the plain present negative, the one with the *-nai* ending, and change the *-nai* to *-nakatta.*

Dictionary Form	Plain Negative	Plain Past Negative	Meaning of Plain Past Negative
kaku	kakanai	kakanakatta	didn't write
kau	kawanai	kawanakatta	didn't buy
taberu	tabenai	tabenakatta	didn't eat
miru	minai	minakatta	didn't see
kuru	konai	konakatta	didn't come
suru	shinai	shinakatta	didn't do
iku	ikanai	ikanakatta	didn't go

Following this same pattern, the past tense of *ja nai* is *ja nakatta.*

So now that you have all the past and present tenses of the dictionary form in both positive and negative, what can you do with them? Of course, you can use them with *deshô:*

> *Ikanatta deshô.*
> Probably didn't go.

> *Wakatta deshô.*
> Probably understood.

These dictionary forms mean the same as the *-masu/ -mashita* forms, and people use them when speaking to close friends and family and sometimes to people who rank below them. For example, a boss may address the lower-ranking staff in the dictionary form, but the lower-ranking workers have to use the *-masu* form when addressing their boss. Young people talking among themselves usually use the dictionary form, especially if they know one another well.

Vocabulary

de mo	でも	even so, still
naa	なあ	very informal, mostly masculine equivalent of *ne*
un (pronounced almost like a grunt)	うん	very informal way to say "yes," more like "yeah"
betsu ni	べつに	not particularly
wa	わ	a sentence particle added mostly to women's speech, mildly emphatic

Examples:

Teramura Chieko has just given Ikeda Masaru directions to a dance club he's heard about.

Teramura: Wakatta?
Ikeda: Un, wakatta yo. De mo, chotto tooi naa!
Teramura: Iie, betsu ni. Chikatetsu de sanjuppun da wa.

Teramura: Did you understand?
Ikeda: Yeah, I did. Even so, it's a bit far, isn't it?
Teramura: Not particularly. It's thirty minutes by subway.

This style of speech may sound more casual and friendly than the *-masu* style, but you need to use it carefully. If you go to Japan as a student and live with a family, you will most likely speak this way with your host family and your classmates, but you will be expected to speak in *-masu/desu* style with your instructors. In a business context, it is considered rude, not friendly, to address the higher-ups in your own company or the employees of another company in the dictionary form. The whole matter of speaking in the dictionary form is rather complicated and beyond the scope of this book, but if you go to live in Japan, you will soon pick up this style. At this point it is more important for you to be able to recognize and respond appropriately to both dictionary forms and honorific speech than to use them yourself.

The dictionary form is also used in impersonal contexts such as the narrative portions of books (that is, the descriptions rather than the dialogues) and in magazine and newspaper articles and scientific papers, as well as in people's diaries.

Finally, further ahead in this chapter, you will learn two more uses for the dictionary form.

Practice 15.1

Vocabulary

osoi	おそい	遅い	late, slow
tabenaide	たべないで	食べないで	without eating
koshô suru	こしょう する	故障 する	have a mechanical breakdown
EVENT ni ma ni au	EVENT に まにあう	間に合う	be on time for EVENT
aikawarazu	あいかわらず		as usual
PERSON ni au	PERSON にあう	会う	meet or see PERSON
ryô	りょう	療	dormitory

As Chan Ngan-fa gets to know the Yamaguchis better, they urge her to speak to them in the plain style. She tries, but sometimes she forgets. Here are some things she said recently to the Yamaguchis. What should she have said in plain form?

EXAMPLE:

Kinô eiga o mimashita. →
Kinô eiga o mita.

1. Abuduuru-san to issho ni Shinjuku e ikimashita.

2. Densha ga koshô shite, osoku narimashita.

3. Kaigi ni ma ni aimasen deshita.

4. Kesa, asagohan o tabenaide koko e kimashita.

5. Honkon no tomodachi ni aimashita.

6. Kyô, kazoku ni tegami o kakimashita.

7. Omoshiroi hon o yomimashita.

8. Ryô no heya o katazukemashita kedo, sentaku wa shimasen deshita.

• The *-naide* ending, which you have already seen in the negative command construction, means "without doing" when it is used by itself, as in *Nani mo iwanaide kaetta.* "Went home without saying anything."

CAN AND CANNOT

There are two ways to say that you can (in the sense of being able, not in the sense of having permission) do a certain action.

1. The first, which is the one most commonly taught to first-year students, because it is supposedly easier, is the construction:

DICTIONARY FORM OF THE VERB + *koto ga dekiru*

Kanji o yomu koto ga dekimasu.
I can read kanji.

Hashi o tsukau koto ga dekiru.
I can use chopsticks.

The negative of this construction is:

DICTIONARY FORM OF THE VERB + *koto ga dekinai*

Oyogu koto ga dekimasen.
I can't swim.

Piano o hiku koto ga dekimasen.
I can't play the piano.

Dekiru all by itself is considered the "can do" form of *suru,* so suru is omitted in these constructions:

Koko de wa benkyô dekimasen.
I can't study here.

As you will remember, the so-called direct object of *dekiru* needs to be marked with *ga,* but in this construction, *koto* is the direct object, so the rest of the sentence (for example, the part about playing the piano) retains its normal particle marking.

Practice 15.2a

Tell your Japanese acquaintance that you can or cannot do the following things:

EXAMPLE:

Can sing songs
Uta o utau koto ga dekimasu.

1. can make a sandwich

2. can't write a novel

3. can go on Saturday

4. can't practice tomorrow

5. can read a Japanese newspaper

6. can't play the guitar

7. can be on time to the meeting

8. can't teach English

2. The second way to talk about abilities is rarely introduced before the second year of study, but it is more commonly used in real life than the *koto ga dekiru* construction and not significantly more difficult. If you go to Japan after only one year of study, you will be glad that you took the time to learn a bit about this construction, even if you may not have to know it in class this year.

    To create this form on a one-step verb, take off the *-ru* and replace it with *-rareru:*

Dictionary Form	Potential ("can do") Form
taberu eat	*taberareru* can eat
okiru get up	*okirareru* can get up

To create this form on a five-step verb, take the *-u* of the dictionary form and replace it with *-eru.*

Dictionary Form	Potential Form
kaku write	*kakeru* can write
oyogu swim	*oyogeru* can swim
dasu send out	*daseru* can send out
matsu wait	*materu* can wait
yomu read	*yomeru* can read
asobu play	*asoberu* can play
wataru cross	*watareru* can cross
kau buy	*kaeru* can buy
iu say	*ieru* can say
kuru come	*korareru* can come
suru do	*dekiru* can do
iku go	*ikeru* can go

• You may meet Japanese people, especially young people, who form the potentials of both one-step and five-step verbs in the same way, so that they say *mireru* instead of *mirareru* and *okireru* instead of *okirareru*. However, not everyone approves of these simplified forms.

You may have noticed that the *-aru* slot was filled by *wakaru* "be clear, understand" in the previous charts in this chapter, while it is filled by *wataru* "cross" here. The reason is that *wakaru* and the other verbs that require *ga* as the object particle do not have potential forms. Instead, you have to use roundabout ways to express the notion of being able. For example, another, fancier way to say "understand" is *rikai suru*, so people say *rikai dekiru* for "can understand."

Whatever their source, these potential forms have two things in common:

1. Whether they started out as one-step, five-step, or irregular verbs, all potential forms are one-step verbs.

    Compare *oyogu, oyogimasu, oyoide, oyoganai* the forms of "swim," which is a five-step verb, with *oyogeru, oyogemasu, oyogete, oyogenai*, "can swim," which is a one-step verb.

2. All of them mark their direct objects with *ga*, although you may hear some people, especially younger people, mark the direct objects with *o*. *Sushi ga tsukureru* "I can make sushi."

Practice 15.2b

Take the statements in Practice 15.2a and write them in the potential form.

EXAMPLE:

Can sing songs
Uta ga utaemasu.

1.

2.

3.

4.

5.

6.

7.

8.

SOME MORE *KO-SO-A-DO* WORDS

You have already met a few members of the so-called *ko-so-a-do* series of words: *kore, sore, are, dore; kono, sono, ano, dono;* and *koko, soko, asoko, doko.* There are still more.

One set is *kochira, sochira, achira, dochira,* or *kotchi, sotchi, atchi, dotchi,* as they are known more informally. You have already seen *dochira* in the construction *Dochira no hô ga ii desu ka?* "Which of the two is better?" The other members of its series mean "this way /side," "that way/side," "that way/side over there" and "which way/side." *Dochira* is often used as a formal, polite equivalent of *doko,* so that instead of asking *Shin Yamato Hoteru wa doko desu ka?* a person might ask *Shin Yamato Hoteru wa dochira deshô ka?* (Replacing *desu* with *deshô* also makes the question more polite. Instead of asking "Where's the hotel?" you're asking "Which way might the hotel be?")

1. *Kochira* is used when introducing people. Introducing someone by saying something like *Kore wa Ishida-san desu* is considered insulting to the person being introduced, so you should always replace *kore* with *kochira* in such cases. To show respect to the person who is being introduced to Ms. Ishida, replace the *desu* with *de gozaimasu*.

   Here is how Ms. Shimizu might introduce Ms. Ishida to her *shamisen* teacher as a prospective student:

   > *Sensei, kochira wa Ishida-san de gozaimasu.*
   > Teacher, this is Ms. Ishida.

   Another common use of *kochira* is in giving instructions telling people which way to go: *Dôzo, kochira e* ("Right this way please.").

2. Another series is *konna, sonna, anna, donna,* "this kind of . . .," "that kind of. . ., " "that kind of . . . over there," and "what kind of. . ."

   > *Donna hito desu ka?*
   > What kind of a person is s/he?

   > *Sonna baka na koto wa dekinai yo.*
   > I can't do a stupid thing like that.

   > *Konna sutereo wa dame desu yo.*
   > This kind of stereo is no good.

3. Still another series, *kô iu, sô iu, aa iu,* and *dô iu,* means nearly the same thing as the *konna, sonna, anna, donna* series.

   > *Dô iu hito desu ka?*
   > What kind of a person is s/he?

   > *Sô iu baka na koto wa dekinai yo.*
   > I can't do a stupid thing like that.

   > *Kô iu sutereo wa dame desu yo.*
   > This kind of stereo is no good.

The main difference between the two series is that they are used in different idioms. For example, the phrase "What does it mean?" is *Dô iu imi desu ka?*, not *Donna imi desu ka?* On the other hand, when reacting with disbelief or dismay to what someone has just said, people exclaim, *Sonna!* or *Sonna koto!* not *Sô iu!* or *Sô iu koto!*

As with all idioms, you just have to learn them as you encounter them, but before nouns, you can usually use either the *konna* series or the *kô iu* series.

Vocabulary

baka (na)	ばか (な)		stupid, crazy
koto	こと		abstract thing or concept, (cf. *mono,* concrete thing or object.)
dame (na)	だめ (な)		no good, worthless, not permitted
poketto	ポケット		pocket
handobaggu	ハンドバッグ		handbag, purse
kossori	こっそり		in secret, sneakily
shitsumon	しつもん	質問	question; *shitsumon o suru* ask a question
kotae	こたえ	答え	an answer to a question
imi	いみ	意味	meaning
ukeru	うける	受ける	undergo, take, be on the receiving end of
o-furo	おふろ		Japanese-style bath

Example:

Zaini Abdul is puzzled by a term she heard on television, so she asks Teramura Chieko about it.

Abuduuru: "Suri" wa dô iu imi?
Teramura: Hito no poketto ya handobaggu kara kossori o-kane o toru to iu imi da wa.
Abuduuru: A, sô? Wakatta.

Abdul: What does *suri* mean?
Teramura: It means sneakily taking money out of people's pockets and handbags.
Abdul: Really? Oh, I see.

• In order to develop your vocabulary, you should ask Japanese people to explain unfamiliar words in Japanese, if possible, instead of just giving you the English equivalent. (There may be no exact English equivalent, for one thing.) Zaini Abdul could have responded to Teramura Chieko's explanation with *Pickpocket desu ka?* but that wouldn't work with someone who didn't speak English well.

• Teramura Chieko and Zaini Abdul have also started speaking to each other in the dictionary form.

Practice 15.3

Pretend that you are asking a Japanese acquaintance what the following words mean. First, frame the question, following the pattern that Zaini Abdul used. Then read the Japanese person's answer and see if you can figure out what the word means.

EXAMPLE:

Tokkyû
Shitsumon: <u>"Tokkyû" wa dô iu imi desu ka?</u>
Kotae: "Totemo hayai densha" to iu imi desu.
Imi: <u>"very fast train"</u>

1. juken
   Shitsumon:_____
   Kotae: "Shiken o ukeru" to iu imi desu.
   Imi: _____

2. taikutsu
   Shitsumon:_____
   Kotae: "Tsumaranai, omoshiroku nai" to iu imi desu.
   Imi: _____

3. kyûkei
   Shitsumon:_____
   Kotae: "Mijikai yasumi" to iu imi desu.
   Imi:_____

4. nyûyoku
   Shitsumon: _____
   Kotae: "O-furo ni hairu" to iu imi desu.
   Imi:_____

5. Same
   Shitsumon:_____
   Kotae: Ookii, kowai sakana desu. Tokidoki hito o tabemasu.
   Imi:_____

THE *NO DA* CONSTRUCTION

Here is another very important construction that few first-year textbooks teach, although in real life, Japanese people can barely get through a minute of conversation without using it. It is difficult to use correctly, but it is so common that you will need to understand it, even if you go to Japan after only one year of Japanese. In fact, many of the dialogues in the previous lessons would have been more natural if it had been possible to use this form.

Japanese grammarians call this construction *no da no bun,* and using it indicates that the sentence is somehow background information or an explanation for the situation at hand. For example, if your acquaintance found you crawling around on the floor, he or she might ask, "What are you doing?" In English, you would answer something like, "I dropped my contact lens." In Japanese, this would require a *no da no bun,* because "I dropped my contact lens" is the explanation for why you are crawling around on the floor.

Similarly, the explanation leading up to a question or request is stated in *no da no bun,* the idea being "This is how things are, and this is what I need or want to know." No one English equivalent will cover all the shades of meaning.

The form of the *no da no bun* is:

> DICTIONARY FORM OF THE VERB + *no da/no desu*
>
>   or   *n da/n desu*
>
>   or   *no*

O-kane ga takusan aru n desu.
O-kane ga takusan aru n da.
O-kane ga takusan aru no.
The fact is, I have a lot of money.

• Using *n da* or *no da* at the end of a sentence when speaking in the dictionary form is considered masculine. The more feminine speech style just uses *no.* (These sorts of distinctions are less rigidly observed than they used to be.)

> *KU*-ADJECTIVE + *n(o) desu/n(o) da*
>
>   or   +*no*

Ano resutoran no ryôri ga oishii n desu.
Ano resutoran no ryôri ga oishii n da.
Ano resutoran no ryôri ga oishii no.
It's that the cuisine at that restaurant is delicious.

NOUN or *NA*-ADJECTIVE + *na* + *n(o) desu/n(o) da*
            or   + *no*

Amerika-jin na n desu.
Amerika-jin na no da.
Amerika-jin na no.
It's that s/he's an American.

Dame na n desu.
Dame na n da.
Dame na no.
It's no good, you see.

The *n desu* version is more common in conversation than *no desu*. Thus the sentence about the contact lens would be

Kontakuto renzu o otoshita n desu.
I dropped a contact lens.

The answer to why you want to go to Japan on a certain airline could be:

Kippu ga yasui n desu.
It's that the tickets are cheap.

"Why" questions are often asked in the *no da no bun* construction, so that a question about why a certain person who looks Japanese can't read a warning sign could be

Dôshite yomenai n desu ka?
Why can't he read it?

and the answer could be

Burajiru kara no Nikkeijin na n desu.
He's a person of Japanese ancestry from Brazil.

Vocabulary

otosu	おとす	落とす	drop
kontakuto renzu	コンタクトレンズ		contact lens
dôshite	どうして		why
Nikkeijin	にっけいじん	日系人	a person of Japanese ancestry, such as a Japanese-American
kusuri-ya	くすりや	薬屋	pharmacist
Burajiru	ブラジル		Brazil
kaoiro	かおいろ	顔色	facial color
Dô nasatta n desu ka?	どうなさったんですか		What's going on? What happened? (polite form of *Dô shita n desu ka?*)
hidoi	ひどい		severe
zutsû ga suru	ずつうがする	頭痛がする	have a headache
dandan	だんだん		gradually
atama ga itai	あたまがいたい	頭が痛い	head hurts
o-naka	おなか		the stomach, abdomen
guai	ぐあい	具合	state, condition
mukamuka suru	むかむかする		feel queasy
geri suru	げりする	下痢	have diarrhea
ase bisshori	あせびっしょり	汗びっしょり	drenched in sweat
Dô shimashô?	どうしましょう?		What should I/we do about it?
atsusa ni mairu	あつさにまいる	暑さにまいる	to be overcome by heat

Example:

Eric Jones has been tramping around Kyôto sightseeing on a hot, muggy, August day. Suddenly during the afternoon he develops a severe headache and nausea. He goes into a pharmacy to buy some aspirin. The pharmacist greets him.

Kusuri-ya:	Irasshaimase.
Joonzu:	Asupirin o kaitai n desu ga. . .
Kusuri-ya:	Ho, kaoiro ga yoku nai desu ne. Dô nasatta n desu ka?
Joonzu:	Hidoi zutsû ga shite iru n desu.
Kusuri-ya:	Sô desu ka? Itsu kara desu ka?
Joonzu:	Sanjuppun gurai mae kara, dandan atama ga itaku natte kita n desu.
Kusuri-ya:	O-naka no guai wa dô desu ka?
Joonzu:	Mukamuka shite imasu.
Kusuri-ya:	Geri shite imasu ka?
Joonzu:	Iie.
Kusuri-ya:	De mo, ase bisshori desu ne. Atsusa ni maitta n deshô.
Joonzu:	Sô desu ka? Dô shimashô ka?

Pharmacist:	Welcome.
Jones:	I want to buy some aspirin, but. . .
Pharmacist:	Oh, your facial color isn't good, is it? What's wrong?
Jones:	I have a terrible headache.
Pharmacist:	Really? Since when?
Jones:	My head gradually began hurting more and more about thirty minutes ago.
Pharmacist:	How's your stomach?
Jones:	It's queasy.
Pharmacist:	Do you have diarrhea?
Jones:	No.
Pharmacist:	Still, you're all drenched in sweat. Well, you've probably been overcome by the heat.
Jones:	Really? What should I do?

• The Japanese often consult pharmacists instead of physicians for minor medical problems.

Practice 15.4

Several situations are described below. Each one requires a speaker to ask a question or give background information in *no da no bun*. The quotations that need to be in *no da no bun* are indented. How would you say them? Don't worry about how to say the other parts of the situations or dialogues, and just give your answers in *-masu/desu* style.

EXAMPLE:

Mr. Green is telling his Japanese employees about the horrible traffic jam he encountered on his way to the office. He asks Ms. Kuroda if she ran into the same kind of traffic. Ms. Kuroda says:
> "No, I came by subway."

Answer: *Iie, watashi wa chikatetsu de kita n desu.*

1. Most people, Japanese and non-Japanese alike, find it easy to get lost in Tôkyô, but Thomas Wilson always seems to know his way around. When asked why, he says:
   (a) "I have a very good map."
   One of his acquaintances asks where he got it, and he explains:
   (b) "Professor Takahashi gave it to me."

2. Most of the international students carry ordinary dictionaries around to their classes, but Amanda Smith has *denshi bukku* (electronic book) editions of several dictionaries that she can read with a device that's the size of a palmtop computer. One of her fellow students admires it and asks:
   (a) "Where did you buy it?"
   After Amanda Smith explains that these are for sale all over Akihabara, the electronics district of Tôkyô, her fellow student asks why she bought it. She replies:
   (b) "It's very convenient."

3. Chan Ngan-fa has asked to leave in the middle of class, and when the instructor asks why, she answers,
   "My stomach hurts."

SUMMING UP
MATOME
まとめ

A. Diaries are customarily written in the dictionary form. Here is an entry from the diary that Amanda Smith is keeping to hand into her Japanese composition teacher at the end of the week. However, she forgot to write this entry in the dictionary form. Correct it for her.

EXAMPLE:

Kyô wa ii tenki deshita. →
Kyô wa ii tenki datta.
It was nice weather today.
Hakubutsukan e atarashii tenrankai o mi ni ikimashita.
Hakubutsukan no shokudô de hirugohan o tabemashita. O-
miyage mo takusan kaimashita. Sore kara, chikatetsu de ryô e
kaerimashita. Chan-san to Abuduuru-san to issho ni bangohan
o tabete kara, shukudai o shimashita. Sore kara, ongaku o
kikimashita. Jûichiji ni nemashita.

B. Ikeda Masaru is asking you about your tastes in music.

Ikeda: Gitaa, hikeru?
You: (You can't play the guitar, but you can play the piano.)
Ikeda: Itsu ka kikitai naa.
You: (Ask him what kind of music he likes.)
Ikeda: Nan de mo suki da yo. Kimi (you) wa? Hôgaku, o-suki?
You: (Ask what *hôgaku* means.)
Ikeda: Nihon no furui ongaku to iu imi da yo.

• Ikeda Masaru is speaking in plain form. *Kimi* is an equivalent
of "you" used by males talking to close friends and subordinates.

C. The drawings on page 238 illustrate situations. Write an explanation of what is happening or what has happened in each one, using *no da no bun.*

Vocabulary

korobu	ころぶ	転ぶ	trip and fall
saifu	さいふ	財布	wallet
nebô suru	ねぼうする	寝坊する	oversleep

1.

2.

3.

4.

5.

6.

1. Give the following directions to a meeting at the Japan YWCA:

    (a) You go to Ichigaya by train.
    (b) Leaving the station, you cross the street.
    (c) Go straight ahead 50 meters.
    (d) Turn right at the corner where the bank is.
    (e) Turn left at the next corner. The YWCA is on the left side.

2. You are in a Japanese culture class giving a report on a very detailed old screen painted with scenes of life in the eighteenth century. You point out the various figures depicted on the screen and describe them. These people are watching *kabuki* (a type of traditional theater), this woman is probably a *geisha*, this man is probably selling fish, this man is making *geta*, this woman is playing the *shamisen*.

3. You are talking with a Japanese acquaintance about your plans for your year in Japan.

Nihonjin:	Kotoshi, nani o shitai desu ka?
You:	(You want to learn calligraphy and karate.)
Nihonjin:	Doko ka ryokô shitai desu ka?
You:	(You'd like to go to Kyûshû.)

4. Your Japanese acquaintance has been visiting you, and as he is about to leave, it suddenly starts raining heavily.

You:	(Offer him this umbrella.)
Nihonjin:	De mo, hontô ni ii desu ka?
You:	(It is. You don't need it, so it's all right for him to use it.)

5. Here's an excerpt from the diary that Thomas Wilson wrote for his Japanese composition class. It concerns a shopping expedition to Akihabara, Tokyo's electronics district. Complete each of the sentences according to the clues given.

EXAMPLE:

Kinô wa (it was raining).→
Kinô wa ame ga futte ita.

Akihabara e (went to buy a computer)_____. Amerika no konpyuuta mo Nihon no konpyuuta mo takusan atta. Amerika no konpyuuta wa (were more expensive than the Japanese computers)_____ kedo, boku wa Amerika no konpyuuta o (bought)_____. Amerika e kaette kara (it's that I want to use it)_____. Kono konpyuuta no Nihongo no opereetingu shisutemu de Nihongo mo eigo mo (can write)_____.

CHAPTER 16

YOYAKU SHITE YOKATTA! (IT'S A GOOD THING WE MADE RESERVATIONS!)

In this chapter you will learn:

1. about verbs of receiving
2. the *-te* forms of negatives and adjectives
3. how to say that you have had a certain experience
4. how to compare more than two things

VERBS OF RECEIVING

You already learned about the verbs of giving in Chapter 14, and you will be happy to find out that there are only two verbs of receiving. The first one, used to talk about receiving from someone who is equal to you or ranks below you, is *morau*. The person from whom the gift or favor is received is marked with either *kara* or *ni*.

> *Ryôshin kara atarashii jitensha o moraimashita.*
> *Ryôshin ni atarashii jitensha o moraimashita.*
> I received a new bicycle from my parents.

The verb for receiving from a superior is *itadaku*.

> *Sensei ni Nihon no jinja ni tsuite no hon o itadakimashita.*
> I received a book about Japan's shrines from the instructor.

A verb in the *-te* form followed by a verb of receiving indicates having someone do something for you.

> *Tomodachi ni shashin o totte moraimashita.*
> I had my friend take pictures.

Sensei ni shukudai no mondai o setsumei shite itadakimashita.
We had the instructor explain the homework problems.

Similarly, a verb in the *-te* form followed by a verb of giving indicates doing something for another person.

Tomodachi wa shashin o totte kuremashita.
My friend took pictures for me.

Sensei ga shukudai no mondai o setsumei shite kudasaimashita.
The instructor explained the homework problems to us.

Note that because of the verbs of giving and receiving, you don't need a direct equivalent for "to us" or "for me."

Practice 16.1

Vocabulary

kasetto teepu	カセット・テープ		cassette tape
-tachi	-たち	-達	(plural suffix for nouns referring to people)
suisenjô	すいせんじょう	推薦状	[letter of] recommendation

Look over the following situations and state each one twice, once as a receiving situation and once as a giving situation.

EXAMPLE:

GIVER: older brother
RECIPIENT: older sister
GIFT: book
Ani wa ane ni hon o agemashita.
Ane wa ani kara hon o moraimashita.

1. GIVER: friend
   RECIPIENT: I
   GIFT: cassette tape

2. GIVER: students
   RECIPIENT: professor
   GIFT: flowers

3. GIVER: Tanaka-san
   RECIPIENT: Suzuki-san
   GIFT: earrings

4. GIVER: professor
   RECIPIENT: I
   GIFT: writing a recommendation

5. GIVER: Mrs. Yamaguchi
   RECIPIENT: Ms. Chan
   GIFT: teaching a Japanese song

THE *-TE* FORMS OF NEGATIVES AND ADJECTIVES

The adjectives and the negative forms have their own *-te* forms; these can be used in many of the same ways as the *-te* forms of the positive verbs.

All of these forms are completely regular. For the *-te* form of a negative verb, simply take the *-nai* ending and change the *-nai* to *-nakute:*

> *ikanai* → *ikanakute* "not going"
> *minai* → *minakute* "not seeing"
> *ja nai* → *ja nakute* "not being"

The *ku-* adjectives are very similar. Just replace the *-i* ending with *-kute:*

> *takai* → *takakute* "being expensive"
> *omoshiroi* → *omoshirokute* "being interesting"

Note that the *-te* form of *ii* is *yokute.*

Since all the *na-* adjectives pattern like nouns, their *-te* forms are made up of the base of the adjective plus *de:*

> *kirei da* → *kirei de* "being pretty"
> *kirei ja nai* → *kirei ja nakute* "not being pretty"

Just as the *-te* form is used when you have two verbs referring to the same subject,

> *Rokuji ni okite, o-furo ni hairimashita.*
> I got up at six o'clock and took a bath.

the *-te* form of the adjective is used when you have two adjectives in a row referring to the same noun.

atarashikute omoshiroi eiga
a new and interesting movie

kantan de benri na hôhô
a simple and convenient method

The combination ADJECTIVE-*te* + *ii* means "nice and . . ."

suzushikute ii heya
a nice, cool room

shizuka de ii uchi
It's a nice and quiet house.

Practice 16.2

Vocabulary

suzushii	すずしい	涼しい	pleasantly cool
amai	あまい	甘い	sweet
shizuka (na)	しずか (な)	静か (な)	quiet
kawaii	かわいい		cute
raku (na)	らく (な)	楽 (な)	comfortable
seikatsu	せいかつ	生活	way of life
kuwashii	くわしい	詳しい	detailed

How would you say it?

1. a nice and warm room

2. a cheap, simple computer

3. an old and famous temple

4. a small, cute child

5. a large, scary dog

6. sweet and delicious oranges

7. a nice and comfortable way of life

8. a complicated and difficult problem

9. a nice and detailed map

10. a long, boring movie

Just as the *-te* form is used in asking or giving permission to do something, the *-te* form of the negative is used to express the idea that it's all right not to do something.

> *Minakute mo ii desu.*
> It's all right not to see it.

The *-te* form of the adjective and NOUN + *de* are used to indicate that the condition described by the adjective or the noun indicated is satisfactory.

> *Takakute mo ii desu.*
> It's all right if it's expensive.
>
> *Fukuzatsu de mo ii desu.*
> It's all right if it's complicated.

Any of these *-te* forms can indicate that the verb or adjective in the *-te* form is the reason for what follows it. For example, if you passed an extremely difficult test, you would obviously be happy about this, and you could say:

> *Shiken ni gôkaku shite yokatta.*
> I'm delighted that I passed the test.

Other examples include:

> *Konna baka na koto o shite hazukashii desu.*
> I'm embarrassed that I did such a stupid thing.
>
> *Atama ga itakute tamarimasen.*
> My head hurts so much that I can't stand it.

By the way, these emotional adjectives such as *ureshii* and *hazukashii* cannot be used when you are talking about the emotions of a third person, the idea being that you can't really know how another person feels.

A *-te* form followed by *yokatta* means "It's a good thing that. . ."

> *Yoyaku shite yokatta!*
> It's a good thing that we made reservations!
>
> *Eigo ga wakatte yokatta!*
> It's a good thing that I understand English!

Practice 16.2

Vocabulary

sôji suru	そうじする	掃除する	do housecleaning
ureshii	うれしい		delighted
koibito	こいびと	恋人	boyfriend, girlfriend
hazukashii	はずかしい	恥ずかしい	embarrassed, ashamed
tamaru	たまる		to be able to tolerate
yoyaku	よやくする	予約する	make reservations

How would you say this?

1. It's a good thing that I did housecleaning!

2. I'm embarrassed that I forgot.

3. It's all right not to make reservations.

4. It's so cold that I can't stand it.

5. I'm delighted that my boyfriend/girlfriend passed the test.

6. Is it all right if I don't go?

7. It's a good thing that I didn't forget.

8. It's so hot that I can't stand it.

9. I'm embarrassed that I tripped and fell.

10. It's all right not to phone.

At first it may seem strange that the *-te* form of the negative can be used to say that one has to do something or that something is required, but it doesn't seem so illogical when you look at the components of this construction. Remember how to say that it's forbidden to do something, such as take photographs?

> *Shashin o totte wa ikemasen.*
> It is forbidden to take photographs.

Now, when you say that it's forbidden not to do something, you are, in effect, saying that it is required. If you were required to take pictures for some reason, you would be told:

Shashin o toranakute wa ikemasen.
It is forbidden not to take photographs.
You have to take photographs.

O-furo ni hairanakute wa ikemasen.
You have to take a bath.

Ashita konakute wa ikemasen.
You have to come tomorrow.

In this case, two negatives add up to a positive.

Note that this *-nakute wa ikemasen* is quite a strong expression, and it should be used only when something is really required or necessary. If you have to do something just because it's the way things are, not because someone is forcing you or because it would be dangerous not to, it's better to use the construction VERB + *koto ni natte imasu.*

Oobun ga nai kara, denshi renji o tsukau koto ni natte imasu.
Because I don't have an oven, I have to use a microwave.

Shû ni ikkai, ikebana no keiko o suru koto ni natte imasu.
I have to take flower arranging lessons once a week.

(Nobody is forcing the speaker, but since she wants to learn flower arranging, she needs to attend the lessons.)

Practice 16.2c

Vocabulary

o-furo ni hairu	おふろに はいる	おふろに 入る	take a bath
oobun	オーブン		oven
denshi renji	でんしレンジ	電子レンジ	microwave oven
ikebana	いけばな	生花	flower arranging
keiko o suru	けいこをする	稽古をする	take lessons or rehearse, especially in the traditional arts
shû ni ikkai	しゅうに いっかい	週に一回	once a week
kusuri o nomu	くすりを のむ		take medicine (Besides meaning "drink," *nomu* refers to ingesting something without chewing, so it is also used for swallowing pills.)
kurejitto kaado	クレジット カード		credit card
nugu	ぬぐ	脱ぐ	take off, remove (clothing or accessories)
ikkai or ichido	いっかい or いちど	一回、一度	once
nikai, nido	にかい、にど	二回、二度	twice
sankai, sando	さんかい、 さんど	三回、三度	three times
yonkai, yondo	よんかい、 よんど	四回、四度	four times
gokai, godo	ごかい、ごど	五回、五度	five times
rokkai, rokudo	ろっかい、 ろくど	六回、六度	six times
nanakai, nanado	ななかい、 ななど	七回、七度	seven times

Vocabulary

hakkai, hachido	はっかい、 はちど	八回、八度	eight times
kyûkai, kyûdo	きゅうかい、 きゅうど	九回、九度	nine times
jukkai, jûdo	じゅっかい、 じゅうど	十回、十度	ten times

Imagine yourself in the following situations. In all of them, you need to tell someone that something is required.

EXAMPLE:

You are explaining certain aspects of Japanese daily life to a student from Indonesia. (Your only common language is Japanese.) The Indonesian student asks if it's all right to go up onto a train station platform to see people off without a ticket. Tell her that it's necessary to buy a ticket.

Kippu o kawanakute wa ikemasen.

1. You are giving cooking lessons. You see that one of your pupils has noticeably dirty hands.

2. You are a hospital nurse, and one of your patients is refusing to take any medicine.

3. A Japanese acquaintance is asking you for advice before traveling to the United States and wants to know if it's possible to pay cash for a rental car.

4. You are an English teaching assistant in a high school, and one of your students wonders if it's possible to turn the homework in the day after tomorrow instead of tomorrow.

5. You've been living in Japan for a while, and a newly arrived acquaintance from Bulgaria (your only common language is Japanese) asks whether it's all right to wear shoes inside a Japanese house in cold weather.

6. You are interviewing an applicant for a school for aspiring professional dancers. The applicant is perhaps not serious enough to be a real professional, because the question of whether it's possible to attend class only twice a week comes up. You tell the applicant that it's required to rehearse six times a week.

HAVE YOU EVER?

You already know how to ask people if they did something on one occasion in the past. For example, if an acquaintance is telling you about a trip around the world, you might ask,

> *Indo e mo ikimashita ka?*
> Did you go to India, too?

Suppose, however, that your acquaintance is talking about how delicious Indian food is and how many interesting historic sites the country has. Then you might want to ask if your acquaintance has ever gone to India, not on some specific occasion, but at any time in the past. The construction for asking this sort of question is:

> PAST DICTIONARY FORM OF THE VERB + *koto ga arimasu.*

> *Indo e itta koto ga arimasu ka?*
> Have you ever gone to India?

> *Suzuki-san ni atta koto ga arimasu ka?*
> Have you ever met Ms. Suzuki?

The construction for saying that you haven't ever done something is:

> PAST DICTIONARY FORM + *koto wa arimasen.*

> *Suzuki-san ni atta koto wa arimasen.*
> I have never met Ms. Suzuki.

The verb before *koto* has to be in the past tense, or else the construction means something different, namely "do occasionally."

> *Suzuki-san ni au koto ga arimasu.*
> I occasionally see Ms. Suzuki.

> *Indo e iku koto ga arimasu.*
> I occasionally go to India.

Changing . . . *koto ga arimasu* to . . . *koto wa arimasu* implies that you are going to compare the activity to something else.

> *Sakana o taberu koto wa arimasu kedo, niku o taberu koto wa arimasen.*
> Ocasionally I eat fish, but I never eat meat.

Changing the *arimasu* to *arimasen*, as in that last sentence, changes the meaning to "never does." (This is one of the ways to say "never" that was mentioned in Chapter 13.)

Suzuki-san ni au koto wa arimasen.
I never see Ms. Suzuki.

Practice 16.3

Vocabulary

Indo	インド		India
tsuki	つき	月	moon
PERSON ni au	PERSON に あう	会う	meet PERSON, see PERSON

• When talking about "seeing" a person socially, always use *au*, not *miru*. *Suzuki-san ni au* means to exchange greetings with Ms. Suzuki and perhaps have a conversation with her. *Suzuki-san o miru* means to see Ms. Suzuki from a distance without any interaction. However, *au* can also carry the meaning of meeting a person for the first time.

Answer the following questions about your own experience.

EXAMPLE:

Tsuki ni itta koto ga arimasu ka? →
Iie, tsuki ni itta koto wa arimasen.
Have you ever gone to the moon?
No, I've never gone to the moon.

1. Nihon e itta koto ga arimasu ka?

2. Nihon no eiga o mita koto ga arimasu ka?

3. Nihonjin ni atta koto ga arimasu ka?

4. Nihon no ongaku o kiita koto ga arimasu ka?

6. Uma ni notta koto ga arimasu ka?

7. Karaoke o shita koto ga arimasu ka?

COMPARING MORE THAN TWO THINGS

In Chapter 13, you learned how to compare two things and to ask questions comparing two things:

> *Nihon to Chûgoku to, dochira ga ookii desu ka?*
> Which is bigger, Japan or China?

> *Chûgoku no hô ga ookii desu.*
> China is bigger.

In order to compare three or more items, you need to use this pattern:

> X *to* Y *to* Z *(no naka) de, dore ga ichiban* ADJECTIVE *desu ka?*
> (or, . . . *dore ga ichiban* VERB PHRASE *desu ka?*)

> *Uma to kuruma to hikôki no naka de, dore ga ichiban hayai desu ka?*
> Which is fastest, a horse, a car, or an airplane?
> (Yes, it's a dumb question, but it's just for purposes of illustration.)

> *Nara to Kyôto to Tôkyô no naka de, dore ga ichiban furui desu ka?*
> Which is the oldest, Nara, Kyôto or Tôkyô?
> (Ah, not as many of you know the answer to this one.)

> *Nara ga ichiban furui desu.*
> Nara is the oldest.

• *Ichiban* literally means "number one," and it's used on lists and the like. *-ban* is completely regular: *ichiban, niban, sanban,* and so on up to infinity.

You don't even have to name the items being compared individually. If you are asking about a large group of similar items or people, you can say something like the following:

> *Dôbutsu no naka de, dore ga ichiban ookii desu ka?*
> Among animals, which one is the largest?

> *Kono resutoran no ryôri no naka de, dore ga ichiban o-suki desu ka?*
> Of the food at this restaurant, what do you like best?

Now here's another construction that may come in handy when comparing things. You're in the computer lab, and you want to know which of the computers is easiest to use. You know how to say "easiest," but not "easiest to use." For that matter, you don't know how to say "hardest to use" or "hard to use" or "easy to write" or "hard to make" or anything along those lines. Fortunately, it's not difficult. All you do is take the -*masu* stem of the verb and add -*nikui* for "difficult to. . ." and -*yasui* (yes, -*yasui*) for "easy to. . ."

> *Koko no hôgen wa wakarinikui desu.*
> The dialect here is hard to understand.

> *Miso shiru wa tsukuriyasui desu.*
> Miso soup is easy to make.

Thus, the way to ask which of these computers is easiest to use is:

> *Kono konpyuuta no naka de, dore ga ichiban tsukaiyasui desu ka?*
> Of these computers, which one is the easiest to use?

You have to be a bit careful with these forms, especially -*nikui*. You might think that *minikui* means "hard to see," and it does in a sense, because it means "ugly."

Practice 16.4

Vocabulary

dôbutsu	どうぶつ	動物	animal
kurasu	クラス		class (a group of students, not a course [*koosu*] or an instructional period [*jugyô*])
hôgen	ほうげん	方言	dialect
miso shiru	みそしる	みそ汁	*miso* soup
yakyû	やきゅう	野球	baseball
sekai	せかい	世界	world
kuni	くに	国	country
toshi	とし	都市	large city
jinkô	じんこう	人口	population
kankôchi	かんこうち	観光地	sightseeing area

Ask comparative questions about the items given.

EXAMPLE:

(a) inu, neko, raion
(kowai)
Inu to neko to raion no naka de, dore ga ichiban kowai desu ka?
Which are the most frightening, dogs, cats, or lions?

(b) koko no hoteru
(takai)
Koko no hoteru no naka de, dore ga ichiban takai desu ka?
Which is the most expensive of the hotels here?

1. sushi, sukiyaki, tenpura
(oishii)

2. yakyû, basukettobooru, futtobooru
(omoshiroi)

3. sekai no kuni
(ookii)

4. Amerika no toshi
(jinkô ga ooi)

5. kanji
(oboeyasui)

6. Nihon no kankôchi
(yûmei)

7. kono kurasu no gakusei
(atama ga ii)

SUMMING UP
MATOME
まとめ

Complete the following dialogues according to the cues given.

1. You are about to mail a letter that is addressed in beautifully written *kanji*, when Ikeda Masaru sees it and asks you about it.

Ikeda: Kimi ga sono kanji o kaita no?

You: (No, you had Teramura Chieko write them for you.)

2. Teramura Chieko is asking about your travels in Japan.

Teramura: Kamakura e itta koto, aru?

You: (Say that you occasionally go to Yokohama, but have never gone to Kamakura.)

3. You want a new camera, so you go to a large discount retailer near Shinjuku Station.

You: (Ask the store clerk which camera is easiest to use.)

Ten'in: Sô desu ne. Kore ga ichiban benri de, tsukaiyasui desu.

You: (Ask how much it is.)

Ten'in: Kamera wa niman gosen en de, keesu wa nisen gohyaku en de, zenbu de niman nanasen gohyaku en ni narimasu ga. . .

You: (Echo the price. Ask if it's all right not to buy the case.)

Ten'in: A, keesu wa iranai n desu ka? Hai, ii desu yo.

4. Your newly arrived Bulgarian acquaintance has heard that there are two types of seats on Japanese trains: *jiyû seki* and *shitei seki*.

Burugariajin: Jiyû seki to shitei seki wa dô chigaimasu ka?

You: (Explain that with ["as for"] *shitei seki*, you have to make reservations.)

CHAPTER 17

AME GA FURU KA MO SHIREMASEN. (IT MAY RAIN.)

In this chapter you will learn to:

1. give advice
2. make guesses and state your opinions

GIVING ADVICE

The form for suggesting to someone what he or she ought to do on a specific occasion is:

PAST TENSE OF THE DICTIONARY FORM + *hô ga ii desu.*

It would be best to . . .
[Someone] should. . .
[Someone] ought to. . .

Sugu chiketto o katta hô ga ii desu.
It would be best to buy tickets soon.

Kono denwa bangô o oboeta hô ga ii desu.
You ought to memorize this telephone number.

If you use the present tense of the verb instead of the past tense, you are giving not advice for a specific situation but a general rule to follow:

Mizu o takusan nomu hô ga ii desu.
It's a good idea to drink a lot of water.

However, when giving someone advice about what not to do, always use the present negative.

Koko no mizu o nomanai hô ga ii desu yo.
It's best not to drink the water here.

Narita-kûkô wa Tôkyô kara tooi desu kara, takushii de ikanai hô ga ii desu. Basu ka densha de itta hô ga ii desu yo.
Narita Airport is far from Tokyo, so it's best not to go by taxi. It's best to go by bus or train.

Practice 17.1

Give the following advice:

EXAMPLE:

To use this map
Kono chizu o tsukatta hô ga ii desu.

1. to ask the store clerk

2. to sell that old car

3. to take off one's shoes

4. to wait a little bit

5. to not argue with the police officer

6. to not eat that kind of fish

7. to study more

8. to exercise every day

9. to learn music

10. to not phone [to] Mr. Morimoto

MAKING GUESSES AND GIVING OPINIONS

Suppose you're making a guess about something, such as this afternoon's weather. If you're fairly sure that it will rain, you can say, as you learned in Chapter 11:

Ame ga furu deshô.
It will probably rain.

But suppose you aren't at all sure, just not ruling out the possibility of rain. Then you use another construction:

DICTIONARY FORM + *ka mo shirenai* or *ka mo shiremasen*
"It may be that. . ."

Even though this construction looks negative, its English
equivalent is positive:

> *Ame ga furu ka mo shiremasen.*
> It may rain.
>
> *Abunai ka mo shirenai.*
> It may be dangerous.
>
> *Ano hito wa Nihonjin ka mo shiremasen.*
> That person may be Japanese.

Note that *da* is dropped before *ka mo shiremasen*, although its
other forms are kept:

> *Jishin datta ka mo shiremasen.*
> It may have been an earthquake.
>
> *Anzen ja nai ka mo shiremasen.*
> It may not be safe.

At the other extreme, if you are almost completely sure of a
situation, you can use another form that looks negative but is
actually positive, the construction:

DICTIONARY FORM + *ni chigai arimasen* or *ni chigai nai*

> *Ame ga furu ni chigai arimasen.*
> It will certainly rain.
> or
> There's no doubt that it will rain.
>
> *Abunai ni chigai arimasen.*
> That just has to be dangerous.
>
> *Ano hito wa Nihonjin ni chigai nai.*
> That person is undoubtedly Japanese.

As you can see, *da* behaves the same as it does with *ka mo
shiremasen* and *deshô*. It disappears, but it reappears in other forms:

> *Anzen ja nai ni chigai arimasen.*
> There's no doubt that it's not safe.

WATCH OUT

When changing a *ku-* adjective from the *-masu* style to the plain (dictionary) style, do **not** change *desu* to *da*. Instead, drop it completely.

Ii desu.
It's good.

WRONG:　*Ii da ka mo shiremasen.*
　　　　Ii da ni chigai arimasen.
RIGHT:　*Ii ka mo shiremasen.*
　　　　Ii ni chigai arimasen.

Practice 17.2a

Vocabulary

taifû	たいふう	台風	typhoon
kôtsû jiko ni au	こうつうじこ にあう	交通事故に 合う	be involved in a traffic accident
dorobô	どろぼう		thief
haitte kuru	はいってくる		come in
jishin	じしん	地震	earthquake

Say that each of the following things may happen or may be true. Then say that each of them will certainly happen or must be true.

EXAMPLE:

Sumisu-san wa Furansugo ga wakarimasu.→
Sumisu-san wa Furansugo ga wakaru ka mo shiremasen.
Ms. Smith may understand French.
Sumisu-san wa Furansugo ga wakaru ni chigai arimasen.
Ms. Smith undoubtedly understands French.

1. Taifû ga kimasu.

2. Date-san wa kekkon shite imasu.

3. Kôtsû jiko ni aimashita.

4. Nani mo wakarimasen.

5. Dorobô wa mado kara haitte kimashita.

6. Ashita wa ii tenki desu.

7. Amari tooku nai desu.

8. Gakusei deshita.

In order to express your opinion, or in other words, to tell people what you think, use the construction:

> SENTENCE (dictionary form) + *to omoimasu/ to omou*
>
> *Ame ga furu to omoimasu.*
> I think it will rain.
>
> *Ano hito wa Nihonjin da to omoimasu.*
> I think that person is Japanese.
>
> *Jishin datta to omoimasu.*
> I think it was an earthquake.
>
> *Anzen ja nai to omoimasu.*
> I think it's not safe.

WATCH OUT

Omou means "think" in the sense of "have an opinion." Thus *omotte imasu* can not be the answer to *Nani o shite imasu ka?* "What are you doing?" The verb for "think" as in "ponder," "mull over" is *kangaeru*, as in *Iroiro na koto o kangaete imasu.* "I'm thinking about various things."

You can even combine *to omou* with the other indications of probability, particularly with *darô*, which is the plain form of *deshô*.

> *Ame ga furu darô to omoimasu.*
> I think it will probably rain.
>
> *Ame ga furu ka mo shirenai to omoimasu.*
> I think that it may rain.

There are two ways to make these expressions negative. Normally, the part before *to omou* is negated:

> *Ame ga furanai to omoimasu.*
> I don't think it will rain.
> (I am of the opinion that it will not rain.)
>
> *Kirei ja nai to omoimasu.*
> I don't think it's pretty.
> (I am of the opinion that it's not pretty)

However, you can also negate *to omou* as *to wa omowanai/to wa omoimasen*. (You need the *wa* in there.) The nuance of this form is "I am not of the opinion. . ." or "I am not inclined to believe. . ."

> *Ame ga furu to wa omoimasen.*
> I am not of the opinion that it will rain.
>
> *Jishin datta to wa omoimasen.*
> I am not inclined to believe that it was an earthquake.

By the way, the dictionary form + *to omou* constructions are not used to talk about what you yourself are going to do. At this point in your study of Japanese, it is easiest to use the dictionary form + *tsumori desu* "It is my intention. . ."

> *Rainen, Nihon e iku tsumori desu.*
> I intend to go to Japan next year.

You can also use *-tai* forms with *to omou.*

> *Kyôshi ni naritai to omoimasu.*
> I think I want to become a teacher.

Practice 17.2b

How would you express the idea that the following statements were your opinion?

EXAMPLE:

Dare mo kimasen.→
Dare mo konai to omoimasu.

1. Omoshiroi eiga desu.

2. Mainichi oyogi ni ikitai desu.

3. Kimura-san wa Nikkeijin desu.

4. Abunai desu.

5. Ano hon wa totemo tsumaranakatta desu.

6. Ano gakkô no senseitachi wa shinsetsu deshô.

7. Sonna koto wa dare de mo dekimasu.

8. Kono depaato de wa nan de mo utte imasu.

9. Suzuki-san wa manshon ni sunde imasu.

10. Sone-san wa go nenkan Amerika ni imashita.

SUMMING UP
MATOME
まとめ

1. Give the following advice using . . .*hô ga ii desu.*
   (a) to practice *kanji*
   (b) to go home
   (c) to not buy a car
   (d) to not take a job at a bank

2. Say that the following things may be true:
   (a) Tamura-san wa Nikkeijin desu.
   (b) Ashita no shiken wa muzukashii desu.
   (c) Sumisu-san wa asoko ni imasu.
   (d) O-kane wa arimasen.

3. Now restate the sentences above so that you are saying that they must be true.

4. Now restate the sentences above so that they are your opinion.

5. Complete the dialogue according to the cues given. You and Chan Ngan-fa are visiting Yokohama's Chinatown. (Yes, Yokohama has a Chinatown!) You've been shopping all afternoon, and now it's time for dinner.

Chan: Ara, resutoran ga takusan aru no nee. Dore ni hairimashô ka?
You: (Suggest that you think it would be a good idea to go [into] a cheap and delicious restaurant.)
Chan: Yasukute oishii mise? Sonna mise wa nai ka mo shirenai kedo. . .
You: (Say that you think that among China's cuisines, *Szechuan* [*Shisen*] cuisine is the most delicious.)
Chan: Hee? Kanton ryôri yori oishii to omou no? Komatta wa nee! Hora! Ano mise wa dô? "*Ngan Fa*" to iu mise.
You: (*Ngan Fa?* You have no doubt that it's delicious.)

CHAPTER 18

DOCHIRASAMA DE IRASSHAIMASU KA? (WHO ARE YOU?)

In this chapter you will learn:

1. to express respect
2. to talk politely on the telephone

HOW TO EXPRESS RESPECT AND TO WHOM

Really mastering the system of humble and honorific speech takes considerable study and experience in living in a Japanese environment. On a practical level, these speech gradations are heard constantly in everyday conversation, so you need to recognize the most common ways of expressing respect and humility, even if you don't know how to use them yourself.

There are two dimensions to expressing politeness in Japanese. The first is the choice between the polite *-masu* form and the plain (dictionary) form. The rules can be complicated, but in general, it is a good idea to use the *-masu* form with all adults who are not either close friends, family members (in the case of students, this usually includes host families), or subordinates on the job. You may think that the plain form sounds friendlier, but, *Japanese culture places a higher value on correct behavior than on appearing friendly and casual.*

You may like your Japanese boss a lot, but using by his or her given name or speaking in plain form will not win you any points and may seriously annoy him or her.

You have already seen a few examples of honorifics. For example, when you refer to your own parents as *ryôshin* and someone else's parents as *go-ryôshin* (Chapter 12), you are using honorifics. When you say *Watashi wa aisu kuriimu ga suki desu* but ask someone else *o-suki desu ka?* you are using honorifics.

Everyone uses honorifics at some time or other. People usually answer the door in honorific style, because they don't know whom they're dealing with, and they don't want to risk offending anyone.

If they then find out that the caller or visitor is someone to whom they don't have to be particularly polite, they can adjust the level of speech to fit the situation.

People in jobs that require meeting the public, such as restaurant servers and receptionists, use honorifics almost constantly in dealing with customers and clients.

In general, use honorifics with people who rank above you in whatever organization or institution you're involved with. In addition, when you are acting as a representative of your organization in dealings with the outside world, use honorifics with the outsiders you encounter. For example, if you are an employee of Widgetronics paying a sales call on Technopoly, you speak to their employees in honorifics, and their employees speak honorifically to you.

There are two forms of honorifics, regular and irregular. One kind of regular honorific is formed by taking the *-masu* stem of the verb, putting an *o-* on the front, and adding ni *naru:*

> *Suzuki-san wa doa o akemashita.*
> Ms. Suzuki opened the door.

> *Shachô wa doa o o-ake ni narimashita.*
> The company president opened the door.

> *Suzuki-san wa repooto o kakimashita.*
> Ms. Suzuki wrote a report yesterday.

> *Sensei wa kyonen kono hon o o-kaki ni narimashita.*
> The professor wrote this book last year.

This won't work with all verbs, however. You can't say *o-tabe ni naru*, because *taberu* is one of several verbs with an irregular honorific. Here are some of the most common irregular forms.

Verb	Irregular Honorifics
iru "be located"	*irassharu (-masu* form: *irasshaimasu, -te* form: *irasshatte* or *irashite*)
iku "go"	*irassharu, o-ide ni naru, ikareru*
kuru "come"	*irassharu, o-ide ni naru, korareru*
miru "see"	*goran ni naru*
taberu "eat"	*meshiagaru*
nomu "drink"	*meshiagaru*
da/desu "be"	*de irassharu* (used in reference to people only)
suru "do"	*nasaru (-masu* form: *nasaimasu, -te* form: *nasatte*)
iu "say"	*ossharu, (-masu* form: *osshaimasu, -te* form: *osshatte*)
shitte iru "know"	*go-zonji desu*

Here are some examples, including a few very common expressions:

> *O-cha o meshiagarimasen ka?*
> Won't you have some tea?

> *Kore o goran ni natte kudasai.*
> Please look at this.

> *Takahashi Sensei wa toshokan ni irasshaimasu.*
> Professor Takahashi is in the library.

> *Ishida-san o go-zonji desu ka?*
> Do you know Ms. Ishida?

> *Shitsurei desu ga, Koyanagi Sensei de irasshaimasu ka?*
> Pardon me for asking, but are you Professor Koyanagi?

Practice 18.1

The following sentences are written in honorific style. What would their neutral equivalents be? Some honorific verbs can stand in for more than one neutral verb, but in these sentences, as in real life, you will find clues to the precise meaning of each one.

1. Yûmei na kata de irasshaimasu.

2. Shachô wa koohii o meshiagatte kara, o-kaeri ni narimashita.

3. Kochira e irashite kudasai.

4. Sushi o meshiagarimasen ka?

5. Shachô wa ashita Sapporo e irassharu deshô.

6. Sensei, hakubutsukan no atarashii tenrankai o goran ni narimashita ka?

7. Kore wa irimasen kara, dôzo, o-tsukai ni natte kudasai.

8. Nanji no densha ni o-nori ni narimashita ka?

9. O-namae o osshatte kudasai.

10. Dô nasatta n desu ka?

11. Tekunoporii no Kimura-san no denwa bangô o go-zonji desu ka?

The humble forms are used when talking about yourself or the people associated with you to someone who ranks above you or comes from outside your in-group. For example, you would use humble forms in reference to yourself and your family when talking to your boss or your instructor. In a business situation, you would use humble forms in reference to all employees of your own company, including the upper management, when talking to someone from another company.

The regular humble form starts out like the regular honorific: You take the *-masu* stem and put an *o-* in front of it, but then you add a form of *suru*, usually *shimasu*. If the verb is already a *suru* verb, such as *sôdan suru* "consult," then simply put a *go-* in front of the noun part and leave the *suru* as it is: *Sensei ni go-sôdan shimashita* "I consulted the instructor." These humble forms often carry the meaning of doing the action described for some higher-ranking person.

> *Shachô no tsukue o o-katazuke shimashita.*
> I straightened up the company president's desk.

> *O-kyaku-san no kooto o o-azukari shimashita.*
> I took charge of the customers' coats.

Kono wain o o-susume shimasu.
I recommend this wine.

And yes, you guessed it, *o-negai shimasu* is a regular humble form, the humble form of *negau* "request, beg," and it has developed into a standard courtesy phrase.

As with the honorifics, there are a number of irregular forms.

Verb	Irregular Humbles
iru "be located, exist"	*orimasu*
aru "be located, exist"	*gozaimasu*
iku "go"	*mairimasu*
kuru "come"	*mairimasu*
miru "see"	*haiken shimasu*
taberu "eat"	*itadakimasu*
nomu "drink"	*itadakimasu*
da/desu "be"	*de gozaimasu* (used for both animates and inanimates)
au "meet"	*o-me ni kakarimasu, o-ai shimasu*
tazuneru (1) "visit"	*ukagaimasu*
kiku "ask"	*ukagaimasu*
suru "do"	*itashimasu*
iu "say"	*môshimasu* (1), *môshiagemasu*
kariru "borrow"	*haishaku shimasu*
shitte iru "know"	*zonjite orimasu* (negative: *zonjimasen*)

These humble verbs have dictionary forms, but they are rarely used in real life. If you want to make any of the *shimasu* forms extra humble, just change the *shimasu* to *itashimasu*. Here are some examples of how the irregular humbles are used:

O-kyaku-sama no yobidashi o môshiagemasu.
I'm paging a customer (in a department store).

Kochira wa otôto de gozaimasu.
This is my younger brother.

O-machi shite orimasu.
I'm waiting/I'll be waiting.

Môshiwake gozaimasen ga, firumu wa gozaimasen.
I'm terribly sorry, but we don't have any film.

No one in Japan will expect you, a non-native speaker, to have a perfect command of honorific and humble speech immediately, but if you study the forms, you will at least know that, for example, both *goran ni naru* and *haiken suru* mean the same thing as *miru*, which isn't something that you'd be able to guess easily on your own.

Practice 18.2

Vocabulary

azukaru	あずかる	預かる	to take charge of, to take care of temporarily
o-kyaku-sama	おきゃくさま	お客さま	customer, guest
susumeru (1)	すすめる (1)	勧める	recommend
todokeru (1)	とどける (1)	届ける	deliver
yobidashi	よびだし	呼び出し	paging, summoning
shôkai suru	しょうかいする	紹介する	introduce
firumu	フィルム		[photographic] film
monitaa	モニター		[computer] monitor

Each of the following sentences is written in the humble style. What is its neutral equivalent?

1. Takahashi Sensei kara kono hon o haishaku shimashita.

2. Fukuzatsu na shitsumon desu ne. Sensei ni ukagatta hô ga ii to omoimasu.

3. Zenbu o-todoke shimashô ka?

4. Kinô, Tekunoporii no Saeki-san to o-hanashi shimashita.

5. Chotto haiken shite mairimasu.

6. Kono chihô no kankôchi wa yoku zonjite orimasu ga, Hokkaidô wa zenzen zonjimasen.

7. Itsu ka Takahashi Sensei ni o-me ni kakaritai to omoimasu.

8. Shitsurei itashimashita.

9. Kore wa totemo ii konpyuuta de gozaimasu ga, monitaa ga gozaimasen kara, yasuku natte orimasu.

10. Ryôshin o shôkai itashimasu.

TALKING ON THE TELEPHONE

Even people who love talking on the telephone in their native language have a hard time adjusting to phone conversations in a foreign language. They can't make do with gestures and facial expressions if they forget a word or phrase, and they can't see the other person's reactions to what they are saying.

Japanese phone conversations can be especially intimidating, because even students who are fairly comfortable with everyday face-to-face interactions may be stumped by the unfamiliar phrases and routines that they encounter. There's nothing to be done about the loss of visual contact with the listener, but at least you can learn a few common expressions that people are likely to say to you.

First let's take the situation of calling someone's home. Sometimes, the person who is calling, not the person who is answering, says *moshimoshi* "hello" first. Then the person answering the phone identifies himself or herself by family name only. The caller then asks for the person he or she wants to talk to.

Vocabulary

Shôshô o machi kudasai.	しょうしょう おまち ください。	少々 お待ち ください。	Please wait a bit. (very polite expression)
dengon	でんごん	伝言	telephone message
kaze o hiku	かぜをひく	風邪をひく	catch a cold or other respiratory infection
tsutaeru (1)	つたえる (1)	伝える	convey [a message]
Gomen kudasai.	ごめん ください。	御免 ください。	a formal way to say goodbye on the telephone
O-daiji ni.	おだいじに。	お大事に。	Take care.

Examples:

Ikeda Masaru has gone home for the weekend, and Thomas Wilson calls him to ask about something that has come up. Masaru's mother answers the phone.

Wilson:	Moshimoshi.
Okaasan:	Moshimoshi, Ikeda desu ga. . .
Wilson:	Kochira wa Tomasu Uiruson desu ga, Masaru-san, irasshaimasu ka?
Okaasan:	Shôshô o-machi kudasai.

Wilson:	Hello.
Mother:	Hello. This is the Ikeda residence.
Wilson:	This is Thomas Wilson. Is Masaru there?
Mother:	Just a minute.

Note that both Thomas Wilson and Ikeda Masaru's mother are being especially polite. In fact, *NAME irasshaimasu ka?* is the standard way to ask for someone on the telephone, no matter whom you're calling. Once Ikeda Masaru picks up the phone, he and Thomas Wilson can speak more informally.

Now suppose that Ikeda Masaru is not at home and Thomas Wilson needs to leave a message for him.

Wilson:	Moshimoshi.
Okaasan:	Moshimoshi, Ikeda desu kedo...
Wilson:	Kochira wa Thomas Wilson desu ga, Masaru-san, irasshaimasu ka?
Okaasan:	A, Masaru wa chotto dekakete orimasu kedo. . .
Wilson:	Sô desu ka? De wa, dengon, o-negai dekimasu ka?
Okaasan:	Hai, dôzo.
Wilson:	Hidoi kaze o hiite. . .
Okasaan:	Ara!
Wilson:	Ashita, oyogi ni ikemasen kara, sô osshatte kudasai.
Okaasan:	Kaze o hiite, oyogi ni ikenai n desu ne. Hai, o-tsutae shimasu.
Wilson:	Yoroshiku o-negai shimasu. De wa, shitsurei shimasu. Gomen kudasai.
Okaasan:	O-daiji ni. Sayonara.

Wilson:	Hello.
Mother:	Hello. This is the Ikeda residence.
Wilson:	This is Thomas Wilson. Is Masaru there?
Mother:	Oh, Masaru has gone out for a bit.
Wilson:	Really? May I ask you to take a message?
Mother:	Yes, go ahead.

Wilson:	I've caught a bad cold. . .
Mother:	Oh, my!
Wilson:	. . . and I can't go swimming tomorrow, so please let him know.
Mother:	You've caught a cold and can't go swimming, right? I'll let him know.
Wilson:	Please take care of it. Well, I'll be hanging up now. Good-bye.
Mother:	Take care. Good-bye.

Note that Mrs. Ikeda refers to her son by just his given name without -*san*, because you are not supposed to add -*san* to the name of a relative when you are talking to a non-family member.

The standard way to leave a message is to give the information, end it with *kara*, and then add *Sô tsutaete kudasai* or *Sô osshatte kudasai*.

Now let's look at a business situation. Ms. Blake has set up the branch sales office of Widgetronics, and Ms. Miller, an old high school classmate of hers, who is now a graduate student doing research in Japan, comes through town. Ms. Miller has seen the phone number for Widgetronics on a billboard near the train station, so she calls that number and gets the receptionist.

Vocabulary

uketsuke	うけつけ	受付	receptionist
Dochirasama de irasshaimasu ka?	どちらさまで いらっしゃい ますか。		the most polite equivalent of "Who are you?"
jidai	じだい	時代	era, days, times
dôkyûsei	どうきゅうせい	同級生	classmate, someone in the same year as you in school

Uketsuke:	Hai, Uijetoronikkusu de gozaimasu.
Miller:	Bureeku-san irasshaimasu ka?
Uketsuke:	Shitsurei desu ga, dochirasama de irasshaimasu ka?
Miller:	Watashi, Jenii Miraa to môshimasu ga. . .
Uketsuke:	Dochira no Miraa-san deshô ka?
Miller:	A, Bureeku-san no kôkô jidai no dôkyûsei na n desu.
Uketsuke:	Wakarimashita. Shôshô o-machi kudasai.

Receptionist: Yes, this is Widgetronics.
Miller: Is Ms. Blake there?
Receptionist: Excuse me, but who are you?
Miller: My name is Jenny Miller.
Receptionist: Ms. Miller from where?
Miller: Oh, I'm a classmate of Ms. Blake's from her high school days.
Receptionist: I see. Please wait a moment.

To avoid the interrogation that Ms. Miller went through, identify yourself right away by name and affiliation (employer or school), as Mr. Morimoto does.

Uketsuke: Hai, Uijetoronikkusu de gozaimasu.
Morimoto: Moshimoshi. Kochira wa Tekunoporii no Morimoto de gozaimasu ga, Bureeku-san, irasshaimasu ka?
Uketsuke: Môshiwake gozaimasen ga, Bureeku wa ima gaishutsu shite orimasu.
Morimoto: De wa, mata o-denwa itashimasu kara. . .

Receptionist: Yes, this is Widgetronics.
Morimoto: Hello. This is Morimoto from Technopoly. Is Ms. Blake there?
Receptionist: I'm sorry, but Ms. Blake is out of the office.
Morimoto: Is that so? Well, I'll call again, so. . .

Note that even though the receptionist ranks below Ms. Blake, she refers to her without *-san* and uses humble verbs in talking about her. This is because she and Ms. Blake are part of the same company, and Mr. Morimoto is an outsider. When talking about Ms. Blake to a fellow employee, the receptionist would use honorific verbs and always add *-san* or some form of address related to her job title.

Receptionists or switchboard operators may also tell you that the person you are calling is:

gaishutsu shite orimasu	がいしゅつ しております	外出して おります	out of the office
seki o hazushite orimasu	せきを はずして おります	席を 外して おります	away from his/her desk
kyûka o totte orimasu	きゅうかを とって おります	休暇を 取って おります	on vacation
yasunde orimasu	やすんで おります	休んで おります	taking some time off
shutchôchû de gozaimasu	しゅっちょう ちゅうで ございます	出張中で ございます	on a business trip
hanashichû de gozaimasu	はなしちゅう でございます	話中で ございます	on the phone

If you are aware of these expressions and routines, you should be able to handle most of the normal telephone situations on some level.

In this and other respects, the best ways to make further progress are to study hard, expose yourself to the language and culture as much as possible, and keep your eyes and ears open for the ways in which Japanese people speak and write.

May River Festival

ANSWERS TO THE EXERCISES

CHAPTER 3

3.1. a. morning, nice weather   b. afternoon, hot   c. evening, raining or snowing

3.2. (Answers will vary but should consist entirely of phrases introduced so far.)

Summing Up:

A. 1. Sô desu ne.   2. Iie, dô itashimashite. 3. Ee, okagesama de.   4. Kochira koso yoroshiku o-negai itashimasu.   5. Itte irasshai.

B. 1. You: Hai, sô desu. ... You: Watakushi wa, (name of company or school) no Miraa de gozaimasu. Kochira koso yoroshiku o-negai itashimasu.   2. Tomita: Koohii o dôzo. You: Okamai naku. Tomita: Dôzo, dôzo. You: De wa, itadakimasu.   3. Wada: Chotto o-negai shimasu. You: Dôzo. Wada: Dômo. You: Iie, (dô itashimashite).   4. You: Gochisôsama deshita.   Sayonara.

CHAPTER 4

4.1. 1. Iie, chigaimasu. Sore wa sandaru ja arimasen (Remember, you may use any of the negatives). Geta desu.   2. Iie, chigaimasu. Sore wa puuru ja nai desu. O-furo desu.   3. Iie, chigaimasu. Sore wa beruto de wa arimasen. Obi desu. 4. Iie, chigaimasu. Sore wa sokkusu ja nai desu. Tabi desu.   5. Iie chigaimasu. Sore wa kabin ja arimasen. Tokkuri desu.   6. Iie, chigaimasu. Sore wa makura ja nai desu. Zabuton desu.

4.2. 1. (Kaigi wa) ashita desu.   2. (Shiken wa) asatte desu.   3. (Ano hito wa) Suzuki-san desu.   4. Ano kata wa Iwasaki-sensei desu.   5. Ano kyandii wa ichi doru desu.
6. Are wa jinja desu.   7. Sore wa sashimi desu.

4.3. 1. ichi-ni-san-no-yon-go-roku-nana-ban   2. nana-roku-go-no-yon-san-ni-ichi-ban   3. go-yon-san-ni-no-ichi-zero (OR rei)-kyû-hachi-ban.   4. kyû-hachi-nana-no-roku-go-yon-san-ban
5. hachi-zero-zero (OR rei-rei)-no-ichi-ni-san-no-nana-roku-go-yon-ban   6 and 7. (answers will vary).

4.4. 1. Kôhii wa nihyaku en desu.   2. Kono geta wa gosen yonhyaku sanjû ni en desu.
3. Kono kyandii wa sen gohyaku rokujû nana en desu.   4. Kono sokkusu wa nanahyaku gojû en desu.   5. Kono mikan wa rokujû go en desu.   6. Sono nattô wa yonhyaku jûhachi en desu.   7. Ano obi wa hassen happyaku sanjû en desu.   8. Ano sandaru wa sanzen sanbyaku yonjû en desu.   9. (Answers will vary)

4.5. Answers will vary but will all follow the format (PROGRAM) wa gogo (OR gozen) ___ ji kara ____ ji made desu.

Summing Up: (The parts in parentheses are not wrong, but could be omitted.)

1. Aoki: Ano kata wa donata desu ka? You: (Ano kata wa) Sumisu-sensei desu.
2. You: Konsaato wa itsu desu ka? Ikeda: (Konsaato wa) asatte desu. You: Kippu wa ikura desu ka? Ikeda: Sanzen en desu. You: Konsaato wa nanji kara desu ka? Ikeda: Gogo hachiji kara desu.   3. You: Sumimasen ga, kore wa kimono desu ka? Clerk: Iie, chigaimasu. Sore wa nemaki desu. You: Kono nemaki wa ikura desu ka? Clerk: Nisen sanbyaku en desu. You: Jaa, kore o kudasai. Hai, sanzen en. Clerk: Otsuri (wa) nanahyaku en desu. Arigatô gozaimashita.

CHAPTER 5

5.1. 1. watashi no kasa   2. Sumisu-san no hon   3. Tanaka-san no denwa bangô   4.Chan-san no nooto   5. Morimoto-san no rajio   6. ashita no kaigi   7. Shingapooru no doru
8. Nihon no okane   9. Kôbe no kokusai bôeki sentaa   10. Hoteru no hito

5.2. 1. Abuduuru-san wa doko ni imasu ka? Asoko ni imasu.   2. Kasa wa doko ni arimasu ka? Soko ni arimasu.   3. Nooto wa doko ni arimasu ka? Toshokan ni arimasu.   4. Resutoran wa doko ni arimasu ka? Kamakura ni arimasu.   5. Sumisu-san wa doko ni imasu ka? Daigaku ni imasu.

5.3. (In all cases, you may repeat the NOUN wa phrase in your answer, but you don't have to.) 1. Beddo no shita ni arimasu.   2. Beddo no ue ni arimasu.   3. Tsukue no ue ni arimasu. 4. Tsukue no shita ni arimasu.   5. Tsukue no yoko ni arimasu OR Tsukue to beddo no aida ni arimasu.   6. Kuzukago no naka ni arimasu.   7. Isu no ushiro ni imasu.   8. Hondana no ue ni arimasu.   9. Tansu no ue ni arimasu.   10. Suisô no naka ni imasu.   11. Yuka no ue ni arimasu.   12. Hikidashi no naka ni arimasu.

Summing Up:

1. ...You: Kinyôbi made Kyôto ni imasu.   2. You: Sumimasen ga, yûbinkyoku wa doko ni arimasu ka?   Ekiin: Ano depaato no tonari ni arimasu.   (It's next to that department store over there.)   3. ... You: Ano kabe to hondana no aida ni arimasu.

REVIEW CHAPTERS 1–5

A. 1. d 2. e 3. a 4. f 5. b 6. c 7. h 8. i 9. g

B. 1. Denwa wa eki no yoko ni arimasu.   2. Basu no ushiro ni arimasu.   3. Eki no mukô ni daigaku ga arimasu.   4. Apaato wa hon'ya no ue ni arimasu.   5. Kôen wa eki no mae ni arimasu.

C. 1. kiosk or newsstand   2. bicycle   3. roof   4. furniture   5. bench   6. pond   7. trees

CHAPTER 6

6.1. 1. Sore wa chiisai hon desu.   2. Kore wa shiroi nooto desu.   3. Are wa akai ryukku desu. 4. Kore wa ookii tsukue desu.   5. Sore wa omoshiroi tegami desu.   6. Kore wa aoi seetaa desu.   7. Sore wa yasui kutsu desu.   8. Sono hon wa chiisai desu.   9. Sono nooto wa shiroi desu.   10. Watashi no ryukku wa akai desu.   11. Ikeda-san no tsukue wa ookii desu. 12. Suzuki-san no tegami wa omoshiroi desu.   13. Kono seetaa wa aoi desu.   14. Sono kutsu wa yasui desu.

6.2a. (In all cases, it is permissible to use *arimasen* instead of *nai desu* and vice versa. 1. Atatakaku nai desu.   2. Amari abunaku nai desu.   3. Amari nagaku nai desu. 4. Mezurashiku nai desu.   5. Suzushiku nai desu.   6. Amari yasuku nai desu.   7. Samuku nai desu.   8. Osoku arimasen.   9. Amari yoku nai desu.

6.2b. 1. shimasen   2. ikimasen   3. tabemasen   4. nomimasen   5. nemasen   6. mimasen 7. kikimasen   8. kaerimasen   9. yomimasen   10. okimasen

6.3. 1. Beddo no shita ni kutsu ga arimasu.   2. Tsukue no yoko ni kuzukago ga arimasu. 3. Tsukue no ue ni konpyuuta to sutando ga arimasu.   4. Mado no mae ni hondana ga arimasu.   5. Yuka ni seetaa ga arimasu.   6. Suisô no naka ni sakana ga imasu.   7. Hondana no mae ni ryukku ga arimasu.   8. Isu no ushiro ni neko ga imasu.   9. Beddo no ue ni bôshi ga arimasu.   10. Hikidashi no naka ni jiinzu ga arimasu.   11. Tsukue no shita ni konsento ga arimasu.   12. Kabe ni posutaa ga arimasu.

6.4. 1. ichiman   2. ichiman nisen   3. niman   4. niman gosen   5. yonman hassen roppyaku sanjûni   6. goman go   7. jûman   8. nijûsan-man yonsen   9. hyakuman   10. gohyaku-man 11. senman   12. issen-nihyaku-sanjû-yonman gosen roppyaku nanajûhachi   13. ichioku 14. nioku gosen-man   15. kyûoku issen-happyaku-nijû-nanaman sanzen roppyaku nijûichi 16. jûoku

Summing Up:

1. Takahashi echoes Date's comment that La Couronne isn't very good, so he asks which restaurant has good food. After some thought, Date suggests La France. Takahashi asks how much the set menu there is. Date says that he thinks it's about 8,000 yen.   2. a. You: Nanaman gosen en desu.   b. You: Ee, totemo tsumaranai desu.   c. You: Yôfuku ga arimasu. You: Hon to nooto ga arimasu.   d. You: Enpitsu ga arimasu. You: (Pen wa) arimasen.

CHAPTER 7

7.1. (Answers will vary, but they should follow the patterns given in the example.)

7.2a. 1. six o'clock.   2. He eats toast and eggs and drinks milk.   3. nine hours   4. He cooks for himself, because he goes shopping and eats dinner after returning home.   5. After dinner he goes jogging and watches television.   6. He takes a shower.

7.2b. (Answers will vary but should follow this format:) 1. ——ji ni okimasu.   2. NOUN (to NOUN) o tabemasu. NOUN o nomimasu. (If you don't eat breakfast, you would say *Asagohan wa tabemasen.*)   3. ——ji ni dekakemasu.   4. ——ji ni hirugohan o tabemasu. 5. ——ji ni kaerimasu.   6. (examples:) Joggingu o shimasu. Terebi o mimasu. Shinbun o yomimasu. Tegami o kakimasu. etc.   7. ——ji ni nemasu.

7.2c. 1. Kaban no naka ni wa arimasen.   2. Terebi wa mimasen.   3. Joggingu wa shimasen. 4. Gozen rokuji ni wa okimasen.   5. Sashimi wa tabemasen.   6. Tôkyô ni wa arimasen. 7. Kariforunia ni wa arimasen.   8. Kaisha ni wa imasen.

7.3. 1. gozen niji nijuppun   2. gogo yoji jûroppun   3. gozen goji yonjuppun or rokuji nijuppun mae   4. gogo rokuji han or rokuji sanjuppun   5. gozen sanji gojûnana fun or yoji sanpun mae   6. gogo shichiji nifun   7. gozen hachiji yonjûgo fun or kuji jûgo fun mae 8. gogo kuji nijûkyû fun

Summing Up:

1. You: Gogo kuji juppun kara desu. . . . You: Jûji gojuppun made desu (OR Jûichiji juppun mae made desu.)   2. You: Watashi wa itsumo shichiji yonjûgo fun no densha ni norimasu. . . . You: Hachiji jûgo fun ni tsukimasu. (Here you start off with *watashi wa* because you are comparing yourself to Mr. Sone.)   3. You: Hai, tabemasu. . . . You: Sumisu-san wa niku o tabemasu ga, Uiruson-san wa tabemasen.

CHAPTER 8

8.1a. 1. Kinô, tegami o kakimashita.   2. Kinô, atarashii rajio o kaimashita.   3. Kinô, Furansu ryôri o tabemashita.   4. Kinô, Kyôto ni dekakemashita.   5. Kinô, sushi o tsukurimashita.   6. Kinô, gozen goji ni okimashita.   7. Kinô, omoshiroi eiga o mimashita. 8. Kinô, tomodachi ni shashin o misemashita.   9. Kinô, dekimashita.   10. Kinô wa nichiyôbi deshita.

8.1b. 1. Iie, kakimasen deshita.   2. Iie, tabemasen deshita.   3. Iie, kaimasen deshita. 4. Iie, shimasen deshita.   5. Iie, nomimasen deshita.   6. Iie, ikimasen deshita.   6. Iie, ikimasen deshita.   7. Iie, imasen deshita.   8. Iie, yomimasen deshita.

8.1c. 1. Samukatta desu.   2. Atsukatta desu.   3. Nagakatta desu.   4. Mijikakatta desu. 5. Yasukatta desu.   6. Muzukashikatta desu.   7. Omokatta desu.   8. Akarukatta desu.

8.1d. 1. Samuku nakatta desu OR Samuku arimasen deshita. (Either form is fine in all cases.)   2. Atsuku nakatta desu.   3. Nagaku arimasen deshita.   4. Mijikaku nakatta desu. 5. Yasuku arimasen deshita.   6. Muzukashiku nakatta desu.   7. Omoku arimasen deshita. 8. Akaruku nakatta desu.

8.2a. 1. Shokudô de hirugohan o tabemashita.   2. Kôen de tenisu o shimashita.   3. Nagisa de hon o yomimashita.   4. Suupaa de niku o kaimashita.   5. Kuruma no naka de ongaku o kikimashita.   6. Nihon de karate o naraimashita.   7. Terebi de eiga o mimashita.   8. Kuji kara sanji made ginkô de shigoto o shimashita.   9. Hoteru de o-cha o nomimashita.
10. Uchi de sushi o tsukurimashita.
8.3. 1. F   2. F   3. T   4. T   5. F   6. F   7. T   8. F

Summing Up:

1. a. wa, ni, ni.   b. wa, no.   c. ga, o,   d. wa, o   e. wa, kara, made   f. no, ni, ga, no   g. wa
h. wa, ni, wa, ni,   i. no, wa, no, ni   2. a. You: Okinawa e ikimashita. . . .You: Totemo tanoshikatta desu. Mainichi oyogimashita. .... You: Iie, kikimasen deshita.   b. You: Shinjuku de eiga o mimashita. ...You: Amari omoshiroku nakatta desu (OR Amari omoshiroku arimasen deshita). ... You: Uchi e kaerimashita.

CHAPTER 9

9.1. 1. Takushii noriba mo arimasu ka?   2. Eki no mae ni mo arimasu ka?   3. Shibuya de mo kaimono o shimashita ka?   4. Nomimono mo urimashita ka?   5. Doitsugo mo benkyô shimashita ka?   6. Furansu de mo (Furansugo o) benkyô shimashita ka?   7. Ishida-san mo Suisu de Furansugo o benkyô shimashita ka?   8. Kyôto mo Nara mo omoshirokatta desu ka?
9.2. 1. November 3   2. May 5   3. April 29   4. September 15   5. Ichigatsu tsuitachi desu.
6. Nigatsu jûyokka desu.   7. (Answers will vary)   8. Shichigatsu yokka desu.   9. Jûgatsu sanjûichinichi desu.   10–14. (Answers will vary.)
9.3. 1. (Hotchikissu wa) mittsu arimasu.   2. Rooru pan o muttsu kaimashita.   3. (Kono kamibukuro no naka ni) booru ga nanatsu arimasu.   4. Kono koohii-jawan o futatsu tsukaimashita.   5. Iie, hitotsu (dake) tabemashita.   6. Ee, (ano bideo o) zenbu mimashita.
7. . . . Sandoitchi o yottsu kudasai.   8. Ee, takusan kikimashita.
9.4. 1. Okane ga arimasen kara...   2. Takakatta desu kara....   3. Hasegawa-san ga ikimashita kara...   4. Minna shiken ni shippai shimashita kara. . .   5. Minna shiken ni gôkaku shimashita kara...   6. Kyô wa ano gakusei wa daigaku ni ikimasen deshita kara...

Summing Up:

1. You: Raigetsu no futsuka desu. (OR Raigetsu no futsuka ni dekakemasu.) . . . Nogata-san to (issho ni) ikimasu.   2. You: Rokugatsu tooka ni dekakemasu. ... You: Kugatsu nijûyokka ni modorimasu. ... You: Mochiron, hikôki de ikimasu.   3. You: Sumimasen ga, sono rooru pan wa ikura desuka? ....You: Jaa, (OR Sô desu ne.) Itsutsu kudasai (OR Itsutsu o-negai shimasu).

CHAPTER 10

10.1. 1. Kore wa fukuzatsu na kikai desu.   2. Kore wa kantan na mondai desu.   3. Kore wa kirei na doresu desu.   4. Kore wa taisetsu na shorui desu.   5. Kore wa kanpeki na chakuriku deshita.   6. Kono kikai wa fukuzatsu desu.   7. Kono mondai wa kantan desu.   8. Kono doresu wa kirei desu.   9. Kono shorui wa taisetsu desu.   10. Kono chakuriku wa kanpeki deshita.
10.2. (These are all opinion questions, so there are no established right answers.)

10.3a.

Polite Form	Dictionary Form	-*te* Form	Meaning
iremasu	ireru	irete	put in, include
shimemasu	shimeru	shimete	close
akemasu	akeru	akete	open
tarimasu	tariru	tarite	be sufficient
kimasu	kiru	kite	wear
karimasu	kariru	karite	borrow, rent

10.3b.

Polite Form	Dictionary Form	-*te* Form	Meaning
keshimasu	kesu	keshite	extinguish, turn off
naoshimasu	naosu	naoshite	fix, repair
otoshimasu	otosu	otoshite	drop
kashimasu	kasu	kashite	lend, rent out
sagashimasu	sagasu	sagashite	look for

10.3c.

Polite Form	Dictionary Form	-*te* Form	Meaning
nakimasu	naku	naite	cry
manekimasu	maneku	maneite	beckon
arukimasu	aruku	aruite	walk
ugokimasu	ugoku	ugoite	move around
nozokimasu	nozoku	nozoite	omit

10.3d.

Polite Form	Dictionary Form	-*te* Form	Meaning
oyogimasu	oyogu	oyoide	swim
isogimasu	isogu	isoide	hurry
kogimasu	kogu	koide	row
kasegimasu	kasegu	kaseide	earn
nugimasu	nugu	nuide	take off shoes or clothing

10.3e.

Polite Form	Dictionary Form	-*te* Form	Meaning
yomimasu	yomu	yonde	read
yorokobimasu	yorokobu	yorokonde	be happy
shinimasu	shinu	shinde	die
nomimasu	nomu	nonde	drink
hagemimasu	hagemu	hagende	make an effort
fumimasu	fumu	funde	step on
narabimasu	narabu	narande	get in line
musubimasu	musubu	musunde	bind
asobimasu	asobu	asonde	play, goof off

10.3f.

Polite Form	Dictionary Form	-*te* Form	Meaning
arimasu	aru	atte	be located
urimasu	uru	utte	sell
norimasu	noru	notte	ride, board
hashirimasu	hashiru	hashitte	run
kaerimasu	kaeru	kaette	return home
machimasu	matsu	matte	wait
narimasu	naru	natte	become
magarimasu	magaru	magatte	turn (a corner)
mekurimasu	mekuru	mekutte	turn [pages]
kezurimasu	kezuru	kezutte	sharpen
orimasu	oru	otte	break, bend
toorimasu	tooru	tootte	pass through
okorimasu	okoru	okotte	get angry
tachimasu	tatsu	tatte	stand up
kirimasu	kiru	kitte	cut
majirimasu	majiru	majitte	be mixed
kerimasu	keru	kette	kick
shaberimasu	shaberu	shabette	talk

10.3g.

Polite Form	Dictionary Form	-*te* Form	Meaning
araimasu	arau	aratte	wash
iimasu	iu	itte	say
nuguimasu	nuguu	nugutte	wipe
omoimasu	omou	omotte	think, have an opinion
aimasu	au	atte	meet
waraimasu	warau	waratte	laugh
tsukaimasu	tsukau	tsukatte	use
chigaimasu	chigau	chigatte	be different
suimasu	suu	sutte	sip
nuimasu	nuu	nutte	sew
hiroimasu	hirou	hirotte	pick up
sasoimasu	sasou	sasotte	invite
mayoimasu	mayou	mayotte	wander

10.4a. 1. Basu ni notte kudasai.   2. Basu o orite kudasai.   3. Kippu o katte kudasai.   4. Ano tatemono o mite kudasai.   5. Kono teepu o kiite kudasai.   6. O-namae o kaite kudasai. 7. Pasupooto o misete kudasai.   8. Hayaku nete kudasai.   9. Gozen rokuji ni okite kudasai. **10.4b.** 1. Enpitsu ya nooto o katte (kara), jugyô ni demashita.   2. Daigaku o sotsugyô shite kara, Nihon no kaisha ni shûshoku shimashita.   3. Kitte o katte kara, tegami o yûbin de dashimashita.   4. Kitte o takusan shûshû shite kara, urimashita.   5. Toshokan e itte benkyô shimashita.   6. Terebi o mite kara, nemashita.   7. Puuru de oyoide kara, atama o araimashita.   8. Hikôki o orite kara, tomodachi ni denwa shimashita.

Summing Up:

1. You: Iie, amari taisetsu ja arimasen (nai desu).   2. You: Iie, suiei wa suki desu ga, amari jôzu ja nai desu.   3. You: Densha de Kamakura e itte kimashita. . . . You: Ee, mimashita. Soshite Daibutsu o mite kara, chiisai resutoran de hirugohan o tabemashita. ... You: Sore kara, kirei na o-tera ya jinja o takusan mimashita.   4. a. oyonde   b. moide   c. yaite   d. tashite   e. kikoete   f. agatte   g. They don't end in -iru or -eru.

REVIEW CHAPTERS 6–10

1. Kayôbi to mokuyôbi deshita.   2. Itsuka ni (ronbun o) dashimashita.   3. Jûhachi nichi deshita. Nichiyôbi deshita.   4. Jûkunichi deshita. Getsuyôbi deshita.   5. Nijûyokka ni haikingu ni ikimashita. Doyôbi deshita.   6. Jûyokka deshita.   7. Paatii wa mikka deshita. 8. Sanjûnichi deshita. Kin'yôbi deshita.   9 a. uso   b. uso   c. uso   d. hontô   e. hontô   f. uso   10. You: Kaimono o shimashita. ....You: Shatsu o takusan kaimashita. ...You: Marui de suteki na buutsu mo mimashita ga. ..   You: Demo, totemo takakatta desu kara, kaimasen deshita. . . . You: Niman gosen en deshita. .... You: Kimu-san to issho ni ikimashita. 11. You: Yattsu arimasu. .... You: Tonari no kyôshitsu ni mo isu ga arimasu yo.

CHAPTER 11

11.1a. 1. Nijô-jô desu ka? Totemo chikai desu ne.   2. Asoko ni shingô ga arimasu ne? 3. Kono michi o watatte, hyaku meetoru massugu ikimasu.   4. Eki no aru kôsaten o hidari e magarimasu.   5. Gasorin sutando no tonari no tatemono ga hon'ya desu.
11.1b. 1. Tsugi no kado o hidari e magarimasu.   2. Shingô o migi e magatte, hyaku meetoru ikimasu.   3. Tsukiatari o hidari e magatte, happyaku meetoru massugu ikimasu.
4. Nibanme no shingô o migi e magatte, tsugi no chiisai yokomichi ni hairimasu.   5. Asoko ni hoteru ga arimasu ne? Yum Yum Resutoran wa ano hoteru no naka ni arimasu.
11.1c. 1. Kono ginkô no mukaigawa ni hon'ya ga arimasu yo.   2. Denki seihin no mise wa kono hon'ya no tonari ni arimasu.   3. Denki seihin no mise o dete, hidari e magariasu. Yamato Hoteru wa sanbanme no kôsaten ni arimasu.   4. Hoteru o dete, migi e magaraisu. Tsukiatari o migi e magarimasu. Nandemo-ya Depaato wa tsugi no kado ni arimasu.
5. Depaato o dete, migi e magarimasu. Gofukuten wa nibanme no kado no hidarigawa ni arimasu.
11.2. 1. Amanda Sumisu wa teepu o kiite imasu.   2. Zaini Abuduuru wa hon o yonde imasu. 3. Mekishikojin no gakusei wa sakkaa o shite imasu.   4. Kimu Byon Iru wa koora o nonde imasu.   5. Pooru du Pon wa gitaa o hiite imasu.   6. Wan Pei Jin wa Nuuin Mi Ramu to hanashite imasu.   7. Kaato Shumitto wa benkyô shite imasu.   8. Tove Hansen wa nete imasu.   9. Jooji Masaera wa sakkaa no shiai o mite imasu.   10. Teramura Chieko wa Takao e itte imasu.   11. Ikeda Masaru wa Mitaka e kaette imasu.
11.3. 1. d   2. c   3. d   4. b   5. a   6. f   7. d   8. e
11.4. 1. Hai, ame ga furu deshô.   2. Hai, Furansugo ga wakaru deshô.   3. Hai, gôkaku suru deshô.   4. Hai, nete iru deshô.   5. Hai, sukii ga dekiru deshô.   6. Hai, muzukashii deshô. 7. Hai, benri ja nai deshô.   8. Hai, Takahashi sensei deshô.   9. Hai, shashin o toru deshô.

Summing Up:

1. a. Ano basu ni notte, Naitokyappu Hoteru no mae de orite kudasai.   b. Hoteru ni haitte, hidari e magatte kudasai.   c. Michi o watatte, asoko de matte ite kudasai.
2. You: Kikoemasu ga, wakarimasen. Kankoku go o hanashite imasu ka? .... You: Ikeda-san wa erai desu ne.

CHAPTER 12

12.1. Sasaki-san no o-kaasan no Kei-san to o-tôsan no Ichirô-san wa (o-)futari to mo (go-)kenzai desu. O-neesan no Michiko-san wa nijû nen mae ni Yamada Kenji-san to kekkon shite, o-kosan ga futari imasu. Ue no o-kosan wa otoko no ko de, Yôichi-san to iimasu. Shita no o-kosan wa onna no ko de, Emi-san to iimasu. Sasaki-san no oigosan no Yôichi-san wa mô sugu daigaku ni hairimasu ga, meigosan no Emi-san wa mada kôkôsei desu. Sasaki-san wa okusan no Etsuko-san to o-jôsan no Mika-san to sannin de Yokohama no manshon ni sunde imasu. (You could also refer to Yôichi as Yôichi kun and Emi and Mika as Emi-chan and Mika-chan.)

12.2. 1. Kei-san wa nanajussai desu.   2. Kenji-san wa yonjû nanasai desu.   3. Michiko-san wa yonjû gosai desu.   4. Yoshimasa-san wa yonjussai desu.   5. Etsuko-san wa sanjû go sai desu. 6. Yôichi-san wa jûhassai desu.   7. Emi-san wa jûgosai desu.   8. Mika-san wa jûissai desu. 9. Aoki-san wa nijû nanasai de kekkon shimashita.   10. Hatachi de hajimete Nihon e kimashita.   11. Kyûjû kyûsai de nakunarimashita.

12.3 1. Nihon e ikitai desu.   2. Byôin e ikitaku nai desu.   3. Tomodachi wa Yooroppa e ikitagatte imasu.   4. Koora o nomitaku nai desu.   5. Shamisen o naraitai desu ka? 6. Gakuseitachi wa kaeritagatte imasu.   7. Yukata ga hoshii desu.   8. Keitai denwa wa hoshiku nai desu.   9. Imôto wa jitensha o hoshigatte imasu.   10. Dentaku ga hoshii desu.

12.4. 1. Chizu o kaimashô.   2. Chikatetsu de ikimashô.   3. Rajio o kikimashô.   4. Kono mise ni hairimashô.   5. Hyaku meetoru oyogimashô.   6. Tegami o kakimashô ka?   7. Kono kyôkasho o benkyô shimashô ka?   8. Shodô o renshû shimashô ka?   9. Kono bideo o mimashô ka?   10. Kono densha ni norimashô ka?

Summing Up:

1. You: Sô desu ne. Sutereo ga hoshii desu ne. ...You: Ano atarashii eiga mo mitai desu ne. 2. You: Iie, Amerika ni imasu (or orimasu). . . . You: Chichi wa isha de, haha wa kyôshi desu. ... You: Ani to imôto ga hitori zutsu imasu. ... You: Chigaimasu. Bengoshi desu. ... You: Mada kôkôsei desu.

CHAPTER 13

13.1. 1. takaku narimashita   2. omoshiroku natte imasu   3. muzukashiku narimasu 4. bengoshi ni narimashita   5. okotte imasu   6. sensei ni natte imasu   7. tsukarete imasu 8. shitsurei ni natte imasu   9. fukuzatsu ni narimasu   10. kaeru ni narimashita

13.2. 1. Shashin o totte mo ii desu ka?   2. Enpitsu o karite mo ii desu ka?   3. Kono sandoitchi o tabete mo ii desu ka?   4. Kono heya de benkyô shite mo ii desu ka?   5. Kôen de sakkaa o shite mo ii desu ka?   6. Kono shinbun o yonde mo ii desu ka?   7. Enpitsu de kaite mo ii desu ka?   8. Kuruma o aratte mo ii desu ka?   9. Denwa o tsukatte mo ii desu ka? 10. Bengoshi ni sôdan shite mo ii desu ka?

13.3a. 1. Doko ni mo imasen.   2. Dare mo tsukatte imasen.   3. Nani mo tabemasen deshita. 4. Dore mo mimasen deshita.   5. Dare mo araimasen deshita.   6. Nani mo kiite imasen.

13.3b. 1. Nani mo mimasen deshita.   2. Doko de mo utte imasen.   3. Eigo wa dare mo hanashimasen.   4. Nani mo kaimasen.   5. Nani mo kakimasen deshita.

13.4a. 1. Kono kyôkasho to sono kyôkasho to, dochira ga ii deus ka?   2. Sukiyaki to tenpura to, dochira no hô ga o-suki desu ka?   3. Furansugo to Supeingo to, dochira ga o-jôzu desu ka?   4. Chikatetsu to basu to, dochira no hô ga hayai desu ka?   5. Sapporo wa Tôkyô yori samui desu. (No context is given for these sentences, so the pattern exemplified by Tôkyô yori Sapporo no hô ga samui desu is also fine for all the rest of these sentences.) 6. Chikatetsu wa basu yori hayai desu.   7. Ryokan wa hoteru yori omoshiroi desu.   8. Kanji wa hiragana yori fukuzatsu desu.   9. Nihonjin no sensei wa Amerikajin no sensei yori ooi desu.

13.4b. 1. Kanji wa hiragana yori muzukashii desu. Hiragana wa kanji hodo muzukashiku arimasen.   2. Paatii wa shukudai yori tanoshii desu. Shukudai wa paatii hodo tanoshiku arimasen.   3. Hawai wa Nihon yori chikai desu. Nihon wa Hawai hodo chikaku nai desu. 4. Raion wa nezumi yori kowai desu. Nezumi wa raion hodo kowaku nai desu.   5. Kono shashin wa hoka no shashin yori kirei desu. Hoka no shashin wa kono shashin hodo kirei ja arimasen.

Summing Up:

A. 1. Shiroi inu wa kuroi inu yori chiisai desu. or Kuroi inu wa shiroi inu hodo chiisaku nai desu.   2. Sumisu-san no uchi wa Joonzu-san no uchi yori furui desu. or Joonzu-san no uchi wa Sumisu-san no uchi hodo furuku arimasen.   3. Kono nezumi wa sono nezumi yori atama ga ii desu. or Sono nezumi wa kono nezumi hodo atama ga yoku nai desu.   4. Kono uma wa hoka no uma yori hayai desu. or Hoka no uma wa kono uma hodo hayaku arimasen. 5. Hokkaidô wa Okinawa yori samui desu. or Okinawa wa Hokkaidô hodo samuku arimasen. B. 1. You: Sô desu ka? .... You: Môshiwake gozaimasen. Nido to shimasen.   2. You: Sô desu ne. You: Ee, Minesota wa Tôkyô yori samui desu. ... You: Iie, Shiberia hodo samuku arimasen.

CHAPTER 14

14.1a. 1. Dare de mo wakarimasu.   2. Doko e de mo aruite ikimasu.   3. Nan de mo utte imasu.   4. Dore de mo tsukatte imasu.   5. Itsu de mo uchi e kite kudasai.   6. Dochira de mo suki desu.   7. Dore de mo suki desu.   8. Dono Nihonjin de mo shitte imasu.
14.1b.1. doko ka   2. nani ka   3. dare ka   4. dare ka   5. nani ka   6. dare ka
14.2a. 1. yakanai   2. ugokanai   3. kasanai   4. sagasanai   5. tatanai   6. nomanai 7. erabanai 8. yobanai 9. naranai   10. noranai   11. kaeranai   12. uranai   13. awanai 14. hirowanai 15. nuguwanai 16. misenai   17. akinai   18. hashiranai
14.2b. 1. Mainichi hirune o suru deshô.   2. Piza wa tabenai deshô.   3. Kaisha ni ikanai deshô.   4. Denwa ni denai deshô.   5. Rajio o kiku deshô.   6. Sake wa nomanai deshô. 7. Apaato wa katazukenai deshô.   8. Oyoganai deshô.   9. O-kaasan to issho ni terebi o miru deshô.   10. Hon o yomu deshô.
14.2c. 1. E ni sawaranaide kudasai.   2. Uma ni esa o yaranaide kudasai.   3. Kenka shinaide kudasai.   4. Kamera o wasurenaide kudasai.   5. Asagohan ni okurenaide kudasai. 6. Sono takushii ni noranaide kudasai.
14.3. 1. agemashita   2. agemashita   3. kuremashita   4. sashiagemashita   5. yarimashita 6. kudasaimashita   7. kuremashita   8. agemashita (or yarimashita)
14.4. 1. Hakubutsukan e tenrankai o mi ni ikimashita.   2. Boroichi e furui hon o uri ni ikimashita.   3. Puuru e oyogi ni ikimashita.   4. Kurabu e odori ni kimashita.   5. Kankoku e eigo o oshie ni ikiashita.   6. Karaoke kurabu e uta o utai ni kimashita.   7. Hawai e shôsetsu o kaki ni kaerimashita.   8. Toshokan e atarashii zasshi o yomi ni kimashita.

Summing Up:

1. Dare mo wakarimasen or Dare de mo wakarimasu.   2. Eigakan e eiga o mi ni ikimasen ka? 3. Neko ni sakana o yarimashita.   4. Ame ga futte imasu kara, dare mo ikanai deshô. 5. Otôto wa watashi ni suteki na shatsu o kuremashita.   6. Ishida-san wa Tanaka-san ni chokoreeto o agemashita.   7. Asoko de wa nani mo tsukurimasen.   8. Doko ka (Nani ka) oishii resutoran wa arimasen ka?   9. Dare mo shirimasen.   10. Takahashi Sensei wa

watashitachi ryûgakusei ni kirei na sensu o kudasaimashita.   11. Abunai desu kara, tsukawanaide kudasai.   12. Abuduuru-san wa hamu o tabenai deshô.

CHAPTER 15

15.1. 1. —itta   2. —osoku natta   3. ...ma ni awanakatta   4. ... kita.   5. .... tomodachi ni atta.   6. ...tegami o kaita   7. ...yonda.   8. ...katazuketa....shinakatta.

15.2a. 1. Sandoitchi o tsukuru koto ga dekimasu.   2. Shôsetsu o kaku koto wa dekimasen.   3. Doyôbi ni iku koto ga dekimasu.   4. Ashita wa renshû dekimasen. 5. Nihongo no shinbun o yomu koto ga dekimasu.   6. Gitaa o hiku koto wa dekimasen. 7. Kaigi ni ma ni au koto ga dekimasu.   8. Eigo o oshieru koto wa dekimasen.

15.2b. 1. Sandoitchi ga tsuremasu.   2. Shôsetsu wa kakemasen.   3. Doyôbi ni ikemasu. 4. Ashita wa renshû dekimasen. (The potential of suru is dekiru in both constructions.) 5. Nihongo no shinbun ga yomemasu.   6. Gitaa wa hikemasen.   7. Kaigi ni ma ni aemasu. 8. Eigo wa oshieraremasen.

15.3. 1. "Juken" wa dô iu imi desu ka? (The word means "taking tests.")   2. "Taikutsu" wa dô iu imi desu ka? (The word means "tedium.")   3. "Kyûkei" wa dô iu imi desu ka? (The word means "rest period" or "break.")   4. "Nyûyoku" wa dô iu imi desu ka? (The word means "taking a Japanese-style bath.")   5. "Same" wa dô iu imi desu ka? (The word means "shark.")

15.4. 1. a. Totemo ii chizu ga aru n desu.   b. Takahashi Sensei ga kudasatta n desu. 2. a. Doko de katta n desu ka?   b. Totemo benri na n desu.   3. O-naka ga itai n desu.

Summing Up:

A. 1. Hakubutsukan e atarashii tenrankai o mi ni itta. Hakubutsukan no shokudô de hirugohan o tabeta. O-miyage mo takusan katta. Sore kara, chikatetsu de ryô e kaetta. Chan-san to Abuduuru-san to issho ni bangohan o tabete kara, shukudai o shita. Sore kara, ongaku o kiita. Jûichiji ni neta.

B. ...You: Gitaa wa hikemasen ga (or hikenai kedo), piano wa hikemasu (or hikeru). ...You: Donna ongaku ga o-suki (desu ka)? ... You: Hôgaku wa dô iu imi (desu ka)?

C. 1. Neko ga sakana o tabeta n desu.   2. Kodomo ga koronda n desu.   3. Kono hito wa saifu o wasureta n desu or Kono hito wa o-kane ga nai n desu.   4. Kono hito wa nebô shita n desu.   5. Basu ga konai n desu or Basu ga osoi n desu.   6. Kono futari wa Hawai e itte kita n desu or Kono futari wa Hawai kara kita n desu or Kono futari wa Hawai ni ryokô shite kita n desu.

REVIEW CHAPTERS 11–15

1. a. Densha de Ichigaya e ikimasu.   b. Eki o dete, michi o watarimasu.   c. Gojû meetoru massugu ikimasu.   d. Ginkô no aru kado o migi e magarimasu.   e. Tsugi no kado o hidari e magarimasu. YWCA wa hidarigawa ni arimasu.   2. Kono hitotachi wa Kabuki o mite imasu. Kono onna no hito wa geisha deshô. Kono otoko no hito wa sakana o utte iru deshô. Kono otoko no hito wa geta o tsukutte imasu. Kono onna no hito wa shamisen o hiite imasu.

3. You: Shodô to karate o naraitai desu. ....You: Kyûshû e ikitai desu.   4. You: Kono kasa o dôzo. ...You: Ii desu yo. Watashi wa irimasen kara, tsukatte mo ii desu.   5. Akihabara e konpyuuta o kai ni itta. Amerika no konpyuuta mo Nihon no konpyuuta mo takusan atta. Amerika no konpyuuta wa Nihon no konpyuuta yori takakatta kedo, boku wa Amerika no konpyuuta o katta. Amerika e kaette kara tsukaitai n(o) da. Kono konpyuuta no Nihongo no opereetingu shisutemu de wa Nihongo mo Eigo mo kaku koto ga dekiru (or kakeru).

CHAPTER 16

16.1. 1 (giving) Tomodachi ga kasetto teepu o kuremashita. (receiving) Watashi wa tomodachi ni kasetto teepu o moraimashita.   2. (giving) Gakuseitachi wa sensei ni hana o sashiagemashita. (receiving) Sensei wa gakuseitachi ni hana o moraimashita.   3. (giving) Tanaka-san wa Suzuki-san ni iyaringu o agemashita. (receiving) Suzuki-san wa Tanaka-san ni iyaringu o moraimashita.   4. (giving) Sensei wa suisenjô o kaite kudasaimashita. (receiving) Watashi wa sensei ni suisenjô o kaite itadakimashita.   5. (giving) Yamaguchi-san wa Chan-san ni Nihon no uta o oshiete agemashita. (receiving) Chan-san wa Yamaguchi-san ni Nihon no uta o oshiete moraimashita.

16.2a. 1. atatakakute ii heya   2. yasukute kantan na konpyuuta   3. furukute yûmei na o-tera   4. chiisakute kawaii kodomo   5. ookikute kowai inu   6. amakute oishii orenji   7. raku de ii seikatsu   8. fukuzatsu de muzukashii mondai   9. kuwashikute ii chizu   10. nagakute tsumaranai eiga

16.2b. 1. Sôji shite yokatta!   2. Wasurete hazukashii desu.   3. Yoyaku shinakute mo ii desu.   4. Samukute tamarimasen.   5. Koibito ga shiken ni gôkaku shite ureshii desu.   6. Ikanakute mo ii desu ka?   7. Wasurenakute yokatta!   8. Atsukute tamarimasen.   9. Koronde hazukashii desu.   10. Denwa shinakute mo ii desu.

16.2c. 1. Te o arawanakute wa ikemasen.   2. Kusuri o nomanakute wa ikemasen.   3. Iie, kurejitto kaado o tsukawanakute wa ikemasen.   4. Iie, ashita shukudai o dasanakute wa ikemasen.   5. Iie, kutsu o nuganakute wa ikemasen.   6. Shû ni rokkai keiko shinakute wa ikemasen.

16.3. Answers will vary, but all of them should be in one of the following two forms: 1) PAST TENSE OF THE DICTIONARY FORM + *koto ga arimasu* or 2) PAST TENSE OF THE DICTIONARY FORM + *koto wa arimasen.*

16.4. 1. Sushi to sukiyaki to tenpura no naka de, dore ga ichiban oishii desu ka?   2. Yakyû to basukettobooru to futtobooru no naka de, dore ga ichiban omoshiroi desu ka?   3. Sekai no kuni no naka de, dore ga ichiban ookii desu ka?   4. Amerika no toshi no naka de, dore ga ichiban jinkô ga ooi desu ka?   5. Kanji no naka de, dore ga ichiban oboeyasui desu ka?   6. Nihon no kankôchi no naka de, dore ga ichiban yûmei desu ka?   7. Kono kurasu no gakusei no naka de, dare ga ichiban atama ga ii desu ka?

Summing Up:

In the first two exercises, the first alternative given is the dictionary form with the expected *no da no bun.* The second alternative is in the *-masu* form.)

1. You: Iie, Teramura-san ni kaite moratta no. (or ...kaite moratta n desu or...kaite moraimashita.)

2. You: Yokohama ni iku koto wa aru kedo, Kamakura ni itta koto wa nai. (Yokohama e iku koto wa arimasu kedo, Kamakura ni itta koto wa arimasen.)

3. You: Dono kamera ga ichiban tsukaiyasui desu ka? ... You: Ikura desu ka? .... You: Niman nanasen gohyaku en desu ka? Keesu wa kawanakute mo ii desu ka?

4. You: Shitei seki wa yoyaku shinakute wa ikenai n desu. (...shinakute wa ikemasen.)

CHAPTER 17

17.1. 1. Ten'in ni kiita hô ga ii desu.   2. Sono furui kuruma o utta hô ga ii desu.   3. Kutsu o nuida hô ga ii desu.   4. Chotto matta hô ga ii desu.   5. O-mawari-san to kenka shinai hô ga ii desu.   6. Sonna (or, sô iu) sakana o tabenai hô ga ii desu.   7. Motto benkyô shita hô ga ii desu.   8. Mainichi undô shita hô ga ii desu.   9. Ongaku o naratta hô ga ii desu. 10. Morimoto-san ni denwa shita hô ga ii desu.

17.2a. (answers given alternately in dictionary form and *-masu* form, but either is correct)

1. Taifû ga kuru ka mo shiremasen. Taifû ga kuru ni chigai arimasen.   2. Date-san wa kekkon shite iru ka mo shirenai. Date-san wa kekkon shite iru ni chigai nai.   3. Kôtsû jiko ni atta ka mo shiremasen. Kôtsû jiko ni atta ni chigai arimasen.   4. Nani mo wakaranai ka mo shirenai. Nani mo wakaranai ni chigai nai.   5. Dorobô wa mado kara haitte kita ka mo shiremasen. Dorobô wa mado kara haitte kita ni chigai arimasen.   6. Ashita wa ii tenki ka mo shirenai. Ashita wa ii tenki ni chigai nai.   7. Amari tooku nai ka mo shiremasen. Amari tooku nai ni chigai arimasen.   8. Gakusei datta ka mo shirenai. Gakusei datta ni chigai nai.
17.2b. 1. Omoshiroi eiga da to omoimasu.   2. Mainichi oyogi ni ikitai to omoimasu. 3. Kimura-san wa Nikkeijin da to omoimasu.   4. Abunai to omimasu.   5. Ano hon wa totemo tsumaranakatta to omoimasu.   6. Ano gakkô no senseitachi wa totemo shinsetsu darô to omoimasu.   7. Sonna koto wa dare de mo dekiru to omoimasu.   8. Ano depaato de wa nan de mo utte iru to omoimasu.   9. Suzuki-san wa manshon ni sunde iru to omoimasu. 10. Sone-san wa go nenkan Amerika ni ita to omoimasu.

Summing Up:
1. a. Kanji o renshû shita hô ga ii desu.   b. Kaetta hô ga ii desu.   c. Kuruma o kawanai hô ga ii desu.   d. Ginkô ni shûshoku shinai hô ga ii desu.   2. a. Tamura-san wa Nikkeijin ka mo shiremasen.   b. Ashita no shiken wa muzukashii ka mo shiremasen.   c. Sumisu-san wa asoko ni iru ka mo shiremasen.   d. O-kane wa nai ka mo shiremasen.
3. a. Tamura-san wa Nikkeijin ni chigai arimasen.   b. Ashita no shiken wa muzukashii ni chigai arimasen.   c. Sumisu-san wa asoko ni iru ni chigai arimasen.   d. O-kane wa nai ni chigai arimasen.   4. a. Tamura-san wa Nikkeijin da to omoimasu.   b. Ashita no shiken wa muzukashii to omoimasu.   c. Sumisu-san wa asoko ni iru to omoimasu.   d. O-kane wa nai to omoimasu.   5. You: Yasukute oishii resutoran ni haitta hô ga ii to omou. . . .You: Chûgoku ryôri no naka de, Shisen ryôri ga ichiban oishii to omou (wa) yo. ... You: Ngan Fa? Oishii ni chigai nai.

CHAPTER 18

18.1. 1. Yûmei na hito desu.   2. Shachô wa koohii o nonde kara, kaerimashita.   3. Koko e kite kudasai.   4. Sushi o tabemasen ka?   5. Shachô wa ashita Sapporo e iku deshô.
6. Sensei, hakubutsukan no atarashii tenrankai o mimashita ka?   7. Kore wa irimasen kara, dôzo, tsukatte kudasai.   8. Nanji no densha ni norimashita ka?   9. O-namae o itte kudasai. 10. Dô shita n desu ka?   11. Tekunoporii no Kimura-san no denwa bangô o shitte imasu ka?
18.2. 1. Takahashi Sensei kara kono hon o karimashita.   2. Fukuzatsu na shitsumon desu ne. Sensei ni kiita hô ga ii to omoimasu.   3. Zenbu todokemashô ka?   4. Kinô, tekunoporii no Saeki-san to hanashimashita.   5. Chotto mite kimasu.   6. Kono chihô no kankôchi wa yoku shitte imasu ga, Hokkaidô wa zenzen shirimasen.   7. Itsu ka Takahashi Sensei ni aitai to omoimasu.   8. Shitsurei shimashita.   9. Kore wa totemo ii konpyuuta desu ga, monitaa ga arimasen kara, yasuku natte imasu.   10. Ryôshin o shôkai shimasu.

JAPANESE-ENGLISH VOCABULARY

A number (1) after a verb indicates that it is a one-step verb. Five-step verbs are marked only if they could be mistaken for one-step verbs or if there are two verbs, one five-step and the other one-step, that have identical dictionary forms.

abiru (1): to pour something over one's self; *shawaa o abiru*: to take a shower

abunai: dangerous

aida: interval, between; X *to* Y *no aida*: between X and Y

aikawarazu: as usual

akachan: baby

akai: red

Akasaka: a neighborhood in Tokyo

amai: sweet

amari (+ NEGATIVE): not very, not very much

ame: rain; *ame ga furu*: it rains

Amerika: the United States of America

ane: my older sister

ani: my older brother

anko; sweet bean paste

ano (+ NOUN): that (NOUN) over there

anzen (na): safe

aoi: blue, green

apaato: apartment

arau: wash

are: that one, that thing over there

arigatô: thank you; arigatô gozaimasu: thank you (more polite)

aru: [an inanimate object] is located, exists; NOUN₁ *wa* NOUN₂ *ga aru*: NOUN₁ has NOUN₂.

aruku: walk

asatte: the day after tomorrow

ase bisshori: drenched in sweat

ashita: tomorrow

asobu: to play, take it easy, goof around; *asobi ni iku*: to pay an informal visit

asoko: over there

atama: head; *atama ga ii*: is smart;

atama o arau: wash one's hair

atarashii: new

atatakai: pleasantly warm

atsui: hot

atsumaru: to gather into a group

atsusa ni mairu: to be overcome by the heat

azukaru: to take charge of, to take care of temporarily

baka (na): stupid, foolish, crazy

baree: ballet

beddo: Western-style bed

bengoshi: lawyer

benkyô suru: study

benri (na): convenient

bentô: box lunch, packed lunch

beruto: belt

betsu ni: not particularly

biru: Western-style building

biyôin: hair salon

boku: I (used by males only)

booru: ball

boroichi: flea market

bôshi: hat

Bosuton baggu: totebag with two handles

botchan: someone else's son (usually a child)

bukka: consumer prices

Burajiru: Brazil

butiiku: boutique

byôin: hospital

chakuriku: landing (of an airplane)

chichi: my father

chigau: to be different, to be mistaken

chiisai: small, little

chikai: near

chikaku: vicinity, nearby

chikatetsu: subway

chiketto: ticket for a performance

chizu: map

chokoreeto: chocolate

Chûgoku: China; *Chûgokujin*: Chinese person; *Chûgokugo*: Chinese language

da: dictionary form of *desu*

da kara: therefore

daibutsu: Great Buddha (statue)

daigaku: university, college

daigakuin: graduate school

dake: only, just; NOUN *dake*: only NOUN, just NOUN

dame (na): no good, worthless, not permitted

dandan: gradually

dansu paatii: a dance

dare: who; *dare ka*: someone; *dare mo* + NEGATIVE: no one; *dare de mo*: anyone

dasu: send out, put out, turn in

de mo: even so, still, yet; NOUN *de mo*: even NOUN, NOUN or something like it

dekiru (1): be able, be finished; *dekite iru*: is finished

dekiru dake: as much as possible

dengon: message

denki: electricity

denki seihin: electronic products

dentaku: calculator

denwa bangô: telephone number

denwa: telephone; *denwa o kakeru* (1): make a phone call; *denwa ni deru* (1): answer the phone

depaato: department store

dô: how? *Dô shita n desu ka?* What's going on? What happened to you?

Dô shimashô ka? What should I/we do?

dô itashimashite: you're welcome; it's no big deal

dochirasama: who? (most polite form)

Doitsu: Germany

doko: where? *doko ka*: somewhere;

doko de mo: anywhere and everywhere

dôkyûsei: classmate

donata: who? (honorific)

doresu: dress

dorobô: thief

doru: dollar

dôshite: why?

doyôbi: Saturday

dôzo: please do, please feel free, please go ahead

e: drawn or painted picture

ee: yes

eigakan: movie theater

eikaiwa: English conversation

eki: train, bus, or subway station

ekiin: station employee

en: yen

enpitsu: pencil

erai: impressive, distinguished

esa: animal food

Firipin: the Philippines

firumu: film (photographic)

fooku: fork

fuben (na): inconvenient

Fujisan: Mount Fuji

fukuro: bag, sack

fukuzatsu (na): complicated

fune: boat, ship

furu: fall (precipitation); *Ame ga futte iru:* It's raining; *Yuki ga futte iru:* It's snowing.

furui: old (not used in reference to people)

futari: two people

futatsu: two

futsuka: second day of the month

fûtô: envelope

gaikokugo: foreign language

gasorin sutando: gas station

genki (na); healthy, lively; *O-genki desu ka?*: Are you in good health?

geri suru: have diarrhea

geta: traditional Japanese clogs

getsuyôbi: Monday

ginkô: bank

gitaa: guitar

go: five

go-chisôsama deshita: Thank you for the food or drink.

Go-enryo kudasai.: Please refrain. Please don't do.

gofukuten: traditional clothing store

gogatsu: May

gogo: afternoon, P.M.

gôkaku suru: pass; *shiken ni gôkaku suru:* pass a test

go-kenzai (na): alive and well (polite)

gomen kudasai: good-bye (formal, on the telephone)

gozen: A.M.

guai: state, condition

hachi: eight

hachigatsu: August

haha: my mother

hai: yes

haikingu: hiking

hairu: enter; *o-furo ni hairu:* take a bath; *haitte kuru:* come in

hajimemashite: pleased to meet you

hajimete: for the first time

hako: box

haku: put on clothing over the legs (pants, shoes, etc.)

hakubutsukan: scientific or historical museum

hamu: ham

hana: flower

handobaggu: handbag, purse

hankachi: handkerchief

hashi (橋): bridge

hashi (箸): chopsticks

hatsuka: twentieth day of the month

hayai: fast, early

hazukashii: embarrassed, ashamed

heta (na): unskilled, bad at

heya: room

hidari: left; *hidarigawa:* left side (of a street, etc.); *hidari no hô:* left side

hidoi: severe

hiki: counter for small animals

hikidashi: drawer

hikôki: airplane

hiku: pull, play a stringed or keyboard instrument; *kaze o hiku:* catch a cold

hirune: nap; *hirune o suru:* take a nap

hito: person

hitori: one person, alone: *hitori de:* alone, by one's self

hitotsu: one

hôgen: dialect

hôhô: method

hoka (no): other; *Hoka ni nani ka?* Anything else?

hon: book

hon: counter for long, narrow objects

hondana: bookshelf

hoomu: railroad station platfom

hora: Look there!

hoteru: Western-style hotel

hyaku: one hundred

ichi: one

ichiban: first, most

ichigatsu: January

ii: good (*yoku, yokatta*)

iie: no

iku: go (*-te* form: *itte*)

ikura?: how much?

ima: now

imi: meaning; *Dô iu imi desu ka?:* What does it mean?

imôto: younger sister; *imôtosan:* someone else's younger sister

inu: dog

irasshaimase: welcome (said by store and restaurant personnel to customers)

ireru (1): put in, include

iru: [person or animal] is located, exists

isha: medical doctor

isogashii: busy

isu: chair

itadaku: humbly receive, humbly eat or drink; *itadakimasu:* (said before eating) itai: painful; *Atama ga itai.:* My head hurts.

itsu: when; *itsu ka:* sometime; *itsu de mo:* any time

itsuka: fifth day of the month

itsumo: always

itsutsu: five

itte irasshai: Good-bye (said by the person staying home to the person leaving)

itte kimasu: Good-bye (said when leaving your home or customary place temporarily)

iyaringu: earring

jaa: Well, then; *Jaa ne:* So long!

ji: o'clock; *ichiji:* one o'clock

jidai: era, years, times

jiinzu: jeans

jishin: earthquake

jisho: dictionary

jitensha: bicycle

jû: ten

jûgatsu: October

jugyô: class session

jûichigatsu: November

jûnigatsu: December

jôzu (na): skilled, good at

ka: (between nouns): or at the end of a sentence: it's a spoken question mark.

kaaten: curtain

kaban: briefcase, totebag

kabe: wall

kabin: vase

kado: corner (on a street)

kaeru (5): return (home or to one's usual place)

kaeru: frog

kagetsu: counter for months

kaidan: stairs

kaigai ryokô : overseas trip

kaigi: meeting

kaikan: a building that rents out rooms for meetings and parties

kaiketsu suru: solve

kaku: write

Kamakura: a small historic city about an hour south of Tokyo by train

kamera: camera

kami: paper

Kanada: Canada

Kankoku: South Korea

kanpeki (na); perfect

kantan (na): simple

Kantongo: Cantonese language

kaoiro: facial coloring

kara: (after NOUN or TIME): from; (after VERB or ADJECTIVE): because; (after *-te :*) after

kariru (1): borrow, rent

karuchaa sentaa: cultural center

kasa: umbrella

kasetto teepu: casette tape

kata: person (honorific)

katakoto gurai: just a few words (of a language)

katazukeru (1): tidy up, straighten up

kau: buy

kawaii: cute

kayôbi: Tuesday

kayou: commute

kaze: a cold or other respiratory infection; *kaze o hiite iru:* have a respiratory infection

keesu: carrying case

kekkon suru: get married; *kekkon shite iru:* is married

kekkô (na): fine; *Iie, kekkô desu.:* No thank you.

kenbutsu: sightseeing

kenka: argument

kenzai (na): alive and well

kesa: this morning

keshigomu: eraser (pencil or ink)

ki o tsukeru (1): be careful

kikai: machine

kikitori: listening comprehension

kikoeru (1): be audible, can hear

kiku: hear, ask, listen

kin'yôbi: Friday

kippu: ticket

kirai (na): disliked; NOUN *ga kirai desu.*: I dislike NOUN.

kirei (na): pretty, clean

kissaten: coffee shop, coffeehouse

kitanai: dirty

kochira koso: same to you; I'm the one who should be saying that

kodomo: child

kôen (公園): park

kôen (講演): lecture

koibito: boyfriend, girlfriend

koko: here, this place

kôkô: senior high school (grades 10–12); *kôkôsei:* high school student

kokonattsu: coconut

kokonoka: ninth day of the month

kokonotsu: nine

kokusai bôeki: international trade

komaru: be upset, be a hassle; *Komarimashita!* I'm upset! Oh, no!

konban wa: good evening

kongetsu: this month

konnichi wa: good day, good afternoon

kono (+ NOUN): this NOUN

konsaato: concert

konsarutanto: consultant

konsento: electrical outlet

konshû: this week

kontakuto renzu: contact lens

koohii: coffee

koohii jawan: coffee cup

koosu: course

kore: this one, this thing

korobu: trip and fall

kôsaten: intersection

koshô suru: have a mechanical breakdown

kossori: sneakily, secretly

kotae: an answer to a question

koto: abstract thing, concept

kotoshi: this year

kôtsû jiko: traffic accident; *kôtsû jiko ni au:* be involved in a traffic accident

kowai: frightening, frightened

kowasu: to break something

ku: nine

kudamono: fruit

kudasai: Please give; VERB-*te kudasai:* Please VERB (command or request)

kudasaru: give (a high-ranking person gives to me or gives to us)

kugatsu: September

kûkô: airport

kurabu: club

kureru: give (an equal or lower-ranking person gives to me or us)

kuruma: car, automobile

kusuri-ya: drugstore, pharmacy

kusuri: medicine

kutsu: shoe

kutsu-ya: shoe store

kuwashii: detailed

kuzukago: wastebasket

kyô: today

kyôdai: siblings, brothers and sisters

kyôkasho: textbook

kyonen: last year

kyôshi: teacher (non-honorific term)

kyôshitsu: classroom

Kyôto: Kyoto (capital of Japan from 794–1868)

kyû: nine

ma ni au: be on time; EVENT *ni ma ni au:* be on time for EVENT

mada: (+ positive verb or adjective): still; (+ negative verb or adjective): not yet

made: until, as far as

mado: window

mae: front, before; NOUN *no mae:* in front of NOUN, before NOUN

magaru: turn

mago: grandchild

mai: counter for flat objects such as paper and clothing

mainichi: every day

makura: pillow

man: ten thousand

manshon: condominium apartment

manten o toru: get a perfect score

Marayago: Malay language

Mareeshia: Malaysia

massugu: straight, straight ahead

mata: again; *mata dôzo:* Please come again (said by store personnel to customers)

matsu: wait; *hito o matsu:* wait for a person

matsuri: festival

meetoru: meter

megane: eyeglasses

mei: niece; *meigosan:* someone else's niece

Mekishiko: Mexico

messe: trade fair

mezurashii: unusual

michi: street, road

mieru (1): can see, be visible

migi: right; *migigawa:* right side (of a street, etc.); *migi no hô:* right side

mijikai: short

mikan: Mandarin orange

mikka: third day of the month

minasan: all of you

mingeihin: folk craft object

minna: all, everyone

miru (1): see, look, watch

mise: store, shop

miseru (1): show

mittsu: three

mizu: water

mô: already, anymore; *mô sugu:* pretty soon

mochiron: of course

modoru: return, back up

mokuyôbi: Thursday

mondai: problem

monitaa: computer monitor

môshiwake arimasen (gozaimasen): I have no excuse, I'm sorry to have to tell you this, I know I was wrong

motto: more

muika: sixth day of the month

mukamuka suru: be nauseated

mukô: beyond, over there; NOUN *no mukô:* beyond NOUN

musuko: my son; *musukosan:* someone else's son

musume: my daughter

muttsu: six

muzukashii: difficult

nagai: long

naifu: table knife

naka: middle, inside; NOUN *no naka:* inside NOUN, in the middle of NOUN, among NOUN

nakunaru: die (polite form)

namae: name

nan: what? *nan de mo:* anything and everything; *nangatsu:* what month? *nanji:* what time? *nansai:* how old? *nannichi:* what day of the month? *nannin:* how many people? *nan'yôbi:* what day of the week? *nani:* what? *nani ka:* something; *nani mo* + NEGATIVE: nothing

nana: seven

nanatsu: seven

nanoka: seventh day of the month

Nara: capital of Japan in the eighth century

naruhodo: of course, that's right, I knew that, etc.

nattô: fermented soybeans

ne(e): right? isn't that so? huh?

nebô suru: oversleep, sleep in

neko: cat

neru (1): lie down, sleep

nezumi: mouse, rat

ni: two

nichiyôbi: Sunday

nigatsu: February

Nihon: Japan; *Nihonjin:* Japanese person; *Nihongo:* Japanese language

Nijô-jô: Nijô Castle

Nikkeijin: person of Japanese ancestry

-nikui: (VERB + *-nikui*): hard to VERB

nimotsu: luggage

nin: counter for people

niwa: garden

no: possessive

nomimono: beverage

nomu: drink, ingest without chewing

nooto: notebook

nyuusu: news

O-daiji ni.: Take care.

o-furo: Japanese-style bath; *o-furo ni hairu:* to take a bath

o-jôsan: someone else's daughter

o-kaasan: someone else's mother

o-kamai naku: Please don't go to any trouble

o-kane: money

o-kyaku-san: customer, guest

o-magosan: someone else's grandchild

o-mawari-san: police officer

o-miyage: souvenir

o-naka: stomach, abdomen

o-neesan: someone else's older sister

O-negai shimasu.: Please.; Please do this for me.

o-niisan: someone else's older brother

o-seibo: year-end gifts

o-shôgatsu: New Year's Day

o-tearai: toilet, restroom

o-tera: Buddist temple

o-tsuri: change (money given back for purchases)

o-tôsan: someone else's father

oba: aunt; *obasan:* someone else's aunt

obaasan: someone else's grandmother

obi: sash for a kimono

odoru: dance

Ohayô.: Good morning.; *Ohayô gozaimasu.:* Good morning (more polite).

oi: my nephew; *oigosan:* someone else's nephew

oishii: delicious, tasty

oji: my uncle; *ojisan:* someone else's uncle

ojiisan: someone else's grandfather

okagesama de: thank you for inquiring about me

okiru (1): wake up, get out of bed

okoru: get angry; *okotte iru:* is angry

okureru (1): be late; EVENT *ni okureru:* be late to EVENT; *okurete iru:* is late

omoi: heavy

omoshiroi: interesting

omou: to think, to have an opinion

onaji: same; *onaji gurai:* approximately the same

ongaku: music

onsen: hot spring resort

ookii: big, large

orenji: orange

oriru (1): to get off a vehicle; *Basu o oriru:* to get off a bus

oru: humble equivalent of *iru*

oshieru (1); teach, inform

osoi: late, slow

otôto: my younger brother; *otôtosan:* someone else's younger brother

otto: husband, my husband

oyogu: to swim

paatii: party

pan-ya: bakery

pasupooto: passport

pen: pen

piano: piano

pikunikku: picnic

poketto: pocket

posutaa: poster

puuru: swimming pool

raigetsu: next month

raion: lion

raishû: next week

rajio: radio

raku (na): comfortable

rebaa: liver (as food)

rekoodo-ya: record store

renshû suru: practice

resutoran: Western-style restaurant

ringo: apple

roku: six

rokugatsu: June

ronbun: research paper

ryô: dormitory

ryokan: traditional Japanese-style inn

ryokô: travel, trip

ryôri: cooking, cuisine

ryôshin: parents; *go-ryôshin:* someone else's parents

ryûgakusei: student studying abroad

ryukku: backpack

saa: hmm

sagasu: look for

sai: counter for years of age; *issai:* one year old

saifu: wallet

sakana: fish

sakkaa: soccer

samui: cold (weather only)

san: three

sandaru: sandal

San Furanshisuko: San Francisco

sangatsu: March

Sapporo: principal city of the northern island of Hokkaidô

sashimi: sliced raw fish

satsu: counter for bound volumes, such as books, magazines, and notebooks

sawaru: touch; NOUN *ni sawaru:* touch NOUN

sayonara: good-bye

seetaa: sweater

seigo: after birth; *seigo ikkagetsu:* one month old

seikatsu: way of life

Sekijûji: Red Cross

sekken: soap

sen: thousand

senkô suru: to major in a subject; *sûgaku o senkô suru:* to major in mathematics

senshû: last week

sensu: folding fan

sentaa: center

sentakuki: washing machine

setsumei suru: explain

shabu-shabu: Japanese-style beef stew

shachô: company president

shamisen: a traditional stringed instrument similar to a banjo

shashin: photograph

shatsu: shirt

shi: (after verb or adjective) and furthermore

shi: four

shiai: game, athletic contest

shibai: theatrical play

Shiberia: Siberia

shichi: seven

shichigatsu: July

shigatsu: April

shigoto: work; *o-shigoto:* work (honorific form)

shiken: test

shimeru (1): close, shut

Shingapooru: Singapore

shingô: traffic light

shinsetsu (na): kindly, nice

shippai suru: fail; *shiken ni shippai suru:* fail a test

shiru: find out; *shitte iru:* know;

shiranai: not know

shita: below, under; NOUN *no shita:* under NOUN, below NOUN

shitsumon: question

shitsurei (na): impolite, rude; *Shitsurei desu ga...:* Excuse me for asking, but... *Shitsurei shimasu:* I'm going to be rude and (leave/come in, etc.); *Shitsurei shimashita:* I'm sorry for what I did

shizuka (na): quiet

shodô: calligraphy

shôkai suru: introduce

shokudô: dining hall

shorui: document

shôsetsu: novel

Shôshô o-machi kudasai.: Please wait a minute. (very polite)

shoten: bookstore

shujin: my husband; *go-shujin:* someone else's husband

shukudai: homework

shûri suru: repair

shûshoku suru: find a job, take a job

shutchô: business trip

soba (蕎麦): buckwheat noodles

soba (傍): vicinity

sobo: my grandmother

sôdan suru: consult; PERSON *ni sôdan suru:* ask the advice of PERSON

sofu: my grandfather

sôji: housecleaning; *sôji o suru:* clean up

sokkusu: socks

soko: there nearby

sono (+NOUN): that NOUN nearby

sore: that one, that thing nearby

sôri daijin: prime minister

soshite: and then

sotsugyô suru: graduate; *daigaku o sotsugyô suru:* graduate from the university

subarashii: wonderful

sûgaku: mathematics

sugu: soon

suisenjô: letter of recommendation

Suisu: Switzerland

suisô: aquarium

suiyôbi: Wednesday

sukeeto: skating

suki (na): liked; NOUN *ga suki desu:* I like NOUN

sukii: ski, skiing

sukoshi: a little bit; *mô sukoshi de:* in a little bit

sumimasen: Excuse me for bothering you; Thank you for the unexpected favor

sumu: live, dwell; PLACE *ni sunde iru:* lives at/in PLACE

Supein: Spain; *Supeingo:* Spanish language

suru: do; SPORT *o suru:* play SPORT

susumeru (1): recommend

susumu: advance; *tokei ga susumu:* a watch runs fast

sutando: lamp

suteki (na): great, fantastic

sutereo: stereo

suupaa: supermarket

suutsukeesu: suitcase

suwaru: sit

suzushii: pleasantly cool

tabako: cigarette; *tabako o suu:* smoke a cigarette

taberu (1): eat

tabi: split-toed socks for wearing with *geta*

taifû: typhoon

taiikukan: gymnasium

taisetsu (na): important

taitei: usually

takai: high, expensive

tamaru: be able to put up with, tolerate

tanomu: request, order; PERSON *ni tanomu:* make a request of a person, order a person

tansu: chest of drawers

tatemono: building

teeburu: Western-style table

teepu: tape

tegami: letter

ten'in: store clerk

tenisu: tennis

tenki: weather

tera: Buddhist temple

terebi: television; *terebi bangumi:* television program

to: and, with

tô: counter for large animals

todokeru (1): deliver

tokei: clock, watch

tokidoki: sometimes

tokkuri: sake flask

tokoro: place

tomaru: stop (one's self)

tonari: neighboring; NOUN *no tonari:* next to NOUN

too: ten

tooi: far

tooka: tenth day of the month

toru: take

toshi: year, age; t*oshi o toru:* grow old; *toshi o totte iru:* is old

toshokan: library

totemo: very

tsugi (no): next

tsuitachi: first day of the month

tsukareru (1): become tired; *tsukarete iru:* is tired

tsukau: use

tsukiatari: T-shaped intersection

tsukue: desk

tsukuru: make

tsuma: my wife

tsumaranai: boring

tsumetai: cold to the touch

tsutaeru (1): convey a message

uchi: house, within

ue: top, above; NOUN *no ue:* on top of
    NOUN, above NOUN

ukeru: undergo, take, be on the
    receiving end of

uketsuke: receptionist

uma: horse

umareru (1): be born

un: yeah

undô (suru): physical exercise

ureshii: delighted

uru: sell

urusai: annoyingly noisy

ushiro: behind, rear; NOUN *no ushiro:*
    behind NOUN

uso: false, lie

uta: song

utau: sing

wa: topic particle

watakushi: I

wakaru: to be clear, to be
    understandable; NOUN *ga wakaru:*
    I understand NOUN

wasureru (1): forget

wataru: go across

watashi: I (less formal)

watashitachi: we

ya: and things like that

yama: mountain; *yama ni noboru:*
    climb a mountain

yappari: after all, now that I think
    about it

yasai: vegetable

yasui: cheap; (VERB + *-yasui*); easy to
    VERB

yasumi: time off, vacation, break

yattsu: eight

yobidashi: paging, summoning

yôfuku: Western-style clothes

yôka: eighth day of the month

Yokatta!: (past tense of *ii*) Oh, good!

yokka: fourth day of the month

yoko: side; NOUN *no yoko:* alongside
    NOUN

yokomichi: side street

yoku: (*-ku* form of *ii*) well, often

yomu: read

yon: four

Yooroppa: Europe

yorokobu: be happy about something

yoru: evening

yottsu: four

yoyaku: reservation

yûbin de dasu: mail; *tegami o yûbin de
    dasu:* mail a letter

yûbinkyoku: post office

yuka: floor

zabuton: floor cushion

zasshi: magazine

zehi: by all means

zenbu: the whole thing

zutsu: each, apiece, at a time

zutsû: headache; *zutsû ga suru:* have a
    headache

ENGLISH-JAPANESE VOCABULARY

This is a list of some of the English equivalents of the Japanese words and phrases used in this book. It is **not** a dictionary, and it should not be used as such. Instead, it should be used only as a reminder of forgotten vocabulary for students working on the exercises. The listings are written to be amenable to the way students in real life look up words .

A number (1) after a verb indicates that it is a one-step verb. Five-step verbs are marked only if they could be mistaken for one-step verbs or if there are two verbs, one five-step and the other one-step, that have identical dictionary forms.

A.M.: gozen
able, be: dekiru (1)
above: ue; above NOUN: NOUN no ue
across: ...from NOUN: NOUN no mukaigawa; go across: wataru
add (...ingredients) ireru (1)
advance: (move fast) susumu
after: after NOUN: NOUN no ato de; (after VERB): VERB-*te* kara; (after that): sore kara
after all: yappari
afternoon: gogo
again: mata; (once more): mô ichido
airplane: hikôki
airport: kûkô
alive and well: kenzai (na), go-kenzai (na) (polite)
all: (the whole thing): zenbu; (every individual): minna
alone: hitori de
already: mô (+ positive)
always: itsumo
America, United States of: Amerika
and (between nouns): to; (. . .things like that): ya; ("and" between verbs): VERB₁ *te* + VERB₂; (and furthermore): shi; and then: soshite
angry (get angry): okoru; (is angry): okotte iru
answer (to a question): kotae
anymore: mô (+ negative)
apiece: zutsu; (five hundred yen each): gohyaku en zutsu

apple: ringo
April: shigatsu
aquarium: suisô
argument: kenka; argue: kenka o suru
August: hachigatsu
aunt: (my...): oba; (someone else's...): obasan

baby: akachan
bag: fukuro
bakery: pan-ya
ball: booru
bank: ginkô
bath: (Japanese-style): o-furo; take a bath: o-furo ni hairu (1)
be (is equivalent to): da, desu; (inanimate object is located): aru; (person or animal is located): iru (1) (humble form oru [5])
bed: beddo
before: mae; (before NOUN): NOUN no mae
behind: ushiro; (behind NOUN): NOUN no ushiro
below: shita; (below NOUN): NOUN no shita
belt: beruto
between: aida; (between NOUN₁ and NOUN₂): NOUN₁ to NOUN₂ no aida
beverage: nomimono
beyond: mukô; (beyond NOUN): NOUN no mukô

bicycle: jitensha
bit, a little: sukoshi
boat, ship: fune
book: hon
bookshelf: hondana
bookstore: hon-ya
boring: tsumaranai
born, be: umareru (1)
borrow: kariru (1)
boutique: butiiku
box: hako
boyfriend: koibito
Brazil: Burajiru
breakdown, have a mechanical: koshô
    suru
bridge: hashi
briefcase: kaban
brother, older: (my. . .): ani; (someone
    else's ...): o-niisan;
brother, younger: (my...) otôto;
    (someone else's...) otôtosan
building: tatemono; (Western
    style...): biru
busy: isogashii
buy: kau
by all means: zehi

calculator, electronic: dentaku
calligraphy: shodô
camera: kamera
can: dekiru (1)
Canada: Kanada
Cantonese language: Kantongo
car: kuruma
careful, be careful: ki o tsukeru (1)
case, carrying: keesu
cassette tape: kasetto teepu
cat: neko
center: sentaa
chair: isu
change (money returned): o-tsuri
chest of drawers: tansu
child: kodomo; (someone else's child
    [honorific]): o-kosan
China: Chûgoku; Chinese language:
    Chûgokugo; Chinese person:
    Chûgokujin

chocolate: chokoreeto
chopsticks: hashi
class (students in the same year):
    kurasu
class session: jugyô
classmate: dôkyûsei
clean: kirei (na); clean house: sôji
    suru
clock: tokei
clogs, traditional Japanese: geta
close (near): chikai
close (shut): shimeru (1)
clothes (Western-style...): yôfuku
club: kurabu
coffee: koohii
coffee cup: koohii jawan
coffee shop: kissaten
cold: (weather): samui; (to the
    touch): tsumetai; (illness): kaze
college: daigaku
comfortable: raku (na)
complicated: fukuzatsu (na)
concert: konsaato
condition (state): guai
condominium apartment: manshon
confer: sôdan suru; (to confer with a
    person): PERSON to sôdan suru
consult: sôdan suru; (consult a
    person): PERSON ni sôdan suru
consultant: konsarutanto
consumer prices: bukka
contact lens: kontakuto renzu
convenient: benri (na)
convey (a message): tsutaeru (1)
cooking: ryôri
cool (pleasantly cool): suzushii
corner (street corner): kado
course: koosu
crazy: baka (na)
cuisine: ryôri
culture center: karuchaa sentaa
curtain: kaaten
cute: kawaii

dance: odoru; (a dance): dansu paatii
daughter: (my...): musume; (someone
    else's ..): o-jôsan

day: hi; (day after tomorrow): asatte
December: jûnigatsu
delighted: ureshii
deliver: todokeru (1)
department store: depaato
desk: tsukue
detailed: kuwashii
diarrhea, have: geri suru
dictionary: jisho
die: nakunaru (polite); shinu
different, be: chigau
dining hall: shokudô
dirty: kitanai
dislike: (I dislike NOUN): NOUN ga
   kirai desu
distinguished: erai
doctor (medical): isha, o-ishasan
   (honorific)
document: shorui
dog: inu
dollar: doru
dormitory: ryô
drawer: hikidashi
drugstore: kusuri-ya

each: -zutsu; (one person at a time,
   one person each): hitori zutsu
earring: iyaringu
easy to. . .: VERB + -yasui
eight: hachi, yattsu
eighth day: yôka
electrical outlet: konsento
electronic products: denki seihin
embarrassed: hazukashii
English: (. . . conversation): eikaiwa;
   (. . . language): eigo
enter: hairu
era: jidai
eraser (pencil or ink): keshigomu
Europe: Yooroppa
even so: de mo
evening: ban; (good evening):
   konban wa
every day: mainichi
exercise (physical): undô
eyeglasses: megane
facial coloring: kaoiro

fail (a test): shiken ni shippai suru
fan (Japanese-style folding fan): sensu
fantastic: suteki (na)
far: tooi
father: (my...): chichi; (someone
   else's...): o-tôsan
February: nigatsu
festival: matsuri, o-matsuri
fifth day: itsuka
film (photographic): firumu
find out: shiru (5)
first day: tsuitachi
first time, for the: hajimete
first: ichibanme no; daiichi
fish: sakana; (sliced raw fish):
   sashimi
five: go, itsutsu
fix: naosu; shûri suru
flea market: boroichi
floor: yuka; (story of a building): -kai
floor cushion: zabuton
flower: hana
folk craft item: mingeihin
food: tabemono; (cuisine): ryôri;
   (animal food): esa
foolish: baka (na)
foreign language: gaikokugo
forget: wasureru (1)
fork: fooku
four: shi, yon, yottsu
fourth day: yokka
Friday: kin'yôbi
frightened: kowai
frightening: kowai
frog: kaeru
front: mae; (in front of NOUN):
   NOUN no mae
fruit: kudamono

garden: niwa
gas station: gasorin sutando
gather (into a group): atsumaru
Germany: Doitsu
get (take): toru; (receive) morau,
   itadaku: (get angry): okoru; (get
   married): kekkon suru; (get off a
   vehicle): oriru (1); (get up): okiru (1)

girlfriend: koibito

give (...to me or us): kureru (1), kudasaru (from a higher ranking person); (...to someone else) ageru (1), sashiageru (1) (to a higher ranking person); (Please give me NOUN): NOUN o kudasai

go: iku

go across: wataru

good afternoon: konnichi wa

good bye: sayonara; (when leaving home temporarily): Itte kimasu; (when seeing off someone who is leaving home) Itte irasshai; (when leaving the presence of a superior): shitsurei shimasu

good evening: konban wa

good morning: ohayô (gozaimasu)

good: ii (yoku); good at: jôzu (na)

gradually: dandan

graduate school: daigakuin

graduate: sotsugyô suru; (...from the university): daigaku o sotsugyô suru

grandchild: (my...) mago (someone else's...) o-magosan

grandfather: (my...) sofu; (someone else's...): ojiisan

grandmother: (my...):sobo; (someone else's...): o-baasan

great: suteki (na)

guitar: gitaa

gymnasium: taiikukan

hair salon: biyôin

hair: kami

ham: hamu

handbag: handobaggu

handkerchief: hankachi

happy: ureshii; (be happy about): yorokobu

hard to. . .: VERB + -nikui

hat: bôshi

head: atama

headache: zutsû; (have a ...): zutsû ga suru

healthy: genki (na)

hear: kiku; (can hear): kikoeru (1), (I can hear NOUN): NOUN ga kikoeru

heat: atsusa; (be overcome by the heat): atsusa ni mairu (5)

here: koko

high school: kôkô

hiking: haikingu

homework: shukudai

horse: uma

hospital: byôin

hot spring resort: onsen

hot: atsui

hotel (Western-style): hoteru

house: uchi, ie; (your ...) o-taku

housecleaning: sôji

how old: nansai?, o-ikutsu?

how: dô?; how much: ikura? how many: ikutsu?

hundred: hyaku

husband: otto; (my...) shujin; (someone else's...) go-shujin

I: watakushi, watashi(less formal), boku (least formal and used by males only)

impolite: shitsurei na

important: taisetsu (na)

impressive (in reference to people): erai

inconvenient: fuben (na)

inn, traditional Japanese-style: ryokan

inside: naka; (inside NOUN): NOUN no naka

international student: ryûgakusei

international trade: kokusai bôeki

intersection: kôsaten

interval: aida

introduce: shôkai suru

January: ichigatsu

Japan: Nihon; (Japanese person): Nihonjin; (Japanese language): Nihongo

Japanese ancestry, person of: Nikkeijin

jeans: jiinzu

job, find a: shûshoku suru

July: shichigatsu

June: rokugatsu
just: (just NOUN): NOUN dake

kindly: shinsetsu (na)
knife (table knife): naifu
know(s): shitte iru; (do(es)n't know):
  shiranai
Korea, South: Kankoku

lamp: sutando
landing (airplane): chakuriku
last month: sengetsu
last week: senshû
last year: kyonen
late, be: osoi, okureru (1); (is late):
  okurete iru; (be late to EVENT):
  EVENT ni okureru
lecture: kôen
left: hidari; (left side): hidari no hô,
  hidarigawa
letter: tegami
library: toshokan
life (way of life): seikatsu
liked: suki (na); (I like NOUN):
  NOUN ga suki desu
lion: raion
listening comprehension: kikitori
live (dwell): sumu; (live at PLACE):
  PLACE ni sunde iru
liver (meat): rebaa
long: nagai
look: miru (1), (Look there!): Hora!
look for: sagasu

machine: kikai
magazine: zasshi
mail a letter: tegami o yûbin de dasu
major: senkô suru; (major in
  mathematics): sûgaku o senkô suru
make: tsukuru
Malay language: Marayago
Malaysia: Mareeshia
man: otoko no hito, dansei
Mandarin orange: mikan
March: sangatsu
married, get: kekkon suru; (is
  married): kekkon shite iru

mathematics: sûgaku
meaning: imi; (What does it mean?):
  Dô iu imi desu ka?
meeting: kaigi
message: dengon
meter: meetoru
method: hôhô
Mexico: Mekishiko
Monday: getsuyôbi
money: o-kane
monitor: monitaa
month (counter for months): -kagetsu
more: motto
most: ichiban + ADJECTIVE
mother: (my...) haha; (someone
  else's...) o-kaasan
mountain: yama
mouse: nezumi
movie: eiga; (movie theater): eigakan
Mt. Fuji: Fujisan
much: takusan: (how. . .?): ikura?
museum (scientific and historical):
  hakubutsukan
music: ongaku

name: namae; (your name): o-namae
nap: hirune; (take a nap): hirune o
  suru
nauseated, be: mukamuka suru
near: chikai
neighboring: tonari (no)
nephew: (my...) oi; (someone else's...)
  oigosan
New Year's Day: o-shôgatsu
news: nyuusu
next month: raigetsu
next week: raishû
next: tsugi (no),
next to: yoko; (next to NOUN):
  NOUN no yoko
niece: (my...) mei; (someone else's...)
  meigosan
nine: ku, kyû, kokonotsu
ninth day: kokonoka
no: iie
no good: dame (na)
noisy (annoyingly noisy): urusai

not particularly: betsu ni
notebook: nooto
novel: shôsetsu
November: jûichigatsu
now: ima

o' clock: -ji; (ten o'clock): juji
October: jûgatsu
of course: mochiron
often: yoku
on time, be: ma ni au; (be on time for
    EVENT): EVENT ni ma ni au
one person: hitori
one: ichi, hitotsu; (ADJECTIVE+one):
    . . .no
only: (only NOUN) NOUN dake
or: ka
orange: orenji; (orange-colored):
    orenjiiro (no)
order: tanomu
overseas travel: kaigai ryokô
oversleep: nebô suru

paging: yobidashi
painful: itai
parents: (my...): ryôshin; (someone
    else's...) : go-ryôshin
park: kôen
party: paatii
pass (a test): (shiken ni) gôkaku
    suru
passport: pasupooto
pen: pen
pencil: enpitsu
perfect score, get a: manten o toru
perfect: kanpeki (na)
person: hito, kata
    (honorific form)
pharmacy: kusuri-ya
Philippines: Firipin
photograph: shashin
piano: piano
picture (drawn or painted): e
pillow: makura
pink: pinku (no)
place: tokoro
platform (railroad station): hoomu

play (amuse one's self): asobu;
    (...a stringed or keyboard
    instrument): hiku; (..a sport) suru,
    yaru
pleased to meet you: hajimemashite,
    dôzo yoroshiku
pocket: poketto
police booth: kôban
police officer: o-mawari-san
possible (as much as possible): dekiru
    dake
post office: yûbinkyoku
poster: posutaa
president (of a company): shachô
pretty: kirei (na)
pretty soon: mô sugu
prime minister: sôri daijin
problem: mondai
put in: ireru (1)
put up with, be able to: taeru

question: shitsumon
quickly: hayaku
quiet: shizuka (na)

radio: rajio
rain: ame; (It's raining): ame ga futte
    iru
rat: nezumi
raw fish: sashimi
receive: morau, itadaku (humble)
recommend: susumeru (1)
recommendation: (letter of. . .)
    suisenjô
record store: rekoodo-ya
Red Cross: Sekijûji
refrain (not do): enryo suru; (Please
    refrain): go-enryo kudasai
rent: kariru (1)
repair: shûri suru
request: tanomu, o-negai suru
    (humble); (make a request of
    PERSON): PERSON
    ni tanomu
reservation: yoyaku; (to reserve):
    yoyaku suru
respiratory infection: kaze

restaurant (Western-style...):
resutoran; (traditional Japanese...)
ryôri-ya

restroom: o-tearai, toire, keshôshitsu

return (to one's customary place):
kaeru (5); (to some other place)
modoru

right (direction): migi; (right side):
migigawa, migi no hô

road: michi

room: hcya

rude: shitsurei (na)

run fast (clocks, watches, etc.): susumu

sack: fukuro

safe: anzen (na)

sake: sake; (sake flask): tokkuri

same: onaji; (same person): onaji
hito: (not the same): onaji ja nai

San Francisco: San Furanshisuko

sandal: sandaru

sash (for a kimono): obi

Saturday: doyôbi

second day: futsuka

secretly: kossori

see: miru (1); (can see) mieru (1),
(I can see NOUN): NOUN ga mieru;
(see a PERSON): PERSON ni au

send out: dasu

September: kugatsu

seven: shichi, nana, nanatsu

seventh day: nanoka

severe: hidoi

shirt: shatsu

shoe: kutsu; (shoe store): kutsu-ya

shop: mise

shopping: kaimono; (go shopping):
kaimono ni iku

short: mijikai

show (verb): miseru (1)

shrine (Shinto): jinja

shut: shimeru (1)

siblings: kyôdai, go-kyôdai (honorific);
(How many siblings do you have?):
Go-kyôdai wa nannin desu ka?

side: yoko; (at the side of NOUN):
NOUN no yoko

side street: yokomichi

sightseeing: kenbutsu; (... area):
kankôchi

simple: kantan (na)

sing: uta o utau

Singapore: Shingapooru

sister, older: (my...): ane; (someone
else's ...): o-neesan

sister, younger: (my...): imôto;
(someone else's...): imôtosan

sit: suwaru

six: roku, muttsu

sixth day: muika

ski, skiing: sukii

skilled: jôzu (na), tokui (na)

slow: osoi

smart: atama ga ii

smoke (cigarettes): tabako o suu

snow: yuki; (it's snowing): yuki ga
futte iru

soap: sekken

soccer: sakkaa

socks: sokkusu; (split-toed Japanese
socks): tabi

solve: kaiketsu suru

sometimes: tokidoki

son: (my...): musuko; (someone
else's...): musukosan, bottchan

song: uta

soon: sugu

sorry, I'm: sumimasen; (I'm sorry for
having been rude): shitsurei
shimashita; (I'm sorry and I was in
the wrong or I'm sorry, and I know
you're disappointed): môshiwake
arimasen or môshiwake gozaimasen

souvenir: o-miyage

Spain: Supein; (Spanish language):
Supeingo

stairs: kaidan

state (condition): guai

station (train, subway): eki;
(... employee): ekiin

stereo: sutereo

still: mada (with positive verbs and
adjectives)

stomach: o-naka

stop: (. . .one's self): tomaru(5);
   (. . .something else) tomeru (1)
store: mise
store clerk: ten'in
straight ahead: massugu
straighten up: katazukeru (1)
street: michi
study: benkyô suru
stupid: baka (na)
Sunday: nichiyôbi
supermarket: suupaa
sweat: ase; (drenched in sweat): ase
   bisshori
sweater: seetaa
sweet: amai
sweet bean paste: anko
swim: oyogu
swimming pool: puuru
Switzerland: Suisu

T-shaped intersection: tsukiatari
table: teeburu
Take care!: Ki o tsukete!
   O-daiji ni!
take charge of: azukaru
take: toru; (. . . a shower): shawaa o
   abiru
tape: teepu
taxi: takushii; (taxi stand): takushii
   noriba
teach: oshieru (1)
teacher: sensei (honorific), kyôshi
   (non-honorific)
telephone: denwa; (. . . number):
   denwa bangô; (call PERSON on the
   telephone): PERSON ni denwa o
   suru/kakeru
television: terebi;
   (. . . program):
   terebi bangumi
temple (Buddhist): tera, o-tera
ten thousand: man (ichiman)
ten: jû, too
tennis: tenisu
tenth day: tooka
test: shiken
textbook: kyôkasho

thank you: arigatô (gozaimasu);
   (thank you for the food or drink):
   go-chisôsama deshita; (thank you for
   the unexpected favor): sumimasen
that: (nearby): sono + NOUN; (. . .one
   nearby) sore; (over there) ano +
   NOUN; (. . .one over there) are
   there: (...nearby) soko; (over...) asoko
therefore: da kara
thief: dorobô
thing: koto (abstract); mono
   (concrete)
third day: mikka
this: kono + NOUN; (...one) kore
this month: kongetsu
this week: konshû
this year: kotoshi
three: san, mittsu
Thursday: mokuyôbi
ticket: kippu, chiketto
tidy up: katazukeru (1)
tired, become: tsukareru (1); (is tired):
   tsukarete iru
today: kyô
toilet: o-tearai, toire, keshôshitsu
tolerate: taeru
tomorrow: ashita; (the day after. . .):
   asatte
top: ue; (on top of NOUN): NOUN
   no ue
totebag: kaban; (luggage-style...)
   Bosuton baggu
touch: sawaru; (touch NOUN):
   NOUN ni sawaru
trade fair: messe
traditional clothing store: gofukuten
traffic accident: kôtsû jiko; (be
   involved in a . . .): kôtsû jiko ni au
traffic light: shingô
translator: honyakuka
travel: ryokô suru
trip (and fall): korobu
Tuesday: kayôbi
turn in: dasu
turn: magaru; (. . . right): migi e
   magaru; (. . . at the corner): kado o
   magaru

two people: futari
two: ni, futatsu
typhoon: taifû

umbrella: kasa
uncle: (my...): oji; (someone else's...)
    ojisan
under: shita; (under NOUN): NOUN
    no shita
undergo: ukeru (1)
understand: wakaru; (I understand
    NOUN): Watashi wa NOUN ga
    wakaru
university: daigaku
unskilled: heta (na), nigate (na)
until: made
upset, be: komaru; (I'm upset.):
    Komatta!, Komarimashita!
use: tsukau
usual, as usual: aikawarazu
usually: taitei

vacation: yasumi, kyûka
vase: kabin
vegetable: yasai
vicinity: chikaku

wait: matsu; (. . .for PERSON):
    PERSON o matsu; (please wait a
    moment [very polite]):
    shôshô o-machi kudasai
wake up: okiru (1)
walk: aruku
wall: kabe
wallet: saifu
warm (pleasantly warm): atatakai
wash: arau
washing machine: sentakuki
wastebasket: kuzukago
watch (timepiece): tokei

water: mizu
we: watashitachi
wear (. . .over the legs): haku;
    (. . .clothing that touches the
    shoulders) kiru (1); (on the head):
    kaburu; (. . .eyeglasses) megane o
    kakeru; (. . .accessories) suru
weather: tenki
Wednesday: suiyôbi
Welcome!: Irasshaimase!
well (adverb): yoku, jôzu ni;
    (interjection): jaa, saa, maa, de wa, sô
    desu ne
what: nan, nani; (what time): nanji?
what day: (. . .of the month): nannichi?
    (. . . of the week) nan'yôbi?
what month: nangatsu?
where: doko?
who: dare?, donata? (honorific),
    dochirasama? (most polite)
why: dôshite
wife: tsuma; (my...) kanai; (someone
    else's...) okusan
window: mado
woman: onna no hito, josei
wonderful: subarashii, suteki (na)
work: shigoto; (to work): shigoto o
    suru, hataraku
write: kaku

yeah: un
year: toshi, nen, (the year 1997): sen
    kyûhyaku kyûjû nana nen
year-end gift: o-seibo
yen: en; (Japanese yen): Nihon en.
yes: hai, ee (informal)
you: (using the person's name or title is
    most common); anata, kimi (used by
    males only)
you're welcome: dô itashimashite